Social Actions for Classroom
Language Learning

NEW PERSPECTIVES ON LANGUAGE AND EDUCATION
Series Editor: Professor Viv Edwards, *University of Reading, Reading, Great Britain*
Series Advisor: Professor Allan Luke, *Nanyang Technological University, Singapore*

Two decades of research and development in language and literacy education have yielded a broad, multidisciplinary focus. Yet education systems face constant economic and technological change, with attendant issues of identity and power, community and culture. This series will feature critical and interpretive, disciplinary and multidisciplinary perspectives on teaching and learning, language and literacy in new times.

Recent Books in the Series
Distance Education and Languages: Evolution and Change
    Börje Holmberg, Monica Shelley and Cynthia White (eds)
Ebonics: The Urban Education Debate (2nd edn)
    J.D. Ramirez, T.G. Wiley, G. de Klerk, E. Lee and W.E. Wright (eds)
Decolonisation, Globalisation: Language-in-Education Policy and Practice
    Angel M. Y. Lin and Peter W. Martin (eds)
Travel Notes from the New Literacy Studies: Instances of Practice
    Kate Pahl and Jennifer Rowsell (eds)
Social Context and Fluency in L2 Learners: The Case of Wales
    Lynda Pritchard Newcombe

Other Books of Interest
Bilingual Education: An Introductory Reader
    Ofelia García and Colin Baker (eds)
Continua of Biliteracy: An Ecological Framework for Educational Policy, Research, and Practice in Multilingual Settings
    Nancy H. Hornberger (ed.)
Developing Minority Language Resources
    Guadalupe Valdés, Joshua A. Fishman, Rebecca Chávez and William Pérez
Language and Identity in a Dual Immersion School
    Kim Potowski
Language and Literacy Teaching for Indigenous Education: A Bilingual Approach
    Norbert Francis and Jon Reyhner
Language Learning and Teacher Education: A Sociocultural Approach
    Margaret R. Hawkins (ed.)
Language, Space and Power: A Critical Look at Bilingual Education
    Samina Hadi-Tabassum
Language Minority Students in the Mainstream Classroom (2nd edn)
    Angela L. Carrasquillo and Vivian Rodríguez
Multilingual Classroom Ecologies
    Angela Creese and Peter Martin (eds)
Disinventing and Reconstituting Languages
    Sinfree Makoni and Alastair Pennycook (eds)
Understanding Deaf Culture: In Search of Deafhood
    Paddy Ladd

For more details of these or any other of our publications, please contact:
**Multilingual Matters, Frankfurt Lodge, Clevedon Hall,
Victoria Road, Clevedon, BS21 7HH, England
http://www.multilingual-matters.com**

NEW PERSPECTIVES ON LANGUAGE AND EDUCATION
Series Editor: Viv Edwards

Social Actions for Classroom Language Learning

John Hellermann

MULTILINGUAL MATTERS LTD
Clevedon • Buffalo • Toronto

To Conny, Nina and Cooper

Library of Congress Cataloging in Publication Data
Hellermann, John
Social Actions for Classroom Language Learning/John Hellermann.
New Perspectives on Language and Education
Includes bibliographical references and index.
1. Language and languages–Study and teaching–Social aspects. 2. Social interaction.
I. Title.
P53.8.H45 2008
418.0071–dc22   2007020106

British Library Cataloguing in Publication Data
A catalogue entry for this book is available from the British Library.

ISBN-13: 978-1-84769-026-5 (hbk)
ISBN-13: 978-1-84769-025-8 (pbk)

Multilingual Matters Ltd
UK: Frankfurt Lodge, Clevedon Hall, Victoria Road, Clevedon BS21 7HH.
USA: UTP, 2250 Military Road, Tonawanda, NY 14150, USA.
Canada: UTP, 5201 Dufferin Street, North York, Ontario M3H 5T8, Canada.

Copyright © 2008 John Hellermann.

All rights reserved. No part of this work may be reproduced in any form or by any means without permission in writing from the publisher.

The policy of Multilingual Matters/Channel View Publications is to use papers that are natural, renewable and recyclable products, made from wood grown in sustainable forests. In the manufacturing process of our books, and to further support our policy, preference is given to printers that have FSC and PEFC Chain of Custody certification. The FSC and/or PEFC logos will appear on those books where full certification has been granted to the printer concerned.

Typeset by Techset Composition Ltd.
Printed and bound in Great Britain by the Cromwell Press Ltd.

Contents

Preface and Acknowledgements. vii

1   Additional Language Learning in a Classroom
    Community of Practice. 1
    Why This Book Now? 1
    Traditional Research on Additional Language Learning 3
    Socio-Cultural Perspectives on Language Learning 4
    Seeing 'Learning' in Traditional Classroom Settings. 17
    Data Collection Context. 22
    An Analytic Tool for Understanding Negotiating
      Meaning and Practice: Conversation Analysis. 27
    Conclusion. 28

2   Conversation Analysis as a Method for Understanding
    Language Learning. 29
    Ethnomethodological Conversation Analysis:
      An Introduction. 29
    Conversation Analysis, Language Learning and
      Membership. 36
    Connecting Members' Local Methods with the
      Community of Practice 39
    Conclusion. 40

3   Opening Dyadic Task Interactions 41
    Openings for Classroom Interactions 41
    Research on Openings in Conversational Interaction. 42
    Openings in the Classroom Community of Practice. 44
    Moves and Sequences for Opening Task Interactions. 46
    Opening Moves and Sequences Characteristic
      of Two Levels of Language Proficiency. 50
    Other Task-Prefatory Opening Sequences 58
    Language Development Seen Comparing Level 'A'
      and Level 'C' Communities of Practice: Turn
      Allocation and Changing Participation. 65

      Language Development Seen Longitudinally
         in Interaction for Task Openings 69
      Conclusion.. 81

4 Story Tellings in Dyadic Task Interactions 83
      Introduction.. 83
      Research on Formats for Conversational Story Telling.......... 84
      Story Tellings in the Adult Language Learning Classroom
         Community of Practice 86
      Similarities of These Tellings to Previous
         Reports of Conversation 87
      Differences Between These Tellings and Previous
         Reports of Conversation 92
      Evidence of Language Development in the Story
         Telling Practices 97
      Story Tellings in the Classroom Communities of Practice 101

5 Disengagements from Dyadic Task Interactions 103
      Introduction... 103
      Local Contexts For and Possible Next Actions
         After Students' Disengagement from Classroom
         Dyadic Interaction 108
      Sequence Types for Talk-in-Interaction for Disengagement
         from Task Interaction.................................. 115
      Disengagement Moves for Serial Dyadic Interaction Tasks..... 123
      Change in Participation: Disengagement Sequences
         in Serial Dyadic Interaction Tasks 125
      Conclusion.. 141

6 Conclusions 143
      Introduction... 143
      How Language Learning is 'Situated'....................... 143
      The Contexts of Classroom Communities of Practice
         and Their Influence on Language Use.................... 145
      Language Learning in Classroom Communities of Practice 150
      Closing Comments on Implications
         for Teaching and Learning 154

Appendix: Transcription Conventions........................... 158

Notes 160

References.. 162

Index 178

Preface and Acknowledgements

The research in this book reflects a convergence of two long-standing interests of mine: language learning and the organization of social interaction. Classrooms represent a unique opportunity to see the intersection of these two interests. The technological capacities of the corpus of data I've had to work with (the Multimedia Adult English Learner Corpus, Reder, 2005) allow for focused investigations of learner–learner interaction in and around language learning tasks. This corpus of classroom video recorded interaction that includes six camera views of each classroom is allow researchers and practitioners new insights into what learning looks like in the classroom.

The research in this book has tried to take advantage of this unique perspective on the classroom by providing micro-level details in the descriptions of social actions that occur between and among learners, actions that classroom teachers (and many researchers) have not been able to see. I hope that these descriptions and analyses will help teachers and researchers (re)consider what we consider to be processes of language learning and the value of face-to-face interaction in that learning. Many of the ideas in this book were influenced by the research done with the Project on Academic Language Socialization at the University of Wisconsin (Zuengler *et al.*, 1998) and the discussions I had with members of that project, particularly, Jane Zuengler, KimMarie Cole, Elizabeth Miller and Ceci Ford. The ideas in the paper also owe much to discussions with Simona Pekarek Doehler, Johannes Wagner, Gabi Kasper and Joan Kelly Hall.

I would like to thank participants in conversation analysis data sessions that took place at Portland State and where many of these ideas were first presented: Dominique Brillanceau, Eunyoung Cho, Luis Perea, as well as Elizabeth Cole and Sarah Albers who helped with translations. I would like to thank the teachers who participated in the data collection, management team members Reuel Kurzet and Sandra Banke, and the support in the data collection and processing from large team of graduate and undergraduate students. Major funding for the project came from the U.S. Department of Education through the National Center for the Study of Adult Learning and Literacy (NCSALL). Additional financial support was provided by Dr Cornelia Wagner.

The research reported on in this volume would not have been possible without the vision of Stephen Reder and Kathryn Harris, the researchers responsible for the establishment of the National Labsite for Adult ESOL at Portland State University (Reder *et al.*, 2003). Their wide-ranging understanding of the factors involved in adult language learning showed them the need for methods and processes for data collection and dissemination that are unprecedented in the field. The video excerpts available via web links in this book only begin to illustrate this innovation. The Multimedia Adult English Learner Corpus and research from this corpus has attracted the attention of a number of scholars interested in researching classroom language learning from socio-cultural perspectives and has significantly added to the theoretical developments in the area of second language learning. Together with NCSALL's director, John Comings, Steve and Kathy allowed the research in this volume to develop without restrictions and persistently asked the questions that helped keep this conversation analysis researcher's eyes on the bigger picture.

Chapter 1
Additional Language Learning in a Classroom Community of Practice

Why This Book Now?

Many potential readers picking up this volume will surely know the rich body of scholarship in the area of classroom discourse, (Cazden, 1988; Cole & Zuengler, 2007; Erickson, 1996; Green & Wallat, 1981; Hester & Francis, 2000; Mehan, 1979; Newman *et al.*, 1989; Nystrand, 1997; Sinclair & Coulthard, 1975; Wells, 1999; among others) and may wonder why they might read yet another study of classroom discourse. Many of those same potential readers will also know that the bulk of the research on classrooms has focused on interaction between the classroom teacher and students. This research has made invaluable contributions to understanding the discourse structures of teacher-led classroom interaction and the relationships between language, teaching and learning. However, because of its focus on the teacher-student cohort interactions (but see Fisher, 1993, 1994; Markee, 2000; Ohta, 2001a, 2001b; among others), this research has not been able to show the turn-by-turn detail of students' interactions with one another and with the subject matter content nor how these interactions lead to learning over time. The lack of focus on learner-learner interaction and development over time has been, for the most part, because of technological limitations.

The vision behind the National Labsite for Adult ESOL (Reder *et al.*, 2003) led technical innovations that allowed for the collection of almost four thousand hours of video recordings of adult ESOL classroom interaction. While some (including the researchers leading the projects) questioned the efficacy of such a massive data collection project (four consecutive years), the rewards are becoming evident as the research findings become public (Brillanceau, 2005; Harris, 2005; Hellermann, 2005b, 2007; Reder, 2005).

The philosophy behind the massive data collection is part of the foundation for the perspective on research and classroom language learning that is taken in this book. Extensive data collection enables a broad and deep empirical vision of a process (learning in a classroom) that occurs through the social interaction of a number of individuals who come together as a collective, mutually goal-oriented enterprise: the Classroom Community of Practice. It is as part of this physical co-presence and the trajectory toward common goals that learning takes place in a classroom. Extensive, long-term data collection through video recordings has allowed researchers to gain insight into both the micro-processes of language development and longer term changes to understand language learning as it happens as part of a community of practice in the classroom.

The availability of a 'full picture' of the breadth and depth of interaction in the classroom has enabled researchers and practitioners to develop a new 'professional vision' (Goodwin, 1994) on the nature of classroom teaching and learning. We have found that practitioners and researchers who see the learning process as it occurs in the classroom, in detail and over time, tend to focus less on what the teacher is doing, less on teaching and learning as a transmission process (Heap, 1985). This richer vision has allowed us to reconsider learning in the classroom as co-constructing knowledge through interaction, 'to be discovered together by the group of human resources in the classroom [and] reflexively constitutive of what indeed is found' (Macbeth, 2003: 258). These opportunities for seeing classrooms anew have enabled empirical studies of the social and situated part of cognition in language learning that has begun in other social scientific disciplines (Cole, 1996; Goodwin, 1995; Hutchins, 1995; Lave & Wenger, 1991; Resnick *et al.*, 1991).

The research reported on in this book takes advantage of new developments in data collection in classrooms (Reder *et al.*, 2003; and described later in this chapter). With this book, I was interested in investigating the ways that particular social actions in adult language learning classrooms, actions that have not been accessible to researchers in the past, are sites for the micro-level practices of language learning and interaction in classroom communities of practice (Lave, 1988, 1996; Lave & Wenger, 1991; Wenger, 1998; Wortham, 2001). These actions are hybrid areas of talk-in-interaction in which practices for organizing face-to-face interaction through language also organize what we think of as the institutional talk of language-learning tasks.

More specifically, using methods for close analysis of language in interaction from Conversation Analysis (CA), the analytic chapters (3, 4 and 5) will focus on the social practices that adult learners of English use to organize their interactions during dyadic language-learning tasks. The chapters each focus on one area of the task interactions: Chapter 3 on the starts of the tasks, Chapter 4 on non-elicited story tellings that occur during the tasks and Chapter 5 on the talk used to organize the students disengagements from their tasks. The rich perspective on interaction in the classroom afforded by the video technology of the data collection (six cameras) allows for the analysis of micro-level language practices as they occur within a classroom community of practice. With the focus of two of these cameras on two pairs of learners engaged in dyadic interaction in each classroom collected over four years, I will address language learning from both microgenetic (Korobov & Bamberg, 2004; Siegler & Crowley, 1991) and longitudinal perspectives.

Traditional Research on Additional Language Learning

The phrase 'additional language learning' is used deliberately to contrast this study of the social practices involved in language development of the adult immigrant learners with a long history of research in the field known as second language acquisition (SLA). The research program of SLA has focused on the acquisition of an abstract grammatical system in learners' second or other language and the linguistic, social, and cognitive factors that influence that acquisition. The field developed in the later half of the 20th century as researchers became interested in using knowledge from linguistics to improve language instruction (Lado, 1957) and was greatly influenced by cognitive psychology and structural linguistics from its inception in the 1950s. These influences include Chomskian formal linguistics (Flynn & O'Neill, 1988; Gass & Schachter, 1989; White, 1985, 1989; and others) and Labovian sociolinguistics on variation within SLA (Bayley & Preston, 1996; Preston, 1996; Tarone, 1988; Young, 1991). The major impact of structural linguistics and cognitive psychology on studies of second language learning can be seen in the catalog of SLA research through current studies (see compendia by Doughty & Long, 2003; Ritchie & Bhatia, 1996). The impact of linguistics and cognitive psychology on SLA has been to concentrate study on additional language learning as the development of a second language formal grammar and the processing of that grammatical system as accomplished by the individual mind-brain. The object of this line of study has often been decontextualized linguistic structures and the subject of quantitative studies (Lazaraton, 2003).

The linguistic and cognitive foci for research on additional language learning is important as basic research to construct formal models of linguistic systems and on the possible organization of those systems in the brain. Applied researchers, however, have started to see the overall research program in the field of SLA as focusing too narrowly on the abstract grammatical systems of learners to the detriment of our understanding of language use and communication by learners of additional languages (Firth, 1996; Firth & Wagner, 1997, 2007; Toohey, 2000; Wagner, 1996).

There have been lines of research in SLA that acknowledge the importance of language as it occurs in interaction between humans (particularly the perspective now known as 'input and interaction' or 'interactionist'). This research (Gass & Varonis, 1985; Hardy & Moore, 2004; Long, 1983, 1996; Varonis & Gass, 1985; and others) has been interested in how the adjustments that learners make in their speech that results from overt prompts from interlocutors in interaction might lead to second language acquisition. However, while the input–interactionist research used expert–learner and learner–learner interactions as a way to collect the data for their studies, the focus of this research has been an individualist, cognitive orientation of learners' acquisition of an individual linguistic competence that results from interaction and not on the social aspects of the interaction in its own right (Seedhouse, 2005; van Lier, 2000).

Socio-Cultural Perspectives on Language Learning

More fully contextualized studies of the social aspects language learning include studies grounded in Vygotskian Sociocultural theory (Brooks & Donato, 1994; Donato, 1994, 2000, 2004; Frawley & Lantolf, 1985; Hall, 1993, 1995, 1997a, 2004; Lantolf, 2000a; Lantolf & Appel, 1994; Lantolf & Thorne, 2006; Ohta, 2000, 2001a; Platt & Brooks, 2002; Vine, 2003; and others), language socialization (Bayley & Schecter, 2003; Kramsch, 2002; Poole, 1990, 1992; van Lier, 2002; Watson-Gegeo, 2004; Willett, 1995) and ethnomethodological conversation analysis (Brouwer & Wagner, 2004; Hellermann, 2007; Markee, 2000; Markee & Kasper, 2004; Mondada & Pekarek Doehler, 2004; Seedhouse, 2004, 2005).

An exchange initiated by Firth and Wagner in the Modern Language Journal (Firth & Wagner, 1997, 2007) first motivated by a call for limiting the number of research perspectives and theories for SLA (Long, 1993) had the effect of encouraging much of this more socially-contextualized research and has given cause for socio-cultural researchers on second language learning to consider to what degree their studies should be considered part of the field known as SLA (Firth, 2007). Some of the criticisms around Firth & Wagner's call for a wider range of research perspectives in SLA suggested that some contextually-focused research (particularly that influenced by conversation analysis) may be valid research but was not research on language 'acquisition' (Gass, 1998; Kasper, 1997).[1]

Although terminological differences such as what is the meaning of 'SLA', in and of themselves, are not particularly important for knowledge production,[2] I raise this particular terminological difference in order to frame my discussion of the theoretical background to this study of additional language learning. The perspective on language and language learning taken in this book sees language as a cognitive and cultural artifact, something that humans have because of our living with and through language. From this perspective, language competence is synonymous with language use and language acquisition is both influenced by and influences the contexts of its use (Goodwin, 1995). Research on language acquisition/learning can gain a great deal of insight from research perspectives that focus on learners, learning and the social actions that language is used to accomplish. With the focus of such a research program on the reflexive contextualization process between language and language use, we can gain new holistic and ecological insight into language and language learning (Kramsch, 2002; Toohey, 2000).

Language competence or membership

Recent work by applied linguists and language learning researchers has been interested in understanding language learning and assessing competence by examining learners' ability to use the language being learned for social practices, often, in real-world contexts. From this perspective, a learner's goal or target for study might be considered some degree of interactional rather than purely grammatical competence (Cekaite, 2007; Cicourel, 1974; Hall, 1993, 1995; Hellermann, 2006; Kanagy, 1999; Kramsch, 1986; Markee, 2000; Young, 1999, 2000, 2002; Young & Miller, 2004). Interactional competence might best be described as the capacity for using language appropriately, for particular routines in particular contexts which might then be relevant for interaction in other equivalent contexts. Such competence does not preclude attention to linguistic form. Rather, assessment of interactional competence in a language focuses on the situationally and interactionally appropriate use of linguistic forms in language use in interaction (McNamara & Roever, 2006).

Given the theoretical perspective on language, learning, and interaction taken in this book (ethnomethodological conversation analysis, see Chapter 2), assessing learners' competence in English will focus on how learners display their various statuses as members of two overlapping communities: the classroom community of practice and the community of English language users. Members using language in social interaction always display a variety of competences for language in social interaction thus (re)defining themselves as members (Heritage, 1984a). We are 'members' of the community of 'English language users' to some degree because we use English. The interaction of focus in this research, an English language classroom, is a context where 'classroom' and the 'English language user' communities overlap. Tracing the development of learners' competence in English in this classroom context will be done by observing video recordings of language routines or discursive practices (Hanks, 1996; Tracy, 2002) that are repeated within a particular class period and over time in equivalent contexts (Brown et al., 1989; Peters & Boggs, 1986). With data focusing on learner dyadic interaction in the moment and over time, change in such practices and change in learners' membership statuses can be observed both as moment-to-moment process and as long-term development.

Community of practice or situated learning theory

From a CA perspective, language use displays our status as members as we use our members' methods to interpret our talk. Membership in and learning through a community of practice is focused on goal-directed action, action that includes talk. Understanding learning within a community of practice came out of anthropological research on learning in a variety of contexts where learning occurred but was not considered the sole focus of the participants in those contexts (Liberian tailors, recovering alcoholics, insurance claims processors, etc.) (Lave & Wenger, 1991; Wenger, 1998). Learning was investigated as it occurred outside of classrooms as part of the socialization into work and society (see also Rogoff, 1990; Scribner & Cole, 1973). Lave and Wenger's theory was proposed and developed as an alternative to a bifurcated understanding of learning. This division would place context-dependent, informal or 'primitive' (Mead, 1943) learning that occurs outside of formal learning contexts on one side and abstract, pan-contextual learning that purportedly occurs in most formal educational settings on the other. The theory suggests that even learning that is usually considered as the collection of abstract, decontextualized conceptual knowledge (learning in formal educational institutions) is mediated by social factors within a community of practice (Lave, 1996). In community of practice theory, learners are active participants in both the shaping of the objects and processes of learning. The interactional dynamic of the situation is seen not just as a conduit for learning but as a stimulus to and raw material for learning. The active aspect of participants in interaction in situated learning theory focuses on participation as a socio-interactive (Mondada & Pekarek Doehler, 2004) indicator of learning.

From this perspective, learning is facilitated by interaction using language practices within a community of practice and can be seen as individuals' changing patterns of participation in the use of those social practices within the community of practice. A community of practice is a group of individuals, usually physically co-present, who come together under the auspices of a common interest or goal and co-construct practices for the interaction that, in turn, constitute the community of practice – their reason for coming together. While some intention in the organizational plan for the community of practice is needed (Wenger *et al.*, 2002), learning occurs in the co-construction of the practices that maintain the community of practice without any overt planning or curriculum. A common example of a community of practice is the workplace. People come together for the common goal of getting some work done and in the process of getting the work done, develop practices for getting that work done that are not overtly instructed and are, to some degree, unique to their own group. In doing this, they model, collaborate with, and mentor one another the practices for getting that work done. Learning, in this situated, community of practice sense, is a process of becoming (McDermott, 1993; Wenger, 1998; Wootton, 1997) rather than a product to be measured against some absolute standard of knowledge.

In the community of practice, learning and knowledge creation is dynamic and shared. For language learning, this means that, while the code necessary for using a language is limited (if not finite), the manifestations of the language for use in various contexts are potentially limitless. Conceptualizing language learning as it occurs within a classroom community of practice shifts the focus for the study of language learning away from the limited structures of the code itself to the contextualized and more open-ended encoding of language as communication.

Language learning classrooms in communities of practice: Some previous research

While community of practice theory has continued to serve as a basis for research on learning in settings outside the classroom (Hutchins, 1995; Wenger *et al.*, 2002) recently it has also served as a framework for research on studies of learning in classroom contexts (Bucholtz, 1999; Leki, 2001; Morita, 2004; Norton, 2001; Toohey, 1996, 2000; Zuengler & Miller, 2007).

See also Rogoff *et al.*, 2001). Toohey's (1996, 2000) ethnographic study of elementary school classrooms incorporates the idea of 'learning as participation' from community of practice theory focusing on voice and identity formation of young language learners in a classroom setting. The ethnographic research methodology incorporates rich descriptions of the backgrounds and lives of each of six learners over the course of three years in elementary school showing how English language minority students socio-historical backgrounds effect participants and, therefore, language learning and identity within a classroom community of practice.

Leki (2001) also focused on issues of identity and role in the classroom in her study of university classroom group work interactions between English second-language university students and their native speaking counterparts. Her findings show how non-native speaker identities were reified by role assignment and participation in these groups. While Leki's context (NS-NNS interaction in university classrooms) is an important area where more research needs to be done, it is questionable to what degree group work in university classrooms constitutes a community of practice. Her findings suggest that the different learners in the group work did not see themselves as participating in a *joint enterprise* and struggled with using a *shared repertoire*[3] for their group interactions but that better instruction might enable communities of practice in such situations to develop.

Morita also focused on English L2 speakers in a multiple case study of international students' academic language socialization in university classroom settings. The focus on international student outsiders' 'negotiation of competence and identity' (Morita, 2004: 583) is drawn from self-reports, interviews and some classroom observation. Morita's study used interpretive ethnographic methods to highlight the reciprocal nature of competence to participate and level of participation in classroom discussion and the complex intersections of culture, gender and identity ascription in the process of university students' academic socialization.

Like Leki (2001) and Morita (2004), Norton (2001) presents examples of lack of full participation within communities of practice. Norton shows how adult language learners may become marginal rather than 'legitimate peripheral' participants. While peripheral but legitimate participants are in the process of becoming full participants in the community of practice, marginal members do not have this trajectory of membership. In Norton's case, because of their marginal status in the community of practice and an imagined community which conflicted with the actual community, these students dropped out of their language learning classes.

These studies of language learners achieving different degrees of participation within classroom communities of practice focus on the social construction of identity through contextual historical and cultural discourses such as race, gender and ethnicity. They consider the term 'negotiation' in the sense of the metaphorical interaction between these big 'D' discourses (Gee, 1996). The research discussed in the next chapters does not deny that these historical and cultural factors influence the identity of individuals and communities. Nor does it deny the role that identity formation (a key aspect of community of practice theory) plays in language learning. Rather, the research here focuses on a recent call (Creese, 2005) for more attention to details of language use in face-to-face interaction to illustrate the interactive processes, the negotiations of meanings, which make up the shifting participation of learners in a community of practice. Focusing on a narrow set of social actions that occur as part of the interaction in learner–learner classroom language learning tasks, we can see the way that patterns of language in interaction create contexts for learning in classroom communities of practice. The goal of the research is to understand how sequences of turns at talk establish local practices for accomplishing particular actions and for participating in and establishing the adult immigrant language learning community of practice. By investigating these practices as they occur in classrooms with learners of different language proficiencies and as they occur over time with individual students, language development can be seen in the change in participation in social practices that are not usually the focus of research on language learning in classrooms.

In further explicating the characteristics of learning within a community of practice, several defining characteristics will be important to highlight. While the boundaries of what constitutes a community of practice are somewhat amorphous, the five concepts outlined below will help to more clearly define how I see a classroom community of practice. These are mutual engagement, joint enterprise, shared repertoire, reification and participation and economies of meaning. Although these concepts are likely relevant for the characterization of many classrooms, as I will explain next, for adult language learning classrooms, they are particularly relevant.

Mutual engagement

It is the mutuality of the participation in the work of the community which commits people to one another and the community. This mutuality enables members to develop local understandings of their individual roles and competences and changes in these roles and competencies within the community of practice. Individuals oriented to one another through their interaction with one another are able to continue that engagement as their level of participation changes.

The mutual engagement of members entails a fluidity in the community of practice for the development, evolution, and management of nebulous boundaries of participation structures (Au, 1980; Erickson & Mohatt, 1982) which occur within a community of practice. One of these participation structures, 'teacher–students' is a massively recurring format for participation in, and some would say, the defining characteristic of, classrooms (Cazden, 1988). In the adult language learning classroom, we see mutual engagement in the attention that the student cohort gives to the teacher and the return attention expected by the teacher. We also see evidence of mutual engagement in students' commitment to one another in their dyadic and small group interaction within the classroom. Student–student mutual engagement is also notable in the adult language learning classroom for the persistence displayed by students in working out meaning in language learning tasks. This mutual commitment of teacher to students and students to teacher and to peers allows for their understanding and negotiation of boundaries for practices within the classroom.

It also allows for the local development of a history of shared experiences in which members understand one another's competencies and roles. Students come to know what to expect of their teacher and their peers by virtue of their being positioned by the institution as a student (they register with the school, pay student fees and are seated in the classroom in the student desks) but also through their mutual engagement in interaction in the community of practice. While students and teachers experienced with schooling bring an understanding of similar communities to a classroom, in order to interact with one another in a particular community of practice, members – students and teacher – must learn in what ways they can communicate and interact with one another through their particular and local mutual engagement in classroom practice.

Joint enterprise

The social contexts of adult language learning classrooms make them especially amenable to understanding them as communities of practice. While children in a classroom may develop a community of practice, it is not true that all young learners, who are by law in a classroom (Rogoff *et al.*, 2001), see their participation as a joint enterprise. On the other hand, while not all adult immigrants to the United States go to language learning classes of their own volition, most do attend voluntarily and have strong instrumental (if not integrative) motivations for participating (see Norton, 2003 for exceptions). These include participating more fully in society, communicating with their children's schools, employment, and work promotion (Hellermann & Brillanceau, 2007). Participants share a common goal of improving their abilities in English and for this reason, the learners see language learning in their language learning classes as a joint enterprise.

Shared repertoire

A third aspect of a community of practice is also particularly relevant for the language learning classroom. Wenger's notion of a shared repertoire is quite broad and includes 'routines, words, tools, ways of doing things, stories, gestures, symbols, genres, actions, or concepts' (Wenger, 1998: 83). And though these are all relevant activities to the adult language learning classroom, particularly transparent for understanding communication in the community of practice are the language practices that are used and develop as part of the shared repertoire of communication in the community of practice. The subject matter being 'language learning', there is a particularly strong reflexive relationship between language use and participation in the development of a shared repertoire of language for communication in the classroom community of practice: use of the shared repertoire facilitates participation while participation facilitates use of the shared repertoire. The development of a shared repertoire of practices in the language learning community of practice is given a high priority being the obvious goal of the language learning classroom.

As the analytic chapters will illustrate, there are different shared repertoires for participation in the different communities of practice that are distinguished by language proficiency. Looking at social practices in and around language learning task interaction, we will see that shared repertoire for language and communication differs in the community of practice for beginning level students (those in the level 'A' and level 'B' classes at the data collection site) and for intermediate level students (those in the level 'C' and level 'D' classes). The different shared repertoires for language and interaction facilitate slightly different communicative practices for language actions in the two communities of practice.

Reification and participation

These preceding three facets of a community of practice are not predefined in established, named communities of practice. Institutions, including schools, do not explicitly list these as rules for members of the institution. Rather, they are co-constructed through the negotiation of practices and meaning by members. The community of practice is an experience lived through practice, enacted in the tension of what is worked out through local practices and what is understood as static, stable institutional products: the dialectic between participation and reification (Wenger, 1998). A group with no shared history or common commitment to sustaining the group (lack of joint enterprise) toward the accomplishment of a goal will find it difficult to engage in the reification part of the dialectic. In the language learning classroom, there will be no commitment to standard texts for language learning or teacher knowledge and expertise. A group with a long shared history that is static and ritualistic and without impetus for change may lack the participatory aspect of the dialectic. A lack of change in participating habits may prevent important refining ideas from entering the community in such a scenario.

The student–student interaction in the adult language learning community of practice offers an ideal site for investigating this dialectic. The focus of the analysis in later chapters is student–student interaction (participation) in around teacher-assigned language learning tasks (reification). The reified aspect of the community of practice is represented in the curriculum of the school, the lesson plan of the teacher, and in the particular task designed to implement the curriculum and lesson plan. The curriculum, lesson plan and task are all designed with an abstract linguistic competency or skill in mind. When the task is presented to students and the students work out the task, in concert, we can see participation with talk-in-interaction and with the teacher-assigned task – the site of the dialectic.

Economies of meaning

Through students mutual orientation, their consideration of the community as a joint enterprise, and the development of a shared repertoire, the dialectic of participation and reification (re)constitutes a community of practice. A key aspect of this dialectic is the notion of 'economies of meaning' (Wenger, 1998), the idea that practices have meaning given by experts as well as novices who are asked to interpret practices. Participants in a community of practice have shared ownership in the meaning of concepts and practices used within that community of practice. In fact, the greater the degree to which meaning is shared within the community, the greater the potential for participation for all those members who share in that ownership. We can imagine this in the classroom when we think of how the meaning of a language routine ('how old are you'), phrase ('my book'), action type (dyadic task interaction) that is learned together and used together in the language classroom, something that becomes part of the language of that community of practice. The greater degree of shared ownership in these routines, the greater the potential for participation by members of the community. A more exclusive ownership of meaning of any one of these routines entails more work needing to be done between participants in the community to enable their performance.

In this respect, understanding meaning and the co-construction or negotiation of meaning within a community of practice as working within economies of meaning recalls ethnomethodology's understanding of members' methods for creating social order as a moral order (Garfinkel, 1967; Jayusi, 1984). We can say there are moral consequences for the degree to which economies of meaning work among participants in social interaction, including the classroom. In ethnomethodological terms, shared ownership of meaning is a moral imperative because to be a member of the language-culture is to work toward intersubjectivity – to negotiate and share meaning. In classroom interaction, without working toward intersubjectivity through shared ownership in meaning, participation and learning is impeded.

Learning in classrooms: Change in participation

The above key characteristics of a community of practice can also be seen as defining the socio-interactive nature of learning in adult language learning classrooms. The dialectic of participation and reification that Wenger (1998) discusses as the tension behind learning are present in all of these constructs. The dialectic is also a focal point for understanding an important feature of community of practice theory, that is, the change in participation by members of the community of practice which constitutes learning. A hallmark of community of practice's theory of learning is understanding learning as members' change in participation in activities within a community of practice over time. An approach to understanding learning as participation will focus on the visible, social and situated way that participants working together make meaning or learn and on how learners learn 'to participate in interactions in ways that succeed over a broad range of situations' (Greeno, 1997: 7).

Social approaches to learning within the field of SLA have been criticized for focusing on language use and not on learning or acquisition (Gass, 1998; Gregg, 1990; Gregg et al., 1997; Long, 1997). This critique starts from the consideration of competence in a language as an innate and implicit knowledge of language (Chomsky, 1986). While a predominant theory in SLA acknowledges that language use in interaction plays an important role in driving acquisition (Swain, 1995; Long, 1996), the study of language acquisition itself is still largely confined to the study of what implicit knowledge of language a learner possesses independent of context, use or social interaction (see Sfard, 1998 for a discussion on the 'acquisition' metaphor for learning).

The perspective of learning taken by community of practice theory, however, shows that some learning or acquisition is not available to individuals alone without a community of practice. This type of learning, therefore, cannot be understood or assessed as an isolated, individual achievement but rather as 'the construction of present versions of past experiences for several persons acting together' (Lave, 1993: 8). In community of practice theory, learning is understood as a dynamic, contextualized process of members' progression from a socio-cognitive identity as inexperienced outsider to that of more experienced or more fully competent member of a particular community. This is described by Lave and Wenger (1991) as the movement from 'legitimate peripheral' participation in the community of practice toward core participation.

A key aspect of this process is the acknowledgement that in a community of practice there are novice members and that a community of practice would not exist without these novices. This understanding of the membership characteristics of a community of practice lends the 'legitimate' status to members who are engaged on the periphery of activity within the community. The notion of competence is seen as an active participatory cohort characteristic, something which members together afford to one another through participation in practices of the community. In the best language learning classrooms, students must participate using the language that they are studying. Students can participate peripherally in the sense that they are observing rather than acting or are using a developmental, somewhat subjective communication system (their 'interlanguage') (Selinker, 1972). The degree to which this idiosyncratic system deviates from the target language of the classroom or of the system which their peers are using might be considered the degree to which a student's participation is peripheral. As students gain experience in the language learning classroom and the language system they use becomes less idiosyncratic and more 'anonymous' (Berger & Luckmann, 1967), they are becoming more core participants in the 'classroom' and 'English language speaker' communities of practice.

'Situated' learning

Such a social and local conception of learning is startling to many (Cole, 1996; Lave, 1993; van Lier, 2000) because of a conception of learning prominent throughout the latter half of the 20th century in cognitive psychology and linguistics that focused on the internal, individual mind-brain's processing and acquisition of some new knowledge that could be taken and used anywhere in any situation. This is known by many as the 'conduit' (Reddy, 1979), or, informational transfer model of learning. In contrast, the formulation of a community of practice by Lave and Wenger and others portrays learning as situated. However, it is 'situated' not in the sense that something learned in a particular context can only be relevant to that particular contextual constellation. This is the heart of the matter of the generalizability or transfer of knowledge and how cognitive and situated perspectives see learning (Anderson *et al.*, 1996; Greeno, 1997; Lave, 1988).

Though the name may imply that in a situated perspective on learning knowledge may not transfer from one context to another, this is not necessarily the case. A situated approach to learning looks for ways that learners improve in the way that they participate in processes or systems that are integrated across contexts (Greeno, 1997; Greeno *et al.*, 1993). Learning works within a community of practice because any community of practice, by definition, is not a discrete, closed entity. The practices and members of one community of practice overlap and are cross-connected with practices and members of other communities of practice. For example, many adult learners of English are members of a classroom community of practice as well as a workplace community of practice, the two communities of practice sharing some interactional and procedural contexts and practices. Considering the possibilities for cross-membership and for learning situations to share features across contexts, we can see how some facet of a particular situated practice can be part of another situated practice (Brown *et al.*, 1989).

This contextualized process perspective on learning considers knowledge (like language) as indexical (Brown *et al.*, 1989; van Lier, 2000; Wortham, 2001). Human language itself is highly indexical. Think of words like 'this' or 'you' and the relative paucity of meaning in these words alone without extra-linguistic contexts for their use.[4] Learning can also be thought of as a highly indexical process in which cognition is partially dependent on the connections to or prompting from interactional and contextual information: a particular concept, a 'denotational text' (Silverstein, 1993), is understood, in part, because at any one time it is part of an activity in which it can 'point to' that context for part of its meaning. While all knowledge is not a rootless, interactional process, knowledge is displayed and learning happens through the interaction on subjective conceptual knowledge. The understanding of the indexical nature of knowledge and learning highlights a reason to study language learning as situated activity and as a process of movement in degree of participation within a community of practice. Greater participation in the community of practice by a member of that community of practice suggests that more cross-contextual indexical connections have been established enabled by and enabling participation/learning.

A focus on the participatory, collaborative and interactive nature of learning may lead one to question the degree to which there is individual agency in learning and teaching. In a community of practice, agency in the community's activities is present but not considered as the foreground to other 'background' situational context. Knowledge production is part of a system for accomplishing action that involves mental, social, and physical processes (Goodwin, 1995, 1996). As such, we can consider learning as the site of continual connections or transformations between inner and external worlds (Bateson, 1972). Individuality is necessary for these connections in a thriving community of practice to exist; without the input of such individuality, a community of practice would become stasis bound.

In researching learning within a community of practice, individual agency in learning, therefore, cannot be separated from practice and participation as an object of study. Local participation is accomplished as part of a physical, local, sequential, and historical context of situation (Wortham, 2005). In classroom settings, agency in learning and teaching is present but is present within the context of a group of people sharing a common physical location, who have shared that location for a particular amount of time, who have come to that place with a common goal in mind, and who have (largely unconsciously) developed ways of interacting within their community of practice. The individual's knowledge and agency allows for the constitution of a community of practice yet the reflexive nature of the structure of the community of practice itself fosters and stimulates individual student agency. It would be a difficult task to try to decide where some kind of separate individual agency begins and ends in understanding learning.

From a situated or community of practice approach to classroom language learning, developing interactional competence is seen in individuals' change in participation at different levels of classroom discourse and interaction. At the level of social interaction, participants in adult immigrant language learning classrooms negotiate their comportment for various participation structures within the classroom (teacher–student, student–student). At the same time, they negotiate the meaning of aspects of the structure of the language code itself and its relationship to the task activity assigned by the teacher (the 'denotational text') (Silverstein, 1993). By investigating the processes of negotiation at each of these (and perhaps other) levels in similar discursive practices over time, it is possible to see how social interaction is part of learning and how change in participation can be evaluated as learning.

An important process through which we can see the negotiation of denotational and interactional texts, of reified and participatory language is through imitation as it occurs in peer–peer interaction. While imitation is an important aspect in Vygotskian sociocultural theory (Lantolf, 2000a), this aspect of learning resonates with more group and social perspectives. As in sociocultural theory, in the situated, community of practice approach to learning, we can see imitation not as mechanical mimicking, but rather, as a mediated use of language. In moments of peer–peer interaction, when a novice or peripheral participant is able to recycle (imitate) a peer's language, the imitator is being allowed to participate peripherally and legitimately. Observing mediated language use such as examples of imitation allows us to see microgenetic movements from peripheral to full participation in a community of practice.

Seeing 'Learning' in Traditional Classroom Settings

Critiques of learning in classrooms reflect a misunderstanding of the different possibilities for learning this context, a misunderstanding due to our limited vision of the classroom (both in the figurative and physical sense). This limited vision sees the classroom (for the most part) as teacher–student interaction without much consideration for interaction among students and between students and tasks during a class period (however, see earlier comments and studies on the importance of such interactions – Erickson, 1982, 1996; Fisher, 1993; Hellermann *et al.*, 2001; Ohta, 2001a). The understanding of learning as it occurs within a community of practice has developed in contexts outside the classroom. Observations about learning, for example, in online gaming communities of practice (Gee, 2003, 2005) suggest the importance of 'affinity spaces' as sites for learning. This discovery has relevance for adult ESOL classrooms and I would guess many other types of classrooms. Adult second language learning classrooms are similar to affinity spaces in that they present opportunities for each group member to learn at an individual pace through their participation within a heterogeneous group. Adult language learning classrooms can also be seen as 'portals' where 'students both interact with signs that constitute the context of the classroom instruction and are able to modify, transform, and add to them' (Gee, 2005: 230).

While, in the classroom, learning does not happen independently of a teacher as it might in an affinity space, in the classroom context that makes up the data for this study, it happens all because of, together with, and beyond the instruction given by the classroom teacher. Research focusing on the relationship between task assignment and learner language has shown how two pairs of learners engaging in the same teacher-assigned language learning task focus on different aspects of the task, aspects which meet their own capabilities at the time they perform the task (Coughlin & Duff, 1994; Foster, 1998; Harris, 2005; Kumaravadivelu, 1991; Willis, 1996).

This research presents empirical evidence for positive ways that traditional teacher-fronted classrooms can take advantage of the heterogeneity inherent in any grouping of students to allow independence of learning and peer mentoring through the engagement in face-to-face (student–student and student–teacher) interaction in the classroom. When a comprehensive view of classrooms is available for empirical study, we see opportunities for learning mediated by a student's peer, by the teacher in private conversation, or by texts available in the classroom. These are opportunities for learning in classroom interaction that occur in addition to the teacher-fronted classroom instruction. Longitudinal research has shown that learners with very different educational experiences in the same classroom become able to participate in the same literacy events in the classroom by utilizing different resources available in the classroom to mediate and individualize their learning (Hellermann, 2006).

The view of learning in a classroom community of practice in the following chapters highlights two particular boundary spaces ('openings' and 'disengagements') in classroom discourse where these 'portals' for the negotiation or co-construction of subject-matter instructional discourse are numerous. To illustrate, consider 'openings' to be illustrated in detail in Chapter 3. When adult learners of English accomplish teacher-assigned tasks in peer dyads, they need to negotiate the meaning of the instructions for the task and the language used in the task itself (Harris, 2005). But they also must negotiate the talk-in-interaction necessary to get that task underway (Hellermann, 2005b, 2007). This negotiation involves the transformation of subject-matter signs (English language) by local deictic cues to enact immediate orientations of the participants in the dyadic task interaction. In this way, a reified aspect of the community of practice, the English-language, teacher-assigned, language-learning task meets the local, situated, and individualized needs for learning of the student members of the community and it is here, at this micro level that change in participation can first be seen. Such language learning tasks, where student peers work together independently of the teacher, are seen as an important site for language learning because of its entire interactive process rather than its static design, or, 'workplan' (Breen, 1989; Coughlin & Duff, 1994; Seedhouse, 2005).

In their early formulations of community of practice theory, Lave and Wenger (1991) deliberately chose not to study classrooms because researchers and theorists tend to think too narrowly in terms of learning as something done formally, in places like classrooms. In contrast to their contexts for learning (work settings), in classrooms, there is an institutional and overt orientation by most if not all participants to learning as the main endeavor of the context. With this primary focus, learning is not intended to be incidental, a byproduct of the classroom as a community of practice. However, empirical research in formal classroom settings (Macbeth, 2000; Mondada & Pekarek Doehler, 2004) has shown that what an instructor intends to be learned is, indeed must be (Garfinkel, 1967, 2002), interpreted differently by different students in the same or different contexts.

The classroom community of practice beyond the dyad

For practitioners and researcher-practitioners interested in how CA studies of the classroom might lead to better teaching and learning, the micro-level analyses in the next chapters present new ways to see language learning as the enactment and formation of communities of practice through talk that occurs as social interaction in their classrooms. The local practices that learners use for opening interactions, engaging in extended tellings, and doing disengagements from interactions will be shown to be sites for the microgenesis of language learning by individual students. This will be shown in the way practices are negotiated and local adjustments to interactions are made. As each of these dyadic interactions happens, it occurs simultaneously within the larger classroom context, with as many as twenty other students. The simultaneous nature of the multiple dyadic interactions allows for a connection between a student dyad and the classroom cohort, between dyadic microgenetic change and cohort socio-genetic (Sfard, 2005) (re)establishment of procedures for talk in a language learning classroom – the classroom community of practice.

Figure 1.1 may help to illustrate that connection. In the figure, the letters represent student dyads engaging in teacher-assigned dyadic language learning tasks. As student dyads engage in those tasks, they use resources including language provided by the teacher, language provided by texts, their own and their partners' understanding of the language co-constructed in their dyad. The dotted lines represent the less fore-grounded interactions that occur across student dyads. This interaction occurs through talk, but more often through one dyad's observation and overhearing of their peers' practices that are going on all around them.

Student dyads working within the classroom cohort develop methods for starting, ending and extended tellings within their teacher-assigned dyadic tasks. The next day, or later in the class, students may not be working with the same peer but bring some shared understanding of how to perform these social interactions to their next interaction. So, while E's participation in language tasks may be being shaped most intensively by the current dyadic interaction with F, E's participation is also being shaped

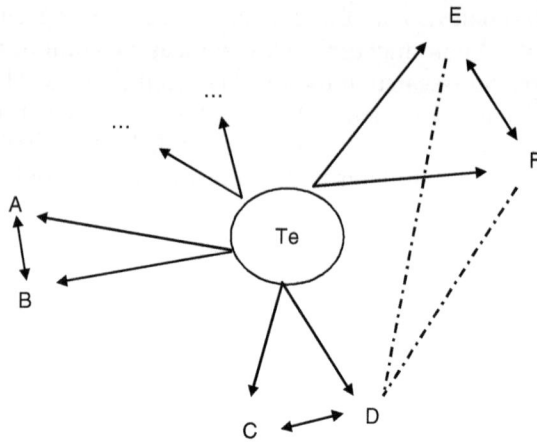

Figure 1.1 Dyadic task interaction in the classroom community of practice

by C and D who are observed doing their task and by past interactions with any and all the students in the class and by the fact that F has also observed C and D doing their task.

Excerpt (1.1) is a concrete example of how this cross-dyadic interaction can work. There, we see the end of a student dyad task interaction, a disengagement sequence in which there is an exchange of closing discourse markers (lines 1–2), Javier offers an appreciation (line 4) and Hui Ying offers the appropriate response (line 5). Afterward, Javier looks to the dyad working at the desk behind him and sees Paula working with Ling. After observing them, he shifts his posture to face the front of the room again as Paula and Ling continue with the task. Some twenty seconds later, Paula taps Javier on the back (line 16) and gives him one of the task directives ('stand up' and in line 19, 'sit down') to model the task for Ling who is having difficulty understanding the task. Javier models each of the directives and then remains at his desk, looking to his right to other students in the class.

(1.1)
9-23-02, 206, A, [46:10-] Javier and Hui Ying
http://www.labschool.pdx.edu/Viewer/viewer.php?pl=JKHCP&cl=1.1
```
1    HY:  okay? eu ⌈h
2    J:              ⌊okay.=
3    HY:  euh hih hih ⌈hih .hhh
4    J:                ⌊thank you
```

```
5    HY: ↑y'elcome.
6    J:  ((looks to table behind him where Paula and Ling are
7        working on the task))
8    J:  ((shifts posture to front of room, folds hands and
9        looks to the right))
10       (10)
11   HY: (    ) ((speaking to herself))
12   P:  stand up
13       (2)
14   P:  <sit do:wn>
15       (4)
16   P:  ((touches J)) please stand up teacher?
17   J:  ((stands))
18   P:  ((looks to Ling))
19   P:  ((looks back to J)) sit down
20       (4)
21   P:  stand up. (.) stand up. (.) ss : tand up. (1) ss : tand up
22       (.) ((stands up))
23       (14)
24   J:  ((shifts posture to face FY who is looking in her
25       bag))
26       (10)
27   HY: ((changes glasses))
28   Te: good. good.
29       (4)
30   Te: stretch
31       (6)
32   J:  (  buena)
33       (2)
34   J:  ((leans toward FY)) excuse me=↑where is you from,
35       (.)
36   J:  where is you from ((pointing at FY))
37   HY: (what is questi⌈on)
38   J:             ⌊where is you from. ((points at FY))
39   HY: FROM >ah ah< from eh Ch- China = Sshanghai ((points to
40       self))
41   J:  Chinese? =
42   HY: yraeh Chinese Shanghai.
43   J:  Shanghay?
44   HY: Shangh<u>ai</u>.
45   J:  Shanghay?
```

46   **HY:**   yeah
47   **J:**   your name?

Javier's interaction with Paula shows learners' ability to 'overhear' (Ohta, 2001a) and orient to their peers situated at other desks in the classroom. In doing so, students can use one another, even in more 'remote' locations, as resources for learning. After seeing the teacher continue to work with a student and commenting on that (line 32), Javier leans over to Hui Ying about her country of origin (line 34).

After disengaging from their task interaction, Javier observes several other classmates and acts as a model for one task interaction occurring just behind him. When he sees that other students continue to be engaged talking in their task interaction, he takes the opportunity, using the time to use English with his deskmate, starting a series of personal questions in line 34.

Students' private speech

An important area of language use in classroom communities of practice that I cannot address in this study but should be mentioned is students' use of spoken language that is not addressed to anyone other than self. Intrapersonal, private speech has been addressed extensively in other research (Lantolf & Yanez, 2003; Ohta, 2000, 2001a) which shows it to be a strategy used by language learners to internalize language from the teacher and an important aspect of the peripheral, but legitimate participation in the language classroom.

Data Collection Context

The data for this research come from a five-year federally funded research project investigating language learning by adult immigrant learners of English in a community college ESOL classroom setting.[5] The adult learners who were part of the study were those who registered for classes (of their own volition) at one site of the community college and paid the community college's nominal registration fee (approximately $50 for a ten-week term). The learners (almost 800 participated in classes during the data collection at the data collection site) ranged in age from 18 to 84 years of age and came from 44 countries speaking 28 different languages. This particular site for the community college classes was a lab school setting in which student full-class and dyadic interactions were recorded in two classrooms designed to collect high quality video and audio data (Reder *et al.*, 2003). Each classroom had six cameras mounted on the ceiling. Every class period, two students and the teacher wore wireless microphones and there were two microphones in the ceiling to capture audio from the entire classroom. Two of the cameras in each classroom focused on the two learner dyads with the wireless microphones. The entire corpus of learner interaction consists of almost 4000 hours of video recordings.

The research reported on in this volume focused on the interactions of learners who participated in classes at the data collection site for five or more terms. After observing data from this subset of the corpus in which the learners and their peer interlocutors were engaged in work on teacher-assigned language learning tasks, it was notable that they were in a particular social context (face-to-face interaction) that necessitated talk-in-interaction between members of the dyad beyond what was assigned by the teacher in any particular language learning task. While these adults were novice users of the English language, they were also adults socialized to interact with others and were seen to be engaging in practices for social organization through language that have been noted in research on everyday conversational interaction between non-learners. I was curious how such conversational social practices might make up foundational practices for engagement in classroom communities of practice and paid attention to (among others) the three social actions outlined in this book: the starts or openings of students' dyadic task interactions, non-elicited story tellings that occurred within language learning tasks, and the endings or disengagements from dyad task interactions.

Interactions in which students were the focus of two of the six cameras in each classroom. The recordings from these camera views were wearing (or seated next to a student wearing) a microphone were observed and transcriptions of the focal practices were made. Approximately 750 minutes of the dyadic interaction of students in four proficiency levels[6] was observed and the phenomena of focus were transcribed. Approximately half of the minutes were from interactions in 'beginning' classroom communities of practice (level 'A' and 'B' classes) and half from interactions in 'intermediate' communities of practice (levels 'C' and 'D' classes). Collections were made of examples of each of these phenomena. The transcribed interactions were then analyzed, focusing on describing the particular ways that the participants co-constructed social order through their talk to achieve a 'beginning', an 'ending' or a 'telling' through sequences of turns at talk. The longitudinal nature of the data allowed me to then look at the same contexts for these social phenomena in consecutive weeks, months, and terms to describe change in the ways that the phenomena were performed within the different classroom communities of practice. The detailed analyses of the sequential order of talk-in-interaction in the classroom follow the precepts of ethnomethodological conversation analysis (Clayman & Maynard, 1995; Goodwin & Heritage, 1990; Hutchby & Wooffitt, 1998; Maynard & Clayman, 2003; Sacks *et al.*, 1974) seeking to

Figure 1.2 Student dyads seated at small tables facing the front of the classroom

uncover participants' orientations to order making in their interaction by focusing on the sequential nature of the learner dyads' talk-in-interaction in their practices for the focal actions.

Like many community college programs for immigrant learners of English in the U.S., these classes were 'all skills' classes meaning that teachers incorporated the study of grammar, reading, writing, speaking and listening into their curricula. The classes met for three hours twice a week. The teachers were experienced practitioners with Masters' degrees in language teaching pedagogy and mixed full class presentation and with small group and pair work activity. To facilitate this pair work, the classrooms at the data collection site were set up so that pairs of students sat side by side at small tables and (during teacher-fronted activities) faced the front of the room where the teacher usually is situated. This is illustrated in Figure 1.2.

Technologies for seeing learning in the classroom community of practice: Video recordings, peer dyadic interaction and conversation analysis

There is a dearth of empirical investigation of classrooms with the goal of understanding change in participation in social practices for language in social interaction as it occurs in a community of practice. Technologically-advanced data collection and processing at the National Labsite has opened up new possibilities for this kind of research. The cameras embedded in the ceiling included four stationary cameras in the corners of the rooms and two mobile cameras at the sides of the classrooms which followed the interactions of two student dyads in each classroom (one of the student in the dyad wore a wireless microphone). The mobile cameras also periodically zoomed in on students' writing and the teacher's writing on the board. Associated written materials from the classes were also collected and stored in a database. Data on 180 self-selecting students including in-home, bilingual interviews were also collected (Hellermann & Brillanceau, 2007).

Software designed specifically for the data (Class Action © Portland State University) allows for viewing transcription and codes together with the six views of the classroom video simultaneously. This allows the researcher as complete a picture of the classroom environment as possible using video recording. The recording and analysis technology have given researchers a comprehensive view of classroom practices and an unprecedented opportunity to observe, in detail, a number of different individual students, student cohorts and entire classrooms through repeated viewings.[7] The ability to see and hear students working in pairs and small groups without the interference of a camera in the room, the teacher or other classroom observer has allowed researchers a new ability to focus research on student learning rather than on teachers' teaching.

The object of study: Social actions through talk in dyadic classroom task interaction

Previous classroom research on language learning has tended to focus on teacher–student interaction because, in part, of the limits of recording technology. The design for data collection facilitated research which focused on learners interacting with one another. The video recordings of learner–learner dyadic interaction has proven to be invaluable to understand meaning making by beginning learners and has suggested the reconsideration of what might be the object of study for research on language learning (Eskildsen & Wagner, 2007), classroom language learning in particular.

By focusing recording on learner–learner interaction, we have been able to see the development of language-learning tasks as they occur in face-to-face interaction between student dyads without the explicit intervention of a teacher. While we have an intuitive understanding of this and some research has shown evidence for the phenomenon (Ford, 1999), early observations of the data showed us how remarkably teachers change the interactional trajectory of a learner-learner dyadic interaction (Garland, 2002). The teachers at the data collection site who were part of the research team were also influenced by this finding and in their subsequent teaching, tried not intervene in student dyadic interaction to the degree they had previously. This allowed for interactional reconfigurations of the dyadic tasks (Mondada & Pekarek Doehler, 2004) as they occurred, without teacher intervention, more organically as a face-to-face interaction between two adults.

This reconfiguration is seen in the way that students co-construct social actions that are made available by students' physical co-presence and common goal orientation to a task. Sites in the interaction that are the boundaries in the shift in participation structure from teacher-cohort to student–student interaction are places where students are engaged in social interaction leading into and out of task-focused interaction. During task-focused interactions, there are also mechanisms for social action through talk that occur in everyday conversational interaction that learners use for social/task interaction (repair, story telling).

Recurring actions through talk, actions that appear in contexts outside the classroom as well as in the classroom, provide a new object of study in additional language learning research. In research on cognitive development in children in schools, because of contextual influences on tasks assigned to elicit particular data, Cole *et al.* (1978) found it necessary to try to define pan-contextual 'linguistic formalisms' (Cole, 1996: 241) to assess that development. Similarly, the research outlined here (and elsewhere: Hellermann, 2007, forthcoming; Wootton, 1997, 2005) has used conversation analytic techniques to uncover and focus on recurring actions that are not task-dependent and the language practices used to accomplish those actions in student dyadic task interaction. Such sites are important for the investigation of language learning as these actions (openings, story tellings and disengagements) are not problems to solve which were given by the instructor. From the perspective of experiential learning (Dewey, 1938), these are sites in which the participants themselves must identify or orient to the problem (starting a task, explicating something within the task, ending the task) and then, through localizing, personalizing and contextualizing their interactions, resolve each issue with language practices.

Research in the field of second language acquisition has suggested the importance of dyadic interaction between language learners with native-speaking experts and with learner peers as facilitative of language acquisition by making language input comprehensible through negotiation (Gass & Varonis, 1985; Krashen, 1977; Long, 1983; Pica *et al.*, 1987; Swain, 1985; and many others). This negotiation of meaning is seen being accomplished in classroom interaction through language-learning 'tasks' (Ellis, 2000, 2003; Skehan, 2003) which also often involve pairs or small groups of students. Given the important role that classroom dyadic and small-group interaction has been shown to play in language learning, the full range contexts and strategies for talk and interaction that occurs in language-learning tasks needs to be investigated to understand the full range of interactional opportunities that are afforded to language learners (Kasper, 2004; van Lier, 2000, 2002; van Lier & Matsuo, 2000).

Ethnomethodological, microethnographic and conversation analytic research has shown how sequences of talk which are usually not the subject of study for classroom discourse researchers, 'side talk' or 'off task talk' are inseparable from what might be considered classroom 'instructional talk' proper (Erickson, 1982; Heap, 1985; Macbeth, 2003; Mehan, 1979; Mori, 2002). These approaches to the study of classroom discourse see the investigation of the contextualization of the talk of the classroom, the meta-talk, talk about learning (Bateson, 1972), as a necessary part of understanding talk, interaction and learning in the classroom. Teachers give explicit instructions for a language-learning task that is designed to engage pairs of learners with the language to be learned and which focuses on particular language forms or target vocabulary. While the explicit pedagogical focus of some tasks may be on pragmatics or phatic communication, the foci of language-learning tasks are not on the mechanics of social interaction inherent in all dyadic or small group interaction. The interactional work of moving from one speech exchange system or participation structure to another is taken for granted as something students can do. Yet this work (shifting from teacher–class cohort interaction to student–student interaction, for example) is a second implied task that students must complete.

I am not sure whether it would be wise to suggest that teachers attempt to explicitly teach students how to make these shifts, or that they could. However, teachers, like researchers, should be aware of this valuable aspect of learner–learner engagement in the language learning classroom. Even in highly-controlled, highly-scripted teacher-assigned language learning tasks, at the start and at the end of these tasks, the learners must negotiate a social interaction with and around their language-learning task performance (Mori, 2002). In doing so, they have the opportunity to creatively co-construct talk for social interaction in a new language, an opportunity which is, for the most part, unmediated by teacher-provided language support.

An Analytic Tool for Understanding Negotiating Meaning and Practice: Conversation Analysis

As discussed previously in this chapter, a community of practice theory of classroom language learning provides a framework for understanding learning processes as well as outcomes. Understanding the process aspect of language learning within a community of practice necessitates methods for the analysis of language and social interaction as learner members participate to different degrees in the work of the classroom community of practice – language learning.

Creese (2005) recently raised the issue of a lack of empirical illustration for the negotiation of meaning within community of practice theory. That critique suggested that more details of language use be given in future studies which use community of practice theory in order to better understand how negotiation of meaning is accomplished in the dialectic between participation and reification. As the next chapter explains, conversation analysis offers a well-developed method for highlighting members' methods for co-constructing social action in the classroom community of practice through language. The ethnomethodological roots of conversation analysis (hereafter, CA) make it consistent with the situated perspective of community of practice learning focusing on uncovering members' co-construction of intersubjectivity through language. As the discussion in Chapter 2 will show, CA's focus on micro-level details of language and sequences of talk-in-interaction in the language learning classroom highlight the individual's microgenesis of language development and can also describe the sociogenesis (Sfard, 2005) of language practices for the entire classroom community of practice.

Conclusion

Since the dissemination of the theoretical principles in community of practice in Lave and Wenger (1991) and Wenger (1998) there have been calls to continue the empirical investigations of learning in practice that use community of practice theory (Barton & Tusting, 2005; Chaiklin, 1993). In the adult language learning classroom, through the use of video recording technology made available by the National Labsite for Adult ESOL, empirical evidence of the process of learning in practice is made visible. The actions available for investigating and practices which accomplish them are made visible by the recording technology are sites for learning not usually viewed as such in research on language learning. They are important sites, however, for the establishment and maintenance of the classroom community of practice. The focus of the recording technology on student interaction, mostly student–student interaction allows the observation of micro-level practices that accomplish the work of establishing intersubjectivity (Garfinkel, 1967; Schegloff, 1992) – the foundational activity for the establishment of understanding between and among humans in social interaction. This understanding of intersubjectivity as socially motivated allows for conversation analysis to be used as a methodology for uncovering the practices in the community of practice that enable change in participation – learning – among its members.

Chapter 2
Conversation Analysis as a Method for Understanding Language Learning

Ethnomethodological Conversation Analysis: An Introduction

The term 'ethnomethodological conversation analysis'[8] is used to refer to a particular theory and method for the analysis of everyday talk that was developed in the mid-1960s by sociologist Harvey Sacks and colleagues. This methods was developed to uncover what was assumed to be the unobservable ways that people make order in their social interactions through talk. Sacks (1992, 1: 28) posited that through careful observation of the language of an interaction that this hidden order could be uncovered and a principled method to analyze these observations could be developed.

As the name suggests, Sacks' ideas were influenced by work in ethnographic sociology (Mead, 1934) and ethnomethodology (Garfinkel, 1967, 2002), an area of sociology which focuses on the methods which 'members' of some culture have for making sense and order out of the mundane, everyday social interactions in which they partake. From an ethnomethodological perspective, mundane activities within a culture (crossing the street, ending a telephone conversation) are seen as locally co-constructed achievements accomplished by the use of common sense 'methods' which are available as part of one's membership in a culture. Researchers working within an ethnomethodological framework are interested in 'the structures that constitute the activity of interest' (Heap, 1985: 267), these structures being particular turns and sequences of turns at talk.

CA has also been influenced by Goffman's (1959, 1961, 1963, 1967, 1971, 1981, 1983) dramaturgical model for understanding face-to-face interaction. Goffman also saw the importance of investigations looking at mundane, micro-level details of human interaction to understand human behavior through its public displays and others' responses to those displays. His ethnographic observations (his method did not make use of electronic recordings) focused on the way that people display different identities in public situations and how those displays are influenced, to a great degree, by the way that person orients to others' perceptions of them.

From these perspectives, the organization for social interactions of two or more people is seen not simply as a scripted role for each person but as a local accomplishment. Ethnomethodology suggests that there is a moral dimension to such organization in that members hold one another accountable for working together to create local intersubjectivity and for maintaining culturally-recognized order (Garfinkel, 1967; Jayusi, 1984). This does not mean that every interaction comes off without disagreement. Norms of engagement can be flouted or broken (Garfinkel, 1967; Grice, 1975), but the orientation to orderly interaction is shown by participants in interactions where some norm has been flouted. In such situations, we see participants try to make sense of the situation as 'normal'. When norms for engagement are egregiously broken, the break is noted and the disrupter of the norms is held accountable.

With this understanding of social order re-enacted and locally adjusted, as a method for understanding social order as it occurs through talk-in-interaction,[9] CA resists the *a priori* attribution of characteristic interactional patterns to members of particular social categories. The categorization of people and events into commonly defined social scientific categories such as gender, race, ethnicity and social class is made only when those categories are oriented to by the participants in a talk-in-interaction. Talk in social interaction is seen as culturally established but locally-preformed social organization worthy of study as much as the large-scale social categories just mentioned. CA seeks to uncover members' or participants' own interpretations of the language and behavior in their interactions that is relevant to making social order in that interaction. Since its inception,[10] a rigorous methodology for doing CA involving recording, transcribing and detailed transcription conventions has developed and been codified (Hutchby & Woofitt, 1998; Schegloff, 2007a; Seedhouse, 2004; ten Have, 1999).

A glance at the transcription of an everyday conversation can make the language used in social interaction between people seem to be quite disorderly. However, through extensive research in the past 30 years, CA studies of everyday, mundane conversation have shown that such language is orderly and worthy of investigation for the insights it gives on social beings negotiating this order, the constitutive 'rules' (Searle, 2002) of talk to make sense of the world. This negotiation or co-construction of the understanding of an unfolding conversation happens continuously in human interaction as people strive to interpret one another's subjective understandings of the world and their interaction. Participants who, together, work out this 'intersubjectivity' are co-constructing social order or processing thought in the mutually shared space of a common language-culture which is a foundation of social interaction. By focusing on participants' orientation to such rules for human interaction as it is done through language, language learning researchers see a method like CA as an exciting possibility for exploring language learning (Brouwer & Wagner, 2004; Huth, 2006; Kasper, 2004; Markee, 2000). The co-constructed language in interaction between language learners in their community of practice is an arena for distributed cognition, for gaining competency in another language and culture, and through this competency for displaying language learning.

One fundamental tenet of CA is that the analysis of talk-in-interaction needs to describe, in meticulous detail, often overlooked aspects of talk and bodily comportment of participants in the talk of participants. To accomplish these descriptions, detailed transcriptions of recordings of talk between participants in an interaction are made using a set of transcription conventions developed first by Gail Jefferson and standardized over the course of 30 years of use by scholars in the field. The detailed transcriptions focus on the sound production, timing and sequential nature of talk-in-interaction and include notations such as the locations of overlapping talk, final phrase intonation, stress, voice quality, tempo and inter- and intra-speaker timed pauses. As an example, some of these details are highlighted in an excerpt (2.1) of a transcription of an interaction between two students in a beginning level adult English language classroom.

(2.1)[11]

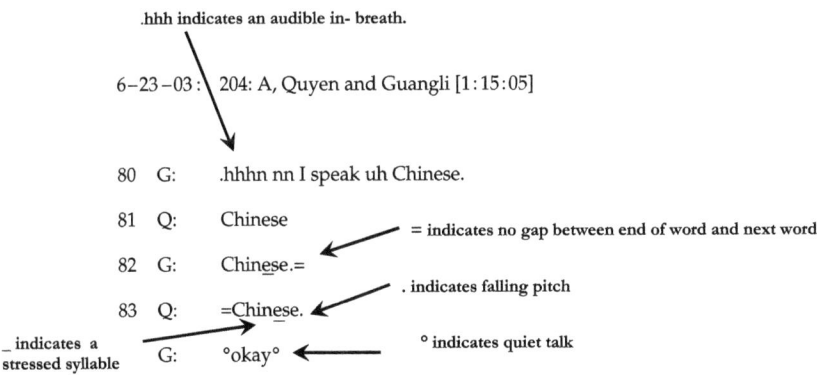

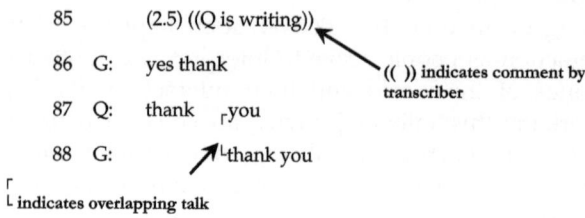

```
         85          (2.5) ((Q is writing))
         86   G:    yes thank
         87   Q:    thank ⌈you
         88   G:         ⌊thank you
⌈
⌊ indicates overlapping talk
```

The detail of the talk exemplified in (2.1) is important for analysts to understand the primary question motivating CA research: 'Why that now?' That is, why are particular forms of language used in an interaction and what type of action are these forms of talk implementing? By focusing on such details, CA tries to uncover the interactional trajectories which emerge from a sequence of turns at talk. The minute details of the timing and relationships of a particular phenomenon of language are relevant to participants as they construct the turns and sequences of turns. Their relevance for participants means they are relevant for researchers as well. Research in CA has shown evidence that often overlooked phenomena in everyday language such as syntactic structure (Ford & Fox, 1996; Ford et al., 2002), laughter (Glenn, 2003; Jefferson, 2004), simultaneous talk (French & Local, 1983; Jefferson, 1973;), pitch (Couper-Kuhlen, 1992, 2001; Ford et al., 2004), gaze and gesture (Goodwin, 1979, 1981; Heath, 1984; Koschmann & LeBaron, 2002; Mori & Hayashi, 2006) are used and oriented to by participants as resources for organizing their talk-in-interaction.

The focus on minute details in the language of the interaction supports a second methodological underpinning of CA methods. Conversation analysts attempt to find evidence for analytical claims made about an interaction in the data themselves by uncovering the orientation of the participants (their interpretations) to the particular instance of talk-in-interaction under study without relying on predefined analytic constructs for interpretation. The methods for basing analytic claims on participants' interpretations, interpretations not elicited by a researcher but uncovered in the language itself, gives CA a unique emic perspective to social scientific research in general, and research on classroom language learning in particular (Kasper, 2004, 2006; Seedhouse, 2005).

Another aspect which makes CA unique from other data-driven qualitative research methods is that it does not rely on researcher-elicited data such as retrospective interviews or other reconstructive interpretive methods for gaining participants' understandings and interpretations of their interactions. Instead, a researcher using CA makes repeated observations of recorded (audio or video) interactions, transcribes the interactions in rigorous detail, and focuses the analysis on uncovering the turn-by-turn sequence of action. The focus on the sequences of turns reveals participants' own orientations and accounts of meaning making in the interaction. The ethnomethodological influences during its development have influenced CA methods to focus analysts' attention on members' methods for ordering their interaction. Such 'methods' are the common-sense ways that ordinary people ('members' of the particular language/culture) in ordinary interactions use to make sense of the micro-actions performed in their talk. Many of the practices uncovered by CA research can be thought of as practices which occur across contexts but which are performed in context-sensitive ways (Sacks *et al.*, 1974). The context-independent practices are the recurring and often minute and mundane facets of interaction that are done in and through talk: turn taking or correcting slight troubles in the stream of a conversation, what is known in CA as 'repair' (Schegloff *et al.*, 1977). These micro-level, inter- or intra-turn organizational practices which, after almost 40 years of empirical analysis, have been shown to be regularly occurring organizational practices in a number of different language-cultures have been characterized as 'molecular sociology' (Lynch, 1993) – the organization of social structure at a very small but very pervasive level.

The close attention to the sequence of utterances in an interaction allows CA to show the reflexive relationship between language and language use. The language of each turn at talk informs and contextualizes the unfolding talk in interaction. Sacks (1992) and other researchers after Wittgenstein (1958) discussed how seemingly 'standard' words, phrases and stretches of talk can be used for different purposes by a speaker in different situations, and by paying careful attention to the sequence of the talk-in-interaction, an analyst can see the implications of current speaker's talk by what happens next in the upcoming slots of the talk-in-interaction. The 'next turn proof procedure' is a shorthand term for one method CA has for uncovering this local contextualization of utterances and indicates that a turn at talk is made conditionally-relevant (Schegloff, 1968) by the talk which preceded it. CA research has posited that the basic talk mechanism for conversational interaction is the adjacency pair (Schegloff, 1968). An adjacency pair consists of two turns at talk, a first pair part (an initiating or eliciting action) after which a second pair part is relevant. For example, a common adjacency pair is question-answer. The first pair part question makes an answer conditionally relevant as a second pair part.

The interactive import or local meaning of an utterance can be uncovered in how a participant responds in a next turn to that utterance. For example, as illustrated in excerpt (2.2), the greeting by S in line 3 of a telephone conversation makes a return greeting by M conditionally relevant in the next turn and in line 4, M returns the greeting.

(2.2[12])

[Crow: Mother & Son 2001]

1		((telephone rings))	1 summons
2	M:	Hello	2 response

3	S:	Hey Ma	3 greeting
4	M:	Hey! How ya doin	4 greeting + inquiry

If the conditionally relevant greeting is not made in the second turn slot (line 4), the first speaker shows the conditional relevance of the second position greeting by repeating the first greeting. Excerpt (2.3) from an interaction between English language learners in a classroom shows how a summons, when not followed by a response, is repeated and oriented to as 'missing' a response.

(2.3)
    10-17-02, 204, A [57:14-57:34], Inez and Jorge
    http://www.labschool.pdx.edu/Viewer/viewer.php?pl=JKHCP&cl=2.3

```
1   J:   ((comes to Inez's desk)) Inez. (     )
2        (3.5)
3   J:   Inez.
4   I:   OH I'm sorry. heh hah hah (.) °heh heh heh°
5        (2)
6   J:   do you live in the northwest?
7   A:   no (.) no I don't. no I don't.
```

In (2.3), Jorge and Inez are about to start a classroom language learning task. Jorge has come over to a desk where Inez is sitting and makes a summons followed by some talk that was not recoverable (line 1). After a pause, Jorge orients to a response turn following his summons as 'missing' and makes a second summons in line 3. Inez follows the second summons with a news token, apology, and laughter indicating she also recognizes being accountable for the 'missing' second turn response in line 2.

Excerpts (2.2) and (2.3) are intended to illustrate the next turn proof procedure showing how a focus on the sequence of talk in the interaction, including a description of gaps between turns, allows the analyst to uncover and rely on the participants' own at-that-moment interpretations of the meaning of the talk for action in their interactions. They also show the localized contextualization of language. In each case, the participants do not rely on 'context' from outside the interaction for its interpretation. The mechanisms behind CAs 'next turn proof procedure' have been described in pragmatics as utterances being made based on presuppositions. The production of an utterance then makes certain interpretations or entailments possible (Silverstein, 1993). In (2.3), we see that the summons offered by Jorge in (3) is not taken up as a summons by Inez but when the second summons if offered, it shows Jorge interprets a response to his first summons to be missing. Inez also orients to that summons as a second summons. From this perspective, linguistic actions are best characterized as 'greeting', 'question', 'promise', 'summons' and the like when there is evidence in the language of the participants which shows they are making that characterization.

CA has been criticized for this radically local perspective on context (Billig, 1999; Rampton *et al.*, 2002; Wetherell, 1998). Interpretive social scientists encountering CA for the first time may wonder why more 'contextual' information about the participants being studied is not collected and, therefore, not reported. CA research does not claim to be using every insight from a full range of possible contextual resources and does not suggest that a researcher should be purposefully ignorant of the wider contextual understanding of an interaction (Hester & Eglin, 1997; Moerman, 1988). However, CA tries to take advantage of readily available and often overlooked locally-provided contextual cues. The method problemitizes the dichotomy within linguistics and discourse analysis between text and context highlighting the micro-level reflexive and (re)-contextualizing nature of language in interaction (McDermott, 1993).

On a larger scale, while the personal histories of participants may be insightful or may play a role in the organization of an interaction, CA researchers believe that having access to a 'full range' of contextualized resources informing particular data one is analyzing is an idealization (Schegloff, 1987a) a researcher cannot hope to achieve. What would be required for inclusion in such a 'full range' of context to absolutely interpret a face-to-face interaction can never be accessible to a researcher. Instead, CA methods try to analyze a narrower, more manageable range of contexts as completely as possible. That leads to the focus on details in language in interaction, minute details that are available, relevant to, and interpreted locally by participants in interaction.

While interpretive, critical discourse analysis may start analyses with predefined social and institutional categories like 'male' or 'teacher' which may be relevant for the interpretation of a particular turn at talk, those categories also may not be relevant to the way that a sequence of talk is performed and interpreted locally (Brown & McNamara, 2004; Schegloff, 1987b).[13] The position of CA is that participants themselves display the degree to which such contextual features of language and interaction are relevant to their interaction. In response to advocates of including wider spectrum of context in an analyses of talk-in-interaction, CA researchers have suggested that after such a thorough analysis of the talk itself and the contextualization of the interaction by that talk has been made, other outside context related to the participants and situation can be examined to answer related but slightly different questions (Seedhouse, 2004, 2005; Silverman, 1999).

Conversation Analysis, Language Learning and Membership

To recap: Research from an ethnomethological CA perspective emphasizes the local co-construction of order and sense making through talk in social interaction. Our understanding of this order-making process is uncovered through the detailed analyses of the sequences of turns at talk. Through such detailed analyses, researchers attempt to show how the participants in the interaction orient to or interpret, moment-by-moment, the meaning of talk in social interaction. Through the examination of large databases of audio or video recordings and collections of similar action types, this method looks for recurring ways that these actions are accomplished through participants' co-constructed language practices.

Since its inception, CA research has uncovered orderly practices, recurring pan-contextual methods that participants use to accomplish social action in mundane interaction such as opening and closing conversations, telling stories and doing repair. More recently, research from a CA perspective has begun to uncover interesting findings on the similar and different methods used by language learners in interaction with first-language speakers (Brouwer & Wagner, 2004; Hosoda, 2001; Kasper, 2004; Wong, 2000). While CA research has focused on understanding the 'context-sensitive' methods involved in co-constructing classroom interaction in general (Ford, 1999; Hellermann, 2005a; Koole, 2003; Lee, 2004; Lerner, 1995; Macbeth, 1990, 1994, 2000, 2004; McHoul, 1978; Mehan, 1979) recent research using CA has started to explore how interaction in the language classroom and how language teaching and learning is accomplished

(He, 2004; Hellermann, 2005b, 2006, 2007; Markee, 2000, 2005; Mori, 2002, 2004; Seedhouse, 1997, 1999, 2004). Mori raised the interesting tension (already some years ago – 2002) between the use of a method designed for 'unmotivated looking' for research on institutional settings, settings in which stakeholders ask for some ameliorative suggestions for their institutional practice – an application of the research findings (Richards & Seedhouse, 2005). For CA, it has been enough to uncover and describe members' practices for social interaction. However, language teachers whose classrooms are studied (and researchers who are teachers themselves) wonder how CA findings can help them teach and help their students learn.

The use of CA methods for understanding learning in general and language learning specifically has been a subject of interest at recent conferences and in thematically-organized journals issues (Markee & Kasper, 2004; *Modern Language Journal*, forthcoming). In one of these issues, calls were made by both Hall (2004) and Larsen-Freeman (2004) for CA researchers to address learning if they choose to work with data from language learners' interactions. Kasper (2006) suggested researchers using CA might follow Mori's advice by engaging in unmotivated observation and analyses of classroom and other learning contexts and then look for connections between the CA outcomes and other research in applied linguistics that addresses language learning. Kasper also suggested that practitioners of CA might use resonant socio-cultural and socio-linguistic theory such as language socialization or situated learning to help create coherence for a research program of CA studies of language learning. Markee, on the other hand, suggests that CA may, in the future, want to ground its studies in a theory of learning, but only after more preliminary descriptive work is done (Markee, 2005).

While some CA practitioners are wary of the use of the term 'learning' with respect to CA practices because of it's roots in psychology (Koschmann *et al.*, 2005), conversation analytic studies have, however, if indirectly, made the notions of 'competence' and 'learning' part of their focus in the way they look for how the moment-by-moment orientations and adjustments which are the competences (Heritage, 1984a; Nguyen, 2006) that participants in talk-in-interaction (including language learners I will argue) must display to one another in order to engage in talk-in-interaction (Forrester & Reason, 2006; Jacoby & McNamara, 1999; Markee, 2005; Schegloff, 1991; Seedhouse, 2004; Wootton, 1997). Recent studies have taken this consideration of members' competence further in considering language learners' competence within a community of practice focusing on interactive practices for learning and the development of these practices both within a particular interaction (microgenetic) and across longer periods of time (longitudinal) (Brouwer & Wagner, 2004; Kasper, 2004; Markee, 2004; Mondada & Pekarek Doehler, 2004; Young & Miller, 2004). Many of these studies have used conversation analysis to understand the micro-level interactive practices of learners with a view toward how these practices may be seen in a participatory framework to discuss learners' interactional competence to participate in second language communication. The degree to which one's participation in particular discursive contexts changes is seen as 'learning'.

The notion of 'membership' in CA (Hester & Eglin, 1997; Jefferson, 2002; Zimmerman, 1978) is particularly relevant to understanding language competence and language learning as it takes place within a community of practice. As conversation analytic work is based on describing 'members' methods' for orienting to and co-constructing social order through talk-in-interaction, it is important to try to understand what defines a 'member' whose 'methods' are being uncovered. Garfinkel and Sacks (1970) give a fairly clear and language-oriented definition of the notion of membership. They characterize membership as not attributable to a personal characteristic but that a member is oriented to as such due to the fact that she/he is engaging in social interaction in a particular 'natural language'. That is, through talk-in-interaction, two or more participants engaged in talk-in-interaction in the same language co-construct themselves as members by the simple fact of this ability to be engaged talk-in-interaction. The status of 'member' for a monolingual speaker of English in an English conversation taking place in English-dominant areas of the United States poses few problems and seems not warrant definition. Yet, Garfinkel and Sacks' describe membership as being locally-occasioned and continually displayed in interaction. This means that to be members, even such monolingual speakers of English in the United States need to do the work, that is, interact in such a way so that in every one of their fluent English–English interactions they are oriented to as being unremarkably, a fluent speaker of English.

For learners of a language who are communicating in that language, defining 'membership' is a bit more difficult, but, quite interesting. Given the definition of membership used by Garfinkel and Sacks, we see that it is possible for one person to be a 'member' of a number of membership categories (Sacks, 1992; Schegloff, 2007b). First, in the particular site where data was collected for this book, the interactional contexts inherent at that site (language classrooms) make relevant certain other memberships for the participants. As adults, they are members of a group we can gloss as 'socialized adults'. As adults taking English classes of their own volition, they declare themselves, with their registration and attendance (and are oriented to), as members of the group 'students of English'. As part of a classroom community of practice, these (and other) identities are (re)constructed in every class period they attend and in every interaction they have with their peers and teacher.

Showing learners' being co-constructed as learners through their talk-in-interaction in the classroom and thus as having statuses as members of a category we know as 'students' has been demonstrated in a great deal of research on classroom discourse. More interesting to uncover, however, through the learners' interactions and orientations to various identities and memberships in the classroom, are displays of, or practices for, some degree of membership in the category 'proficient English language user' (Hellermann, 2007).

As socialized adults, the learners in this study recognize and use (with varying degrees of success) their knowledge of social actions implemented through talk regardless of their novice status as English language speakers. These participants present researchers with a different situation than contexts in which children are learning their first language (Forrester & Reason, 2006; Wootton, 1997). Adult learners use methods for organizing themselves and their language learning tasks that come (in part) from their membership statuses as 'adults' as well as their membership statuses (to varying degrees) as 'proficient English language users'. These adult learners recognize many of the social actions needed for face-to-face interaction in general and for their language learning tasks specifically (starting the task, describing things, telling stories, ending the task). This recognition gives the adult learners some degree of members' knowledge in the membership category of 'English language user', some control of the micro-cultural set of shortcuts (Sacks, 1972) needed for on-the-spot interpretations of talk-in-interaction in some 'natural language'.

Connecting Members' Local Methods with the Community of Practice

Such members' knowledge is used in the learners' processes of 'learning English' – changing their degree of participation in the classroom community of practice through their use of English as a lingua franca. Looking in detail at some of the practices that learners use to accomplish action in their face-to-face interactions in the classroom communities of practice allows us to see the developing methods that define adult learners' language proficiency or degree of membership in their classroom community of practice as well as in the community of practice we might call 'proficient English language users'.

Methods for analysis that focus on the locally co-constructed practices for talk-in-interaction (like CA) can show detailed evidence for several defining characteristics of a community of practice. CA methods are based on the idea that participants work to achieve and continually display 'mutual engagement' and in doing those displays use a 'shared repertoire'. While the local co-construction of talk-in-interaction both creates and is done through a shared repertoire of language practices, we see in longitudinal foci how shared repertoires develop and are different in different classroom communities of practice. Finally, in focusing on students' local co-construction of their interactions using language provided in teacher-assigned tasks, we are able to see the continual intersecting trajectories of reification and participation.

Conclusion

While CA research in the social sciences and in the area of second language acquisition particularly has been criticized for its atheoretical stance, a community of practice theory for learning is quite accommodating of a CA approach to the study of human interaction. As discussed in Chapter 1, community of practice theory conceptualizes learning as the change in a member's level of participation in a community of practice, the movement from legitimate peripheral participation to full participation (Greeno, 1997). With its theoretical background in investigations of ordinary members methods for displaying and accomplishing social action through talk and its analytic methods that focus on turn-by-turn, sequential unfolding of talk-in-interaction, ethnomethodological CA research has discussed language development as it occurs in children (Forrester & Reason, 2006; Tarplee, 1996; Wootton, 1997). As the analyses in the next chapters will show, CA methods also fit well for investigations uncovering the processes (the 'shared repertoire') that adults use to display their mutual engagement with other student members in a joint enterprise – the language learning community of practice. The upcoming analyses describe practices used by adult language learners to accomplish social actions as they occurs within and around their language-learning tasks in their classrooms and how these practices for action change over time through learners' engagement in interaction within a community of practice.

Chapter 3
Opening Dyadic Task Interactions

Openings for Classroom Interactions

As discussed earlier, when studying language learning within a language classroom community of practice, boundary areas, transitions between different participation structures in the classroom organization, are sites where learners' negotiation of participation through language is readily observed. In the language learning classroom, one such site is in the transition from teacher–cohort interaction to student–student interaction that occurs at the beginning of a teacher-assigned language learning task. At these points in the class period, the teacher has modeled a cooperative language learning task that students are to complete working with a peer. These tasks involve various degrees of lexical, grammatical and procedural structure supplied by the teacher. After the teacher gives the instructions and models the task, the students must negotiate the shift from the teacher–student cohort participation structure into the peer dyad participation structure and then together with a peer, using their linguistic, cultural, and local interactional resources through talk-in-interaction must negotiate participation in the task itself. The description of the starts, or, 'openings' of these tasks will allow us a greater understanding of learner-members' methods for ordering their talk-in-interaction within a classroom community of practice.

Opening face-to-face dyadic task interactions is a recurring action that students in many language learning classrooms (those that use small group interaction as part of their pedagogy) must accomplish. Such openings are also a fundamental practice for human interaction in general. Getting a face-to-face interaction started is a practice familiar in some way to all socialized adults. But because of their novice status with the language code and language culture, language learners may find it a challenging area to manage. Investigations of the starts and ends (Chapter 5) of the dyadic task interactions of adult language learners can show the degree to which novice English language speaking adults who have been socialized to interact in other language cultures are able to take advantage of this social competence in developing practices for interaction in a community of practice. As a liminal space (in the sense of being an intersection of competent as novice statuses) openings for dyadic task interactions also prove to be an interesting site for observing changes in participation within the classroom community of practice.

The linguistic, pragmatic and interactional forms and the sequences in which they are deployed to accomplish the boundaries of task interactions are not part of the teacher's explicit instructions for the tasks in which the learner dyads engage and not part of what teachers usually consider a language learning opportunity. As such, these sequences of talk and interaction in the classroom remain an understudied area of the language classroom. While the study of this site of learner–learner interaction is important for such pedagogical reasons, understanding the degree to which the routines for accomplishing these boundary sequences differ from sequences around equivalent boundary actions outside the classroom will show some of the defining features of what makes adult language learning classrooms distinct communities of practice.

Research on Openings in Conversational Interaction

The term 'opening' is borrowed from research will investigated the language and behavior of initial encounters in non-classroom settings. These 'contact signals' (Goffman, 1961, 1981) that participants use to get their social interactions underway have been suggested to be made up of a three-step process of cognitive recognition (the initial 'sorting out' of whether one is known or not known), cognitive displays (usually non-verbal facial displays), and a social recognition display (a greeting) (Goffman, 1963; Schiffrin, 1977). Though this 'impressionistic' research on interaction was done without the benefit of audio or video recordings, it revealed an important site for understanding the organization of human interaction. Some of this discourse analytic research even suggested that rather than the start of something else, openings be considered encounters in and of themselves (Schiffrin, 1977).

Research from a CA perspective, incorporating recordings of interaction for more detailed descriptions showed further evidence that the action of opening an interaction is made up of orderly and recurring practices of talk-in-interaction (Hopper, 1989; Schegloff, 1968, 2002a, 2002b; Zimmerman, 1992). Due to the lack of visual cues, and the potential for various recipients for an opening, opening sequences in telephone talk are made up of intricate recipient design and voice identification sequences. In (3.1) an initial summons (the telephone ringing in line 1) is responded to in line 2 by Sarah's canonical response. Line 2 also serves as a potential voice identification marker (a first turn) which is responded to by Lisa in line 3 with a candidate identification. In the terminology of CA, such a turn is called a 'candidate' identification because of Lisa's rising intonation suggests that she is 'trying' (Sacks & Schegloff, 1979) an identification and not sure of who she is speaking to. Sarah confirms that identification in line 4. It's rising pitch, however, is oriented to by Lisa, suggesting to Lisa that Sarah still has not identified Lisa for certain and Lisa gives her name to completely identify herself in line 5. After the greeting and identification work are completed, Lisa starts in with the reason for the call in line 9.

(3.1[14]) Crow: Lisa and Sarah

```
1                   ((ring))
2    Sarah:         Hello?
3    Lisa:          Sarah?
4    Sarah:         Yeah?
5    Lisa:          Hey it's Li: sa.
6                   (0.3)
7    Sarah:         Hey::a
8                   (0.4)
9    Lisa:          u::m. I::y talked t' Justin,
```

The contexts for and sequences employed in openings of interactions in face-to-face interaction are, of course, much different. But given the technical difficulties of capturing the start of a face-to-face interaction on camera (needing to get permission before the start of the recording), the bulk of CA findings on openings comes from recordings of telephone conversations. When two parties come into physical co-presence, (in an elevator, on a bus, etc.) some degree of joint attention is inevitable, some aspect of the shared environment may be called upon by one party as accessible to another. In such situations, the 'evidential character' (Goffman, 1983) of social life becomes relevant to interactions. Two or more parties together in a social space cannot help but give off (Goffman, 1959) some communicative signs that are then open for reception and interpretation by those in the shared environment. Mutual engagement in some form of communication is so well-facilitated in such situations that in order not to interact in some way, parties must practice civil inattention (looking away, reading, etc.) thereby pre-empting any possible opening for interaction (Goffman, 1963).

In a shared mutual space, if there is no mutual recognition of the two parties, an opening to small talk may occur with a non-committal comment ('nice day' etc.). However, if an opening move of more substance is made, a move which entails some action by a second party (a question), the initiator of the interaction must give some justification for the interaction (Sacks, 1992, vol. 1, part 1, lecture 12) – asking for the time, feigning recognition ('haven't we met before?') and the like.

When face-to-face interactions do get underway, whether between acquaintances or strangers, talk and negotiation at the start of talk-in-interaction is done to ensure mutual engagement, shared understanding among participants, and, to shift from interpersonal to content-focused interaction (Kasper, 1979). This is especially important for participants who do not know one another well (Chafe, 1974; Kasper, 1979), such as adult language learners in a classroom setting.

Learners engaged in classroom interaction and who are explicitly assigned by the teacher to speak to one another as part of a classroom task are not faced with the social work of providing accounts for engaging in an interaction. There is a goal orientation built into their interaction by the teacher's explicit instructions and by the very fact that they both volunteered to take an English class. Nevertheless, the openings of their interactions are important sites for organizing and framing upcoming action between the two participants (Garfinkel & Sacks, 1970). For learners about to engage in a dyadic task interaction, this means that the language that occurs before the task language proper can act to frame and organize both the at-that-time social interaction with a fellow member of the community of practice as well as the language-learning task itself. As we will see, task prefatory talk allows learners to ensure their peer is attending, to clarify task instructions, and to understand to what degree their peer will be able to engage with the task.

Openings in the Classroom Community of Practice

The openings discussed in this chapter occur in student–student pair interactions in which students have been assigned to work together to accomplish some communicative language learning task. In this particular context of classroom dyadic interaction, the openings are bounded by the completion of the teacher's instructions for the task and the undertaking of the task itself (see Table 3.1).

Through the repeated occurrences of teacher-assigned tasks in the classroom I observed, learners are provided with repeated opportunities (Kanagy, 1999; Peters & Boggs, 1986) to co-construct the framing or

Table 3.1 Position of openings with respect to classroom participation structures

Participation structure	Action
Teacher–students	Teacher's task instructions
Student–student	Shifting participation structure and openning task interaction
Student–student	Start of the task

contextualization of the upcoming task in the opening sequences of the interaction. This framing and contextualization involves the production of sequences of physical comportment, gesture and talk to get the student dyad from a teacher–cohort orientation into the peer dyadic participation structure. The repeated situations of student–student pre-task engagement provided by teacher-assigned dyadic task interactions are opportunities for students to develop practices for talk-in-interaction to accomplish this action in the classroom community of practice and for researchers to observe that development. Observing the same student in repeated instances of these actions allows for the uncovering of the microgenesis of learning and the change from legitimate peripheral participation to core participation – the significant move for learning in a community of practice (Lave & Wenger, 1991).

More specifically, in terms of learning in a community of practice, the openings of task interactions are sites where the dialectic of reification and participation (Wenger, 1998) can be seen. The written language support from the teacher and the repetition of language structures that are often part of teacher-assigned tasks for dyadic interaction are the reified aspects of language and the foundation for language practices which are part of the community of practice of the adult language classroom. This reified aspect of discourse is explicitly designed by teachers as a goal, catalyst and support for participation in the dyadic language learning task, a key participation structure of these communities of practice. In the areas around the specific language support and task instructions supplied by the teacher, the openings for the face-to-face dyadic interaction (and as we will see later, the disengagements), there are spaces where students must participate in the negotiation of language practices to move from a situation of no talk to the implementation of the teacher's plan. This negotiation into and out of the teacher's task is not instructed but is part of the development of the shared repertoire of the classroom community of practice. The negotiation of this shared repertoire is the result of the dialectic of reification and participation.

While the discussion of openings for talk-in-interaction to this point has outlined the important implications for theoretical issues such as the structure of social action, classroom discourse and the classroom community of practice, the language of openings in dyadic task interaction also provides evidence of change in participation in a community of practice. This will become evident in the comparisons of the practices for accomplishing openings in two different communities of practice (those made up of beginning and intermediate learners) and by examining the changes in practices for interaction of individual learners.

Moves and Sequences for Opening Task Interactions

The data show there are recurrent non-verbal and verbal moves and sequences that characterize the openings of students' dyadic task interactions whether they are just beginning their study of English (students in level 'A' communities of practice) or have reached a low-intermediate stage of proficiency in English (students in level 'C' communities of practice).

Greetings

While greetings are a common feature of openings in face-to-face encounters (Goffman, 1963, 1981; Sacks, 1992), little empirical evidence has been shown for this feature of social interaction (as discussed earlier) because recording methods necessitate asking for permission before recordings are collected. In contrast to what is expected in face-to-face encounters, at the start of classroom dyadic task interactions, mutual greetings rarely occur. In the collection of 168 task openings, there were a total of 11 greetings offered. However, it should not be surprising that few greetings were used to open dyadic task-focused interactions considering the nature of physical co-presence (Goffman, 1963) and the context or physical co-presence that students in these language learning classrooms find themselves when their dyadic task interactions start.

As illustrated in Chapter 1, in the classrooms at the data collection site, two students are seated next to one another at a small table. Greetings are generally reserved for situations in which participants first enter into a mutual interactional field, at the start of a face engagement (Goffman, 1963; LeBaron & Jones, 2002; Sacks, 1992). In the classroom, contexts and opportunities for such greetings occur when students trickle into the classroom at the start of the class period and typical opening sequences with greetings occur. However, when students have been seated next to one another for even a short period of time, a greeting would seem ironic as part of the opening of a task interaction. The question is, then, why there were even 11 greetings in the collection. This can be explained in a fairly straightforward manner by the type of dyadic interaction in which the greetings occurred. Ten of the 11 greetings in the collection occurred when one student moved to another area of the classroom to interact with a student in a task. Excerpt (3.2) shows one example of a greeting given at the start of such a dyadic task interaction that occurred in a level 'A' classroom.

(3.2) Greeting when a student moves to another's desk
    10-17-02, 204, A, [1:01:27-1:01:42] Inez and Li Meng
    http://www.labschool.pdx.edu/Viewer/viewer.php?pl=JKHCP&cl=3.2
    ((I approaches L's desk))

```
1   I:=>hi:,
2   L:  hi
3   I:  how are you,
4   L:  good.
5   I:  ((laughs))
6   L:  ((gestures for I to sit))
7   I:  eh .hh mm how- what is your name.  ⎤ start of teacher-
8       (.)                                ⎦ assigned task
9   L:  mm ((points to board))
10  I:  name.
11  L:  Li Meng.
```

In (3.2), to start the task interaction, Inez walks over to Li Meng's desk. Starting in line 1, we see the start of a greeting sequence: a greeting followed by return greeting, then an inquiry regarding health and response (lines 3–4). The greeting sequence is followed by laughter and a non-verbal invitation to sit by Li Meng. In line 7, Inez launches the teacher-assigned language learning task.

While greeting sequences are typical in openings for telephone conversations or as part of the opening of face-to-face encounters for recently co-presenced participants (including student peers), they are unwarranted for student peers starting their classroom dyadic task interactions who have been seated side by side, and, in most cases, will remain deskmates for the rest of the class period. Such a point in time in the class period and such a physical context in the classroom make a mutual greeting sequentially marked. This absence of greetings at the start of seated pair tasks shows the students' mutual orientation to their co-presence and to teacher-assigned tasks as one part within the ongoing participation in the community of practice and work that makes up the trajectory and unity of what becomes characterized as one 'class period'.

While the greetings which occurred when one student entered into the presence of another student at the start of a task are well-motivated interactionally, it is not immediately clear why one greeting occurred without movement of one or both students to another area of the classroom. In the following Excerpt (3.3) from a level 'A' class, Jaime and Mai are seated next to one another. The task they have been assigned is to borrow items from one another using the structure 'may I borrow a ...' and respond with the colloquial 'sure, no problem'.

(3.3) Greeting in seated interaction
10-17-02: A: 206, [33:03-33:27], Jaime and Mai
http://www.labschool.pdx.edu/Viewer/viewer.php?pl=JKHCP&cl=3.3

((Students are to ask one another to borrow items and respond with the colloquial, 'sure, no problem'))

```
1  Te: partner says sure, no problem.
2  J:  ((shifts posture)) ↑no problem.
3      (6.0) ((M copies something from board))
4  M:  ((shifts ⌈posture to J))
5  J:=>         ⌊hello Mai,
6  M:  hello:.
7  J:  you teacher? okay.
8  M:  yeah. (.) may I borrow a s- book, ⎫ start of teacher-
9             =your book,                ⎭ assigned task
```

In (3.3), after the teacher's instructions for the task, Jaime shifts his posture toward his deskmate Mai as he repeats the lexical phrase that is the focus of this practice task (line 2) which seems to be a response to the teacher's instructions. Jaime's postural orientation toward Mai is not reciprocated. Rather, there is a six-second gap in which Mai is copying something from the board. After this, she shifts her posture to Jaime who offers an ironic greeting to Mai. Jaime is smiling as he greets Mai and his greeting in this instance seems to indicate Jaime's orientation to and comment on Mai's delay in starting the task interaction. Jaime orients to the lack of immediate start to the task by ironically suggesting, with his greeting, that Mai had not, to some degree, been co-present with Jaime in lines 1–3.

The greeting sequences which occurred in tasks in which a student moved to another student's desk [as in (3.2)] were not designed by the teachers at the data collection site as a required component of these pedagogical tasks and were not explicitly taught by the teachers as part of successfully accomplishing these tasks. For these reasons, the greetings in such task openings (discussed later in this chapter) display quite vividly how, within a community of practice, routines for talk-in-interaction are not always institutionally designed, implemented or mandated, but, are the accomplishment of work by members of the community of practice that can develop organically in the intersection between the constitutive 'rules' of the community and the individual-local co-construction of interactions.

There are also interpersonal implications for such classroom language learning tasks in which students must make contact with one another and start a task interaction. Some teacher-assigned tasks provide a space where a greeting sequence is relevant. In such task interaction, students are afforded the opportunity to engage in such a sequence and thus use language in an authentic way, that is, in a way that they might use the language outside the classroom. In (3.2), we saw how level 'A' classroom communities of practice include both linguistic and interpersonal resources for greeting fellow students when one student moves into a peer's personal space. We see also how in (3.3), a student is able to use that understanding of the working of the community of practice to make an ironic remark by the use of a greeting when a greeting is not interactional expected.

Postural alignment

In both dyadic tasks involving movement to physical co-presence [like that in Excerpt (3.2)] and seated tasks (3.3), one fundamental move in the sequence for opening a dyadic task interaction which follows the teacher instructions is mutual postural orientation and the physical alignment to a mutual workspace. This physical reorientation is especially notable in the seated dyadic task interactions. While students could talk to one another without shifting posture, after the teacher instructions and before the talk is launched by students, they shift posture, often simultaneously but even more often, initiated by one member and then jointly completed. This supports research on language in social interaction which has noted posture shift as a standard component of initiating engagements in face-to-face interaction (Erickson & Schultz, 1981; Streeck, 1995; Goffman, 1961). While there are three openings in the collection in which students did not align their posture before launching the task, each exception is well-motivated. In each, the student who did not orient posture to the deskmate was relying on written information on the board at the front of the class for the task engagement. In these cases, students' system-level constraints of language (Goffman, 1981) necessitated this momentary lack of immediate physical orientation. In each of these three cases, shortly after the task was underway (two to three turns into the task), the non-aligning student shifted posture to face the deskmate. The evidence in the collection analyzed in this study suggests that, as in talk in interaction outside the classroom, mutual postural alignment is an integral part of the dyadic interaction by learners engaged in task interaction in the classroom.

Postural alignment functions in several ways for these beginning adult learners of English. First of all, it marks a break in the participation structure of the classroom talk-in-interaction, a contextualization cue (Gumperz, 1982) bracketing the upcoming talk (Erickson & Schultz, 1982) as an end to the teacher-fronted task instructions to the whole class and beginning of talk between peers. The postural re-alignment is a way that students make themselves and their work materials recognizably available (Kidwell & Zimmerman, 2007) for engagement in the upcoming task. Second, the mutual posture alignment by students creates a spatial field in which gaze, an important communicative signal for the maintenance of face-to-face interaction (Goodwin, 1981, 1986), is shared. The spatial field also enables the dyads to use and orient to one another's gestures, gestures which serve both intra-personal (McNeill, 2000) and interpersonal communicative functions (Koschmann & LeBaron, 2002; Streeck, 1993; Streeck & Hartge, 1992). Finally, this mutually constructed work space enables students to orient to and manipulate objects such as printed material, pencils or other props from the classroom which is especially crucial for facilitating *lingua franca* communication in the language classroom (Davila, 2005; Kress et al., 1998).

Opening Moves and Sequences Characteristic of Two Levels of Language Proficiency

While postural alignment and the lack of greetings illustrate common aspects of methods for opening dyadic task interactions across proficiency levels, there are several notable differences in distribution and frequency of the opening moves used in communities of practice of two proficiency levels.

Direct launch

In the task interactions without greetings, after the teacher instructions and postural alignment by students, a common way for students to get their tasks underway (especially those just beginning their study of English in level 'A' classrooms) is by uttering the first words for the teacher-assigned task. I am calling such a start to dyadic tasks a 'direct launch' and it is illustrated in the next two excerpts.

(3.4)
    7-15-02, 204, A, [57:07-57:26], Larissa and Tina
    http://www.labschool.pdx.edu/Viewer/viewer.php?pl=JKHCP&cl=3.4
(Students are to tell one another to say and spell the words dictated by the other student)

1 Te: in your book. in your book. teacher student.
2   teacher student. in your book.
3 L: ((looks to T who is physically oriented to L))
4 T:=>please say? December.
5 L: December?
6 T: please spell December.

(3.5)
    7-17-03, 204, A, [1:06:10-1:06:22], Quyen and Nasim
    http://www.labschool.pdx.edu/Viewer/viewer.php?pl=JKHCP&cl=3.5
(The teacher has asked the students to fill in a grid with answering questions about rent expenses in their home countries and in the United States. After writing, students are to ask one another the questions.)

1 Q:=> ((after writing, shifts posture to N)) how much is
2   rent now in the you es [U.S.] ((reading the
3   teacher's task prompt from her worksheet))
4   (1)
5   ((points at N's worksheet))
6 N: mm
7 Q: right now,
8 N: (now?)
9 Q: ((nods))

In both Excerpts (3.4) and (3.5) from level 'A' classrooms, students begin their pair task interaction without prefatory talk to one another. In (3.4), immediately following the instructions from the teacher, Larissa shifts her posture toward Tina who is already looking toward Larissa. When Tina has achieved Larissa's gaze, she launches the task in line 4. In (3.5), after the teacher has made her instructions to the class for the task, and after the students do some writing to fill in a grid with questions about rent in their countries and in the United States, Quyen turns to Nasim and asks her a question prompt for the task without any task prefatory talk, reading from her paper (lines 1–2).

Such direct launches are common among student dyads interacting in level 'A' classes: over half of all level 'A' task openings can be characterized as such. This frequency shows how level 'A' students' participation in dyadic tasks is very much oriented to the language provided in the task. The frequency of this type of task opening shows another important aspect of participation in the level 'A' classroom community of practice: the importance of teacher-provided language to mediate interaction between student peers.

In the interactions from level 'C' classrooms investigated, only about one quarter of the openings can be characterized as being direct launched without tasks prefatory talk. The tasks assigned by the teachers observed in both the level 'A' and level 'C' classrooms were introduced by very clear modeling and explicit verbal and non-verbal instructions.[15] It is curious that when tasks are clearly introduced by teachers, when learners are more proficient in the language, there is more task-prefatory talk. The question arises then to the purpose of such task prefatory talk by students with a higher proficiency in the language.

The fact that task-prefatory talk occurs after clear presentations of task instructions shows the inherent incompleteness of language in interaction and the need to overcome a certain level of ambiguity at the start of language learning tasks. Such incompleteness or ambiguity, however, is not a feature exclusive to learner-learner talk. Ambiguity is part of the nature of language and human communication. The so-called 'problem of indexicality' (Garfinkel & Sacks, 1970) in language, the context dependence for interpretation, is what makes spoken interaction for native speakers of a language a constant process of negotiation. More specifically to interaction in teacher-assigned language learning tasks, embodying instructions for a task given by a teacher involves processes in which students make the instructions appropriate for the persons and materials available in their local dyadic interaction (Garfinkel, 2002). For adult learners of English, the developmental trajectory for embodying instructions and working out this local problem of interpretation in classroom task interactions in an additional language is seen in the different ways that learners open their task interactions.

As students increased in proficiency in the language (shown by their progression to level C) their classroom community of practice became characterized by opening interactions with a wider repertoire of verbal negotiations for the immediately forthcoming task. As the excerpts to follow will show, this task-prefatory talk is something different from the negotiation of semantic meaning or linguistic form. It is part of the negotiation of embodied language behavior in the community of practice of the language classroom.

Turn allocation

Turn-allocation, that is, task prefatory talk in which students negotiate who should take the first turn of the teacher-assigned language learning task, occurred as an opening sequence in both level 'A' and level 'C' interactions. In fact, counting the various moves in the collection of task openings showed there to be little difference between the frequency of occurrences of turn-allocation work in level 'A' and level 'C' interactions. However, the differences in how this action is carried out through a sequence of talk-in-interaction gives an interesting picture of the differences in ways learners participate in different classroom communities of practice.

On closer examination of the turn allocation work done in the level 'A' classes, it is apparent that the actions being accomplished in the level 'A' openings are quite different in character from the turn allocation moves in level 'C' openings. The difference in character of the level 'A' instances is another piece of evidence for the strong orientation of the participants to the language and structure of provided in the task itself. Excerpt (3.6) shows how turn allocation is done as part of the opening in a level 'A' classroom when the task is heavily mediated by language support from the teacher. In the task for this excerpt, students have been instructed to carry out a kind of Total Physical Response task in which one member of the dyad give directives (commands such as 'tell me your name', 'stand up' and the like) to the other who carries out the directive through some non-verbal or minimally verbal action.

(3.6)
    7-15-02, 204, A, [2:15:00-2:15:33], Larissa and Tina
    http://www.labschool.pdx.edu/Viewer/viewer.php?pl=JKHCP&cl=3.6
    (Students are to make directives: tell me your name, stand up, etc and the other student is to listen and comply)

3 **Te:** practice together, teacher student, and then

```
4       change. teacher student.=practice. (.) no
5       pictures. only speak and (.) do.
6       (3.0)
7   L:  ((looks to Tina who is looking at Larissa))
8   T:=>do you teacher?
9       (1) ((L leans toward T))
10  L:  what
11  T:=>do you teacher?
12  L:=>((shakes her head and points to Tina))
13  T:  ⌈yes
14  L:=>⌊you teacher.
15  T:  eh:: (2) say (.6) do you name.
```

After the teacher's instructions, Larissa (line 7) orients her posture to her peer, Tina, whose posture is already aligned to Larissa. In line 8, Tina makes a task-prefatory directive to which Larissa, after a pause, offers a repair initiation in line 10 ('what'). Tina's repeat of the task-prefatory directive successfully repairs the misunderstanding as Larissa shakes her head indicating a negative response to Tina's repeated directive. Larissa makes her own directive in line 14 'you teacher'. This is followed by the launch of the task by Tina in line 15.

Looking back to the end of the teacher's instructions (lines 3–5), we can see that as part of the language support provided by the teacher, the task has turn-allocation built into it in the form of roles for taking the first turn. That is, uttering first pair parts for the task involves giving the directives (the role of 'teacher') and responding to those first turns of the task language sequence is the role of 'student'. In line 8, Tina is directing or offering Larissa the first turn, the role of 'teacher'. After Tina repeats that move in line 11, Larissa orients to that meaning and makes her own counter proposal, the directive in line 14 which is accepted by Tina who launches the teacher-assigned task. In the other level 'A' task interactions in which students overtly and verbally perform turn allocation like (3.6), the mediation of the task itself and the task instructions by the teacher provide students opportunities for a type of turn allocation sequence which does not occur in level 'C' task interactions.

When faced with the start of a task in level 'C', students could just directly launch the task (as they did in about one quarter of these interactions). In level 'C' classroom communities of practice, tasks did not carry within them implicit role assignment of the type exhibited in (3.6) that would direct their turn allocation at the start of their tasks. The following two excerpts show the different types of interactional sequences which

Opening Dyadic Task Interactions 55

took place in level 'C' to establish turn allocation for their teacher-assigned tasks. In (3.7), we see one student (Inez) doing task clarification work with the teacher and then two students co-constructing turn allocation (Inez with her peer partner, Sambath).

(3.7) Task clarification with teacher and turn allocation
   11-18-03, 204, C, [1:02:19-1:02:58], Inez and Sambath
   http://www.labschool.pdx.edu/Viewer/viewer.php?pl=JKHCP&cl=3.7
(Students are to practice the reduced form 'going to' for expressing future)

```
1  Te: but read your sentences.  ((Te standing just in
2      front of I))
3  I:  okay.
4  Te: okay?
5  I:  ((reading to self))
6  Te: five minutes
7  I:  with (.) my ((touches Sambath' shoulder))
8  Te: with ⌈your partner.
9  S:       ⌊((aligns posture to I))
10 I:  part⌈ner.
11         ⌊((I aligns posture with S and smiles))
12     (2)
13 I:=>during the- do you reads?
14     (1)
15 S:  pardon me?
16     (.)
17 I:=>you read? (.4) first?
18     (.)
19 S:  okay
20     (8.0)
21 S:  I'm gonna: (1.5) >↑after class<, I'm gonna
22     buy coffee,
23 I:  okay,
24 S:  okay. I'm gonna go buy (.) coffee,
```

In (3.7), after the task clarification work (lines 1–10), Inez turns to face her deskmate and launches the task in line 13. Inez aborts this launch, however, and restarts her turn doing turn allocation work, asking Sambath if she wants to take the first turn in the task. After a repair sequence and clarification of that offer, Sambath accepts (line 19) and after a pause, she launches the task interaction with a statement about her future activity.

In (3.8) students work gradually into the start of their verbal interaction with a sequence of non-verbal behavior including postural shifts before Quyen does task prefatory turn allocation work (lines 14–16) and the task is launched (line 20).

(3.8) task-prefatory alignment sequence with turn allocation
3-02-04, 204, C, [1:18:45-1:19:30], Quyen and Abby
http://www.labschool.pdx.edu/Viewer/viewer.php?pl=JKHCP&cl=3.8

(Students are to tell the other they have a particular malady to task is for one student to give commands to the other student)

```
1   Te:   what should you do for these problems. Think of
2         one or two one or two: pieces of advice, for
3         each, for example, you shou:ld take medicine,
4         you should drink tea. (.) so two: things
5         for each. (.) okay?
6         (3)
7   A:    ((smiles)) ((looks to Q))
8         (2.0)
9   A:    ((leans to Q))
10  Q:    ((turns toward A))
11  A:    ((turns fully to Q))
12  Q:    ((smiles)) eh heh
13  A:    eh heh hah
14  Q:=>  ah: ((looks slightly to board)) uh ((points to
15        A)) ((points to board)) you s- you start with
16        (the) number one (and) ⌈I uh I I advise you.
17  A:                            ⌊((looks toward board))
18        (.)
19  Q:    you
20  A:    ((reading from board)) I have a I have a cold.
21  Q:    uh you should uh: you (should   ) take a
22        medicine
```

After the teacher's task instructions, Abby and Quyen enter into their interaction with non verbal moves including gaze and postural alignment (lines 7–11). In lines 12 and 13 there is an exchange of laughter and in 14, Quyen initiates a turn with a non-lexical vocalization and two gestures which link her peer to the initiation of the task. The task prompt is written on the board and Quyen suggests a first turn task prompt to Abby with the gesture sequence. This elaborate non-verbal sequence for turn allocation is developed verbally just afterward with Quyen's long, multi-clause directive in lines 15–16 in which Quyen tells Abby to take the first turn, to give a hypothetical malady that she, Quyen can respond to. While that turn assigns roles for both participants and implicates turn allocation, Quyen also neatly summarizes at least part of the task in words – the function of the responder: to give advice (line 16).

The two turn allocation excerpts from level 'C' interactions illustrate a shared repertoire for interaction in the level 'C' classroom community of practice that includes more linguistic and turn-taking resources than those used in the level 'A' interactions. In (3.7), Inez uses a discourse marker to bracket a boundary in the classroom discourse and then a prepositional phrase to clarify the task instructions with the teacher. At the same time, she uses the non-verbal move of touching her deskmate's shoulder to both get her peer's attention and to index the object of her ongoing prepositional phrase. Inez starts the task, but cuts off her direct launch to do turn allocation work uttering a fully formed syntactic question. Sambath initiates repair of that directive using the polite phrase 'pardon me' and Inez reformulates the question, making it a two-part directive and temporal locator with rising pitch (line 17) which Sambath understands, making the first task move in line 21. In (3.8), after starting the turn non-verbally, Quyen explicates her directive with a multi-clause turn which accomplishes turn allocation work while partially summarizing the upcoming task. In each case, non-verbal interactional work is supplemented by verbal moves to do turn allocation.

In the excerpt from a level 'A' classroom (3.6), in doing turn allocation work, Tina and Larissa rely on the phrase 'do you teacher' and its reduction 'you teacher', respectively, phrases that orient directly to the names of roles in the task assigned by the teacher. As in the level 'C' Excerpt (3.7), in (3.6), students also co-construct a repair sequence immediately following the first turn allocation move which is successfully resolved and task gets underway following. But unlike the level 'C' interactions, turn allocation work in level 'A' was done either non-verbally or with direct support from teacher task language.

These three excerpts also show both the local and cross-contextual nature of the talk-in-interaction for opening task interactions. The turn allocation work of level A is heavily reliant on the local contextulization of the task language. Although less so, a level 'C' interaction (3.8) also uses a local classroom technology (the board) as a resource for some non-verbal turn allocation work. In both level 'A' interactions (Excerpt 3.6) and level 'C' interactions (Excerpt 3.7), we see pan-contextual interactional work being done in the other-initiated self-repair work done to clarify the turn allocation work. Such 'other' repair sequences have been noted to occur in everyday conversational interaction (Schegloff *et al.*, 1977) regardless of the content of the interaction. The format of the sequences for repair used by the learners in the classroom excerpts are just as noted in the research on native speaker repair. In such 'other repair' sequences, one speaker produces what becomes, for that local interaction, a source of trouble in the talk-in-interaction. Often, there is a pause following the production of the trouble source and another participant in the interaction (an 'other'), initiates a repair of that trouble source. The trouble may then be repaired by 'other' or the producer of the trouble ('self').

This simultaneously local and pan-contextual nature of the language for opening dyadic language learning tasks shows the hybrid nature of the discourse of classroom communities of practice. Structural aspects of talk-in-interaction used in any context appear as part of the negotiation in accomplishing a specific, local language-learning task. The classroom communities of practice for level 'A' and level 'C' classrooms emerge from and as part of these openings of language learning task interactions where the performance of the task is keenly local while some of the interactive practices employed for its performance – greeting, postural alignment, repair are present in contexts beyond language learning task interaction. These excerpts illustrate how co-presence and a catalyst for interaction (language learning tasks) afford opportunities for the use of pan-contextual structures or methods for talk-in-interaction.

Other Task-Prefatory Opening Sequences

Task clarification

One type of interactional work that we might expect to occur before the start of a language learning task is task clarification work. While this occurred in both proficiency levels, surprisingly few of the openings in the collection included such work. The two examples included show that this type of work is part of each proficiency classroom community of practice and give further evidence for how a wider range of linguistic resources can be used by students in level 'C' to clarify and in some cases, make the clarification shorter than similar work which is done in level 'A' classes.

The few task clarifications in level A suggest that it may be that show the difficulty for students at the early stages of learning to express their lack of understanding of a task. In Excerpt (3.9) from level A, the task prefatory talk (lines 13–41) does clarification work when Jin does not understand what to do after Zoya launches the task (line 10).

(3.9) Level A task clarification
4-29-02, 204, A, [2:20:25-2:21:40] Jin & Zoya
(One student is to say the number of a picture; the other is to say what the picture is)
http://www.labschool.pdx.edu/Viewer/viewer.php?pl=JKHCP&cl=3.9

```
1   Te:  Now, please practice together. teacher, (.)
2        teacher and student. ( )
3   J:   ((postural orientation to Z))
4   Te:  teacher and student.
5   J:   ((looks back at teacher))
6   Z:   ((clears throat))
7   Te:  listen,
8   Z:   okay
9   Te:  and say the number. one two
10  Z:   ((postural orientation to J)) two number please?
11  J:   oh ((turns to face Z))
12  Z:   please two number
13  Te:  ((pointing to J)) teacher?
14  Z:   mm teacher okay
15  J:   uh very very (.) busy.
16       very ⌈(write) ((gestures writing))
17  Te:       ⌊very ⌈busy
18  J:              ⌊very busy
19       ((gestures writing)) write
20  Te:  first ⌈listening
21  Z:         ⌊ah:   ah
22  Te:  later writing. (.) right now?
23  J:   no (this) ((gesturing toward board))
24  Z:   okay.
25  J:   (write)
26  Z:   one listen, eh th ⌈writing  okay   okay
27  Te:                    ⌊later yeah later
28       we'll write
29  Z:   ( )
30  Te:  first ⌈(we'll   ) no no no ⌈first speaking and
31  J:         ⌊( ) ((pointing to board))
32  Z:                               ⌊first listen
33  Te:  listening
34  Z:   uh huh ⌈first listen listen and the- uh writing.
35  Te:         ⌊later (    ) yeah ((points to V
```

```
36  Te:  and moves away)) yes
37  J:   oh
38  Z:   ⌈today
39  J:   ⌊( )
40  J:   ((laugh))
41  Z:   today.
42       (1)
43  Z:   okay please, ( . ) ah um eh picture eh  ⎤
44       picture two.                            ⎬  start of the teacher-
45  J:   huh?                                    ⎦  assigned task
46  Z:   picture two what
47  J:   picture two is picture two is he (from) Mexico,
48       from Mexico?
49  Z:   ⌈Mexico
50  J:   ⌊he's from Mexico,
51  Z:   Mexico
52  J:   y⌈es
53  Z:    ⌊okay.
```

In this task, one student is to say the number of a picture in their textbooks and the peer is to say what that picture depicts. After the teacher's instructions for the task (lines 1–3, 5), Zoya, without checking to see if Jin understands the task, launches the task interaction in line 10. As noted earlier, this is the most common way that tasks get underway in level A classes. Zoya's task launch, however, is responded to in line 11 with a news token (Heritage, 1984b) which warrants an upgraded task launch, one which includes a polite request marker by Zoya (line 12). After the teacher intervenes and assigns roles for the task (line 13), Jin begins questioning something on the board which she thinks is relevant to the task (lines 15–16, 18–19). The teacher interprets this attention to the board as a request for a re-explanation of the task and she tells Jin that for the task, students are to listen to one another and (orienting to Jin's gesture in lines 16 and 19) not write (lines 22, 27–28). Jin indicates that what the teacher is explaining is not what she asked about and Zoya gives her candidate explanation for Jin's trouble (line 26). The teacher give her explanation of procedures for the task again (lines 30, 33, 35) which is followed by Zoya's next candidate explanation (line 34). That explanation is ratified by the teacher (line 36) and given uptake by Jin as well (line 37 'oh'), this news token suggesting that she understands now how to do the task. Zoya orients to this as a marker of understanding and restarts the task in lines 38, 41 and 43 with an upgraded launch including the discourse marker 'okay' to introduce the start of a new action and explicit mention of the relevant part of the task which Jin should orient to – the 'picture'.

The lengthy clarification sequence is the result, in part, of students' lack of linguistic proficiency. Interactions such as this highlight students' commitment to one another (mutual engagement) and to the joint enterprise of language learning. This example also shows the early work on the development of a shared repertoire for task engagement that is mediated by the instructor. The direct launch by Zoya in line 12 turns out to not be effective in this instance and after the instructor steps in Zoya works to help Jin understand the task and later, reformulates her task launch showing her orientation to appropriate recipient design, giving Jin more specifics in her second task launch (lines 38–43).

Clarifications of the task before the task launch are not unique to level A interactions, however, they are played out differently in level C classes. In (3.10), Reinaldo clarifies with Xiao Hong the starting point for their task interaction before it gets underway.

(3.10) Level 'C' task clarification
1-20-04, 204, C, [1:22:42] Reinaldo and Xiao Hong
http://www.labschool.pdx.edu/Viewer/viewer.php?pl=JKHCP&cl=3.10

```
1   Te:  so first, check your answers with your partner
2        what you can remember. Then when you're finished,
3        read what she said in the back. okay? let's do
4        this for about ten minutes.
5   X:   okay. first do this.
6        (7.0) ((both students looking at their books))
7   R:   okay.
8   X:   okay first do this.
9   R:   number two?
10  X:   yeah. number two.
11  R:   she can ⌈speak ((reading))
12  X:         ⌊she can't speak English with      start of the teacher-
13       her neighbors.                           assigned task
14  R:   ( ) with her neighbors.
15  X:   Yeah
```

Xiao Hong marks the shift to student–student participation structure in line 5 with a discourse marker 'okay' introducing a new course of action and then a directive to start the task using a pro-term ('this') to point to a shared referent. After a gap of seven seconds when students are looking in their textbooks, Reinaldo uses the discourse marker 'okay' to indicate his readiness which is followed (line 8) by Xiao Hong making the same directive as previously with the same pro-term referent ('this'). Reinaldo offers a candidate referent for 'this' ('number two') which Xiao Hong confirms with an affirmative response and repeat of Reinaldo's candidate referent and Reinaldo launches the task in line 11.

Inquiry into readiness and humor

The community of practice in level C classes is evidenced in several other practices for opening task interactions, practices which do not occur in level A classrooms and require a greater degree of language-cultural proficiency. In (3.9), after the teacher finishes her task instructions, a student inquires as to whether his deskmate is ready to start the task. His deskmate responds with a joke about the difficulty of the task.

(3.11) Inquiry into readiness and joke
2-24-04, 204, C, [45:41-46:23], Reinaldo and Kathryn
http://www.labschool.pdx.edu/Viewer/viewer.php?pl=JKHCP&cl=3.11

```
1   Te:  so, please ask your partner, and talk for about
2        five minutes, (.) what did you need to do
3        yesterday, what do you need to do ⌈today,
4   R:                                     ⌊are you ready
5        Kathryn?
6   K:   (what) what what
7   R:   are you ready?
8   K:   yeah I'm ready. °yeah°. very ea:sy. eh heh
9        ⌈heh heh heh heh
10  R:   ⌊for you not for me
11  K:   .hh no: I just joking. I'm just ↑nahyeah I'm just
12       °joking.°
13       (3.0)
14  R:   what did you do: what did ⌈you do   yesterday
15  K:                              ⌊tchha okay. okay. I ask
16       you I am just (looking) is now, I am just looking
```

In line 4, as the teacher ends her task instructions, Reinaldo makes a direct inquiry to Kathryn about whether she is ready to start the task. Kathryn is focused on some notes in front of her and rather than giving a direct answer to Reinaldo's question, makes what seems like a repair initiation for lack of hearing (line 6). Reinaldo orients to the sequence as in need of repair and repeats his question which then receives a response from Kathryn (line 8). After her response to Reinaldo's query, she makes a self-deprecating ironic remark ('very easy') punctuated with laughter. Reinaldo orients to this remark as humor and responds with return self-deprecation. Kathryn then comments about the nature of her remark, that she was just 'joking' and after a short pause, Reinaldo launches the task in line 14.

The explicit query as to the readiness of a peer partner to start a classroom task has direct sequential consequences for starting the dyadic task. The query implements a sequence before the start of the task itself that helps to ensure that the task will be successfully started. This query sequence also shows how the start of teacher-assigned dyadic task interactions provide sites where language not assigned by the teacher can be tried out. The interpersonal nature of peer dyadic interaction provides a context in which a student might inquire about a peer, to assess some aspect of that peer's condition – regarding a peer's health, well-being or status of task completion. In this instance, Reinaldo displays interactional competence for using language in a grammatically and pragmatically appropriate manner. Kathryn takes the opportunity provided by this task-prefatory sequence to add to the interpersonal nature of the sequence with her humorous comment which is oriented to and joined by Reinaldo.

The use of humor at this point takes the interaction a bit further along the trajectory started by Reinaldo's query into readiness, a trajectory away from explicit orientation to task. This sequence of pre-task talk in lines 4–12 is similar to noticings from casual conversation that main topics of interactions are often preceded by some preliminary topic (Maynard & Zimmerman, 1984; Stokoe, 2000) or 'false first' topic (Sacks, 1992).

Alignment

It is curious that when instructions are clearly explicated and modeled (and we have seen support for that claim in the few examples of task clarification from the collection presented here) that there should be more task-prefatory talk by students in the more advanced proficiency class. Some of these task-prefatory sequences have just been mentioned, but there are other instances in level 'C' task openings, in which task-prefatory talk does not seem to be doing the work of task clarification, turn allocation, or direct inquiry about readiness for the upcoming task. Excerpt (3.10) shows task-prefatory talk that is different in quality from those seen in the students' interactions in level 'A' and which is, perhaps, something more like face-to-face interaction in general. While at first glance, this excerpt might seem like 'task clarification work', after repeated viewing and analysis it became clear that the excerpt is less about clarifying the steps in the task and more about establishing interpersonal alignment for face-to-face interaction. In (3.10), Abby and Tommy engage in a rather lengthy spate of pre-task talk which is made up of a number of self and other repetitions of turns starting in line 13. This opening follows the teacher's instructions to the class (lines 5–9).

(3.12)
10-14-03, 204, C, [2:19:35-2:20:21], Abby and Tommy
http://www.labschool.pdx.edu/Viewer/viewer.php?pl=JKHCP&cl=3.12
(Students are to check their answers for homework with one another)

```
6   Te:  yeah you can look at your old questions but make
7        sure that they are in this order. one, two, three
8        four. Just for five minutes, and then we'll put
9        the questions on the board.
10       ((Abby and T start the physical orientation to a
11       mutual work space))
12       (11.0)
13  A:   from the:: this story,
14  T:   mm one (sixteen).
15  A:   one sixteen.
16  T:   from this story. ((points to A's book))
17  A:   ⌈this story.
18  T:   ⌊write the question five questions.
19  A:   (five/twice),
20  T:   yeah you can write out five questions
21  A:   from this story.
22  T:   yeah.
23  A:   fro⌈m the s⌈tory.
24  T:     ⌊( )    ⌊yeah you can write five (.) five
25       questions
26       ((Students find the page in their books and begin
27       writing out questions))
```

After the teacher's instructions and a lengthy gap (line 12), Abby opens the interaction with an assertion about the material that students should focus on, using the deictic 'this' in coordination with holding her textbook open to the story of reference. At this point, there has been no indication of either student having trouble understanding the instructions. Tommy follows Abby's assertion with a more specific location of the material, giving the page number in the book where the story is located (line 14). In line 15, Abby repeats the page number of the story which she originally pointed out. Tommy follows with an assertion (note the final falling intonation), reformulating the language used by Abby earlier and pointing to Abby's book (line 16). Next, in overlap, Abby repeats the indication of the story to work on while Tommy reads the instructions from the book (to write five questions about the story) which seems to be confirmed by Abby in line 19. Tommy affirms the indication of the number of questions to write with an affirmative response 'yeah' and a paraphrase of the book instructions. Abby repeats her expression of the material to focus on two more times, in lines 21 and 23 around Tommy's token of agreement in line 22 while in lines 24–25, Tommy makes an almost exact repeat of his earlier turn in line 24.

Abby's and Tommy's repetition of the material that the students are focusing on for their task interaction does not seem to be in response to any trouble that the students are having understanding the task. Nor does the work that Tommy is doing (specifying the page number location of the story, reading and paraphrasing the instructions from the textbook) indicate trouble or the need for task clarification. The work being done in this interaction seems to be basic alignment or confirmation work in the absence of trouble, a checking and rechecking in the talk between two competent level 'C' students who understand the task instructions and talk as they set up their materials and physical comportment to start a face-to-face interaction. Such a checking/rechecking routine is a practice of the adult learner community of practice that characterizes it as learner-learner interaction and that enables participation and learning within a community of practice.

Language Development Seen Comparing Level 'A' and Level 'C' Communities of Practice: Turn Allocation and Changing Participation

The following examples of turn allocation work at the start of teacher-assigned tasks illustrate how task openings can be seen as a site for language development. In beginning level classes, we saw how turn allocation was done as part of role assignment. Some tasks in beginning level classes are designed so learners focus their attention on either active or passive roles. In such tasks, one learner plays the active/productive role usually giving a directive while the other learner is not required to produce language, but rather, listens to and carries out the task non-verbally (often, pointing to a picture or making some other physical response like standing). An example of a teacher's instructions for such a task is seen in (3.13):

3.13 (from students' first class period)
1-09-03, 206, A,[59:34-59:46], camera 5
(Wen Ling and Dep are deskmates in this class)

Te: now, please continue ((gesturing toward herself with right hand) teacher and student. You can say sho:w me: capital, (.) ey, or? sho:w me: small?

The instructions by the teacher in (3.13) come from the first class of the term. As we saw in the previous section, students in a level 'A' community of practice use the role assignment inherent in such tasks as a way to do turn allocation for their upcoming task. At times when the teacher did not give the explicit role assignments for a dyadic task, students in level A would use that information as a resource in their current interaction for turn allocation. Excerpt (3.14) occurred in the next lesson four days later.

(3.14)
1-13-03, A, 206, [46:47-47:02], Wen Ling and Dep
http://www.labschool.pdx.edu/Viewer/viewer.php?pl=JKHCP&cl=3.12

```
5   Te:  now. ask your partner.
6   D:   yes ((aligns posture to partner))
7   Te:  ask your partner. Do you have. Do you have a
8        book. do you have ⌈paper.
9   W:=>                   ⌊teacher ((points to peer))
10       student ⌈((points to self))
11  Te:          ⌊Practice with your partner.
12  D:   do you have a paper.
13  W:   yes I do.
```

In (3.14) after modeling the task (to ask yes/no questions and respond with short answers 'yes I do' or 'no I don't'), the teacher instructs the students to work in pairs without telling them explicitly that one student should take the role of 'teacher' and the other the role of 'student'. Wen Ling, however, uses that role assignment language that was part of many previous teacher task instructions for turn allocation work in this task, assigning task roles and turn allocation for herself and her peer in lines 9–10. Her peer (Dep) orients to those directives and complies, taking the role of 'teacher' and starting the first turn of the task in line 12.

As we saw earlier (3.6, 3.13), the teacher uses this type of role assignment as part of the modeling of the task. In the class period before Wen Ling's and Dep's interaction in (3.14), the teacher had also incorporated such a task with these same role assignments. In that next class period, though the teacher did not model that role assignment for the task, Wen Ling used the role assignment the teacher had modeled in the class period before to open her dyadic task interaction. Here, we see the teacher's instructions become resources for students to use at a later time (Hellermann, 2006) as a practice for accomplishing the action of a task opening.

As illustrated in Excerpts (3.7)–(3.14) above, in a level 'C' community of practice, students used more linguistic resources in their dyadic tasks because they were not assigned roles in their tasks and the teacher's language support did not mediate the language of their task openings to the degree that it might have in level 'A'. A shorthand version of a change in participation across the different communities of practice is shown in Table 3.2.

Table 3.2 shows that in level 'A' classes, the teacher may explicitly give roles for students and students may use the language provided by the teacher to start their task interaction. Even when the teacher does not use those role assignments, that language becomes part of students shared repertoire and is available for use in a similar format for an equivalent context in a different activity. In the level 'C' communities of practice, the teacher's instructions do not include explicit role assignments and students negotiate turn allocation using language that is less specific to a particular teacher-assigned task. These examples show how the dialectic between reification (teacher-assigned language learning task) and participation (starting those tasks) in opening language learning tasks facilitates language learning in a community of practice.

The differences in task-opening sequences (verbal and non-verbal) between students' level 'A' and level 'C' interactions highlighted earlier give evidence for the reciprocal nature of language proficiency and classroom talk-in-interaction. The different methods employed for openings by students in the different communities of practice also show the negotiation patterns for talk-in-interaction that are particular to different classroom communities of practice. With a larger repertoire of linguistic resources in English, before the start of their teacher-assigned language learning task interactions, students in level 'C' communities of practice are often engaged in independent learning-focused activities such as skimming through a book, reading task instructions, taking notes or finishing some other writing related to a just previous task. In a level 'A' community

Table 3.2 Change of participation seen in openings from level 'A' and 'C' classes

Level	Teacher talk	Students' talk	Analysis
A	'practice together teacher, student and then change, teacher, student'	'do you teacher?' (Excerpt 3.6)	Students use teacher's language
A	'now, please continue, teacher and student' (3.13)	(you teacher ((gesture)) I student)[1]	
A	'now, ask your partner. Ask your partner. Do you have. Do you have a book. Do you have paper'	'teacher ((points to peer)) student ((points to self))' (Excerpt 3.14)	Students use teacher's language from a previous activity
C	—	'you s- you start with (the) number one (and) I uh I I advise you' (Excerpt 3.8)	Students use their own talk to allocate turns

[1] Wen Ling and Dep are seen starting seen starting the activity but since neither is wearing a wireless microphone that day, the audio is not clear

of practice, due to their more limited proficiency in the language of use, students are more reliant on language provided by the teacher for dyadic interaction and need to be much more focused on the teacher in the moments before a task is assigned. The independent engagement with the language, mediated by written text support and greater language proficiency in level 'C' communities of practice, affords more opportunities for interactive work by students to get together as a dyad, reframing the current classroom participation structure.

The opening moves of the students exhibited previously show that learners in level 'C' classes use a range of practices not used by students for opening interactions in level 'A' classes (and not part of the classroom community of practice of a level 'A' classroom). Some of these moves have been noted to be markers of particular discourse level structure in interaction (turn allocation, task clarification) and to foster particular types of interaction to follow while others display an orientation to the interactions as interpersonal as much as they are instrumental vehicles for task completion.

Language Development Seen Longitudinally in Interaction for Task Openings

After the presentation of an 'inventory', or, ways that students open task interactions in two different communities of practice, it is important to look closely at one student's trajectory of participation in the openings of task activities. Over time, this change in participation is traced across four interaction openings in the student's (Jorge's) second week of ESL classes in a serial dyadic interaction task and then in four interaction openings of the same student in a similar classroom activity from nine months later, Jorge's fortieth week of classes.

In serial dyadic task interactions, students are asked to exchange information with a number of their classmates, for example, name, country of origin or languages spoken. The task involves, in most cases, the students getting out of their seats and moving around the room to collect a limited set of the same information from a number of their classmates. The task is designed to give students the opportunity for repeated interactions and for repeated production of the same language and language forms (often the repeated asking and answering of a set of questions). While not part of their explicit design, these tasks also provide the opportunity for students to practice starting interactions, both when seated and while moving around the room. The tasks provide similar but subtle variations of setting compared to the seated dyadic interactions which require both similar and different formats for opening the particular interaction.

Serial dyadic task interactions in week 2: Jorge

Jorge was a 25-year-old immigrant from Mexico who came to the United States in 2002 and began taking classes several months after arriving. The excerpts in this section come from interactions from a level 'A' classroom, Jorge's second week of ESL classes. In the first series of serial dyadic task interactions (the excerpts in set 3.15), we see Jorge engaging in a task in which students are to ask their peers their names, if they are happy, sad, tired, or shy to elicit yes/no answers with one optional qualifier ('sometimes'). Students were to complete the worksheet (see Figure 3.1), filling out the information for themselves (in line 1) and then asking three more students to fill out the rest of the grid with 'yes' or 'no' in each space. In the row across the top of the grid is 'name' indicating students are to fill in their peers' names in the column below. In the next boxes in the first row are the characteristics they are supposed to find out about: 'happy', 'tired', 'sad' and 'shy'.

Figure 3.1 Student's grid for use in recording information collected in the task

Over the four different interactions, we see Jorge use a number of non-verbal and verbal resources to start each interaction and frame the upcoming task work. In the first interaction of the task (3.15a), after the teacher's instructions, Jorge opens the interaction with a discourse marker, postural alignment and the use of an address term, his peer's name, Vladilen, (which he learned in their previous class period) before another student (Digna) pre-empts that interaction and launches the task with Jorge in line 15.

(3.15a)
    7-1-02, A, 204, [1:21:23–1:21:45], Jorge, Vladilen, and Digna
    http://www.labschool.pdx.edu/Viewer/viewer.php?pl=JKHCP&cl=3.15a

```
2   Jo:  okay ((lifts paper from desk after writing))
3        (1)
4   Jo:  ((glances at V))
5        (4)
6   Jo:  ((turns to V and away quickly))
7        (1)
8   Jo:  ((shifts posture to orient to V))
9        (1)
10  Jo:  Vladilen. (.) ⌈Vladilen.
11  V:                 ⌊((orients to J)) Vladilen (.)
12            ⌈yeah? ((looks over to D))
13  D:        ⌊((moves to V & J's work space))
14  J:   ((looks to D))
```

15 **D:**   Jorge. (.) a:re you happy?
16 **Jo:** yes,

The discourse marker ('okay') in line 2 can be seen as a pivot move (Beach, 1993), a sign of closure or receipt of the teacher's instructions as well as a framing marker opening a new action or participation structure. After making several glances in Vladilen's direction, in line 8, Jorge establishes a postural orientation to Vladilen to start an interaction with him. After using Vladilen's name as a summons, Jorge achieves Vladilen's postural orientation and a response from him (lines 11–12). At the same time, Digna has moved over toward Vladilen's and Jorge's table which both Vladilen and Jorge orient to. Seeing Jorge's postural orientation, she launches the task with Jorge in line 15. She and Jorge complete the task and Jorge re-starts his interaction with Vladilen in (3.15b).

To make that restart, the orientation to the task (line 37), Jorge again uses an address term, and when he receives a confirmation by Vladilen (lines 38 and 41), launches the task with him in line 42.

(3.15b)
   7-1-02, A, 204, [1:22:25–1:22:53], Jorge and Vladilen
   http://www.labschool.pdx.edu/Viewer/viewer.php?pl=JKHCP&cl=3.15b

37 **Jo:** ((orients posture to V)) (   ) Vladilen (   )
38 **V:**   name Vladilen
39   (3) ((J writes))
40 **Jo:** (   ) Vladilen
41 **V:**   Vladilen
42 **Jo:** are you are you happy?
43 **V:**   Jos
44 **Jo:** (no) you ((points at V))
45 **V:**   (you) Jos?
46 **Jo:** you you are you happy?
47   (.5)
48 **V:**   yes
49 **Jo:** yes
50 **V:**   yes

After Jorge's task launch in 42, Vladilen does not offer an answer to the question but initiates another line of action making a candidate saying of Jorge's name (line 43). Jorge does not follow Vladilen's line of action but rather, initiates a repair to maintain his focus on his already launched action (line 44). His repair focuses on recipiency work negating Vladilen's candidate action and repeating the second person pronoun together with an indexical gesture and repeat of the task question (line 46) to get Vladilen's orientation to the action of the task – directives from a student 'asker' to be responded to by the recipient 'you'. Vladilen orients to the task question after this recipiency work by Jorge and responds to the directive in line 48. In this excerpt, some of the task prefatory talk by Jorge comes as a repair, implicated by his peer's shift in course of action and shows an orientation to maintaining an order for the turns at talk for the task.

After completing the task with his deskmate Vladilen, Jorge looks around the room for another student to engage with, sees Digna's name on her name card at the desk next to his and writes that on his own worksheet (Excerpt 3.15c, lines 50–51). He then orients his posture to Digna and makes a summons and the task prompt question in Spanish and English (lines 54–55).

(3.15c)
7-1-02, A, 204, [1:24:26-1:24:55], Jorge and Digna
http://www.labschool.pdx.edu/Viewer/viewer.php?pl=JKHCP&cl=3.15c

50 Jo: ((looks to other students)) (Digna) ((writes other
51   student's name on his worksheet))
52   (5)
53 V: (meese) times
54 Jo: ((shifts posture to Digna)) Digna. Es ( )
55   tu tu estas (.) are you happy?
56 D: happy? Yes.
57 Jo: (3) ((writes))

Jorge's summons in line 54 gets Digna's attention. Jorge believes her to be a speaker of Spanish and starts the task in Spanish before rephrasing the question in English (line 55) to which Digna responds. In 3.15c, Jorge's use of his peer's name acts as a summons for her attention and is a crucial part of the social interaction necessary for such tasks as she, the recipient of the summons, is seated in the adjacent desk and attending elsewhere.

Having worked through the task with his peers in the immediate vicinity of his desk, Jorge has observed other students moving around the classroom and moves out of his chair to interact with another Spanish-speaking student in 3.15d. After arriving at Tina's desk, he says something, possibly in Spanish, and then switches to English to greet Tina and record her name (line 61).

Opening Dyadic Task Interactions

(3.15d)
   7-1-02, A, 204, [1:27:06-1:27:28], Jorge and Tina
   http://www.labschool.pdx.edu/Viewer/viewer.php?pl=
   JKHCP&cl=3.15d

```
60  Jo:  ((gets out of seat moves to Tina's desk))
61       (    ) how are you. (.) Tina?
62  T:   fi:ne
63  Jo:  (3) ((writing)) are you happy?
64       (.)
65  T:   yes I am.
66  Jo:  #yes# (2) ((writing))
```

Tina responds to the greeting and after Jorge finishes writing (probably her name), he launches the task with the first task prompt (line 63). As discussed earlier, though greetings to start dyadic task interactions are rare, when they do occur, they occur when a student has changed location and moved into the vicinity of a peer.

Table 3.3 (below) outlines the sequences of moves in the series of four openings for task interactions from Jorge's first term in a beginning level ESL class.

In the four openings, Jorge uses discourse markers as framing moves between the end of the teacher's instructions and the launch of the task with his peers. Using the names of his peers serves several functions in the task openings. Names are recorded on the students' worksheets in a grid to organize the information they collect on each student. In the pre-task talk, Jorge uses his peers' names for interactive reasons as well. Jorge uses address terms as a way to ensure mutual orientation to the upcoming task (3.15b). When the use of the address term did not achieve mutual

Table 3.3 Summary of moves in Jorge's week 2 openings

Task-prefatory moves				Launch
3.15a	Discourse marker	Posture shift	Address term	Launch
3.15b	—	Posture shift	Address term	Launch: repair work for recipiency
3.15c	—	Posture shift	Address term	Launch
3.15d	Physical alignment	Greeting	Address term	Launch

orientation to the launch of this task in that case, Jorge had to do extra recipiency work (repeated pro-terms, gesture and reformulated task prompt question) to ensure his peer understood that he was launching the task with the first task directive. A name (3.15a, 3.15c) is also used as a summons to get the attention of peers who are not aligned posturally or seated outside Jorge's immediate physical presence. Finally, Jorge uses a name as part of a greeting sequence (3.15d) when moving to work with a peer seated in a different area of the classroom.

The series of interactions from this class period also showed that the change in physical location (3.15d) that is part of the design for serial task interactions has a pedagogical consequence of creating a new context for talk. When Jorge left his seat to interact with a peer (3.15d) and moved into physical co-presence with that peer, other task-prefatory work, a greeting sequence, became conditionally relevant. In that excerpt, the greeting sequence also serves as a place for Jorge to get his peer's name.

Jorge's serial dyadic interaction tasks in week 40

Nine months later, Jorge was in his fourth term of ESL classes when a serial dyadic interaction task was assigned by the teacher. Focusing again on the practices for opening a series of these tasks, while many of the same non-verbal and verbal moves used in his second week in school are also used in this ninth month of study, there is also some evidence of Jorge's change in level of participation in the language use in these contexts.

The four excerpts presented from this class period (3.16) are part of a serial dyadic interaction task in which students were assigned to ask two past tense, yes/no questions to their classmates. Students were provided with task prompts in the form of 'infinitive verb' + 'object', for example, 'drink coffee', 'eat chocolate', 'call relatives'. Students were instructed to form yes/no questions for past tense such as 'did you drink coffee yesterday'? In the first of these excerpts, the teacher finishes her task instructions, Jorge orients his posture to his deskmate, Julia, and utters a discourse marker 'okay' and Julia's name (lines 79–80). Julia responds with a receipt token 'okay' in line 81 and, as Julia is writing, Jorge explicitly checks whether she is prepared to start the task (line 82).

(3.16a)
    4-18-03, B, 206, [34:18-34:46], Jorge and Julia
    http://www.labschool.pdx.edu/Viewer/viewer.php?pl=JKHCP&cl=3.16a

78 **Te:** try to ask many different students.

79 **Jo:** ((Jorge shifts posture toward his deskmate)) okay
80   Julia,
81 **Ju:** okay ((Julia is writing))
82 **Jo:** are you ready?
83 **Ju:** (1) ((stops writing and orients posture to Jorge))
84   (come on)
85 **Jo:** okay ((clears throat))
86   (1)
87 **Jo:** did you (2) °okay° (2) did you call tre- (1) did
88   you call relatives yesterday?
89 **Ju:** yes I ((looks to board)) yes I did.

Julia responds to Jorge's question non-verbally by ending her writing and shifting her posture toward Jorge (line 83) and makes what may be an exhortation to start (line 84) and Jorge, after a framing discourse marker (line 85), launches the task in line 87.

After finishing the interaction with Julia, in (3.16b), Jorge displays his knowledge of the format for serial dyadic interaction tasks by stating the need to speak with other students (line 3) and moving out of his seat to an area where Eduardo and Jing are interacting with one another and the teacher. Upon arriving in that area of the classroom, Jorge repeats some of the instructions that the teacher is giving to Eduardo (lines 7 and 11) and when she models (speaking slowly) the negative response to a past tense yes/no question (line 16), Jorge makes a collaborative completion (Lerner, 1991) of the start of the teacher's model providing the appropriate tense-marked, negative operator (line 17). Eduardo makes a candidate repeat of the teacher's modeling which both the teacher and Jorge orient to as incorrect and Jorge follows the teacher's correction (line 19) with his own (line 20).

(3.16b)
   4-18-03, B, 206, [35:59-36:37], Jorge and Eduardo
   http://www.labschool.pdx.edu/Viewer/viewer.php?pl=JKHCP&cl=3.16b

3 **Jo:** you ask uh (.) different estudents ((rises from
4   chair and moves to another student))
5   (4)
6 **Te:** ((to Eduardo)) question did you
7 **Jo:** did you
8 **Te:** question did you
9 **E:** no I did?

```
10  Te:  yes I did,
11  Jo:  ⌈yes I did,
12  Ji:  ⌊yes I did,
13  Te:  yes I ⌈did
14  Ji:       ⌊no I didn't.
15  E:   ⌈no.
16  Te:  ⌊<no I>
17  Jo:  didn't.
18  E:   did
19  Te:  <didn't>
20  Jo:  <didn't>
21  Te:  didn't (.) didn't
22       (3) ((moves paper onto E's desk, orients posture))
23  Jo:  Eduardo.
24  E:   ((turns head toward Jorge))
25  Te:  did you ((speaking to another student))
26  Jo:  did you: mm ((Jo is locating an action on his
27       worksheet)) cook jesterday?
28       (1)
29  E:   yes I did.
30  Jo:  jes I did.
```

In lines 7–20, Jorge is a peripheral participant to the teacher's interaction with Eduardo. But by moving into this physical space, he is able to participate peripherally and legitimately both repeating the teacher's modeling of the language forms for the task and by collaborating in her explanation to a peer.

After the teacher finishes her work with Eduardo, Jorge opens his interaction with Eduardo with an address term in line 23 which gets his peer's attention. After getting Eduardo's postural orientation, Jorge launches the task with the first question in line 26 repeating the teacher's words (the first two words of the question) and elongating 'you'. He then pauses at a point that is not prosodically, pragmatically or syntactically complete (Ford et al., 1996). This placement of the intra-turn pause at a point that is not a turn transition relevance place (Ford & Thompson, 1996) insures that he can hold the floor to complete his turn. This hold of his turn-in-progress allows him time to find a peer-appropriate action from the choices on his worksheet (we see him scanning the worksheet with his finger during that turn hold) with which to complete the question. He finds 'cook' and asks that question to launch the task. After the task intermezzo language work with the teacher and Eduardo (lines 7–20), Jorge produces a quite fluent task question (lines 26–27).

After ending his interaction with Eduardo and engaging with another student in that area, Jorge moves across the room to the area of Abebe. In (3.16c) we see how face-to-face dyadic interaction provides the opportunity for a student to try out new language, in this case, Jorge's candidate saying of Abebe's name (line 31). The task requires students to record their peer interlocutors' names on their worksheet as they collect information from the task questions. Abebe is seated with his name card in front of him and Jorge could have simply written out Abebe's name by reading it from the name card. The candidate saying of Abebe's name (produced with a rising pitch and oriented to by Abebe as a question) allows him to practice saying the name and serves as a framing address term, a task-prefatory marker opening the interaction.

(3.16c)
4-18-03, B, 206, [39:34-39:52], Jorge and Abebe
http://www.labschool.pdx.edu/Viewer/viewer.php?pl=JKHCP&cl=3.16c

```
28  Jo:  ((moves to Abebe's desk and aligns with him))
29  Jo:  uh ⌈: :m ((leans to look at name card))
30  A:       ⌊((orients posture to Jorge)) Yes sir
31  Jo:  Abebe?
32  A:   yeah that's me (.) (    )
33  Jo:  °okay° ((clears throat))
34       (.5)
35  Jo:  did you: ⌈mm (1) did you tal- talk on the phone
36  A:            ⌊*---------------**
37       yesterday?=
38  A:   yes I did.
```
* = gaze away from speaker
** = gaze on speaker

After receiving a confirmation (line 32) that his candidate name saying is correct, Jorge launches the task in line 35 with a question about talking on the phone. In the task launch, Jorge pauses mid turn (as in 3.16b) to locate an appropriate question on his worksheet. During this pause, his interlocutor, Abebe, moves his gaze to another part of the room when Jorge continues his task launch after the pause and orients to Abebe's lack of gaze, he restarts the turn once he sees that he has achieved his interlocutor's gaze (Goodwin, 1981). Details such as the restart of a turn orienting to recipient gaze shows the effect interaction has on the production of talk and of adult learners' capabilities to make adjustments in their talk noted to occur in the talk of fluent first language speakers.

In the next interaction from this serial task interaction presented here (3.16d), Jin moves into a mutual work area with Jorge and as she erases something from her worksheet, Jorge starts their interaction with an address term (line 68). Almost at the same time as Jorge's addressing of Jin, she greets Jorge and laughs a bit. In line 72, orienting to Jin's erasing work, and, perhaps, her laughter, Jorge asks Jin if she is finished with her task work from her previous engagement.

(3.16d)
4-18-03, B, 206, [43:51-44:05], Jorge and Jin
http://www.labschool.pdx.edu/Viewer/viewer.php?pl=JKHCP&cl=3.16d

```
65 Jo:   ((has moved to the front of the room to wait for a
66        partner to open up))
67 Ji:   ((moves to table near Jorge and erases something))
68 Jo:   Ji ⌈n.
69 Ji:      ⌊hi Jorge
70 Jo:   um::
71 Ji:   heh heh heh heh
72 Jo:   you finish?
73       (2) ((Jin lifts her paper, orients posture to
74       Jorge))
75 Jo:   d- did you ((clears throat)) did you watch tee vee
76       yesterday?
77 Ji:   yes I did.
```

Jorge's pre-task inquiry in line 72 shows how he uses subtly different, context-dependent language for similar framing actions. There is a similarity between the actions accomplished by this question and that asked in the first interaction of the task in (3.16a) when he asked Julia 'are you ready'. In that interaction, Julia had been writing, most likely, the instructions from the teacher prior to the first task interaction of the series. In (3.16d), students have been engaged in the task for some time and Jorge sees that his next task interlocutor, Jin, has been working with another student. The question 'you finish' orients to her possible ongoing task work while 'are you ready' addresses his first partner's preparation for the start of the series of interactions. Jin does not respond verbally to Jorge's question, but adjusts the print materials for the task and orients her posture to Jorge who then launches the task in line 75.

In the final interaction from the series (3.16e), Jorge has returned to his desk and he initiates an interaction with Reinaldo who is standing near his desk.

(3.16e)
4-18-03, B, 206, [46:42-46:59], Jorge and Reinaldo
http://www.labschool.pdx.edu/Viewer/viewer.php?pl=
JKHCP&cl=3.16e

```
85 Jo:  mm Reinaldo.
86      (1) ((R turns to face Jorge))
87 Jo:  (digamos) okay. did you mm ((mumbling to self as
88      he looks through list)) okay ((clears throat)) did
89      you wake up early yesterday?
90 R:   yes I did
```

Before the interaction is opened, Reinaldo is not facing Jorge. Jorge makes a summons to express his availability for the task and to advise Reinaldo's postural orientation and a mutual work space (line 85). After getting Reinaldo's postural alignment, Jorge marks the upcoming task launch with Spanish and English discourse markers (line 87). After launching the task, he holds his turn with the placeholder 'mm' after the subject of the sentence (line 87), a position that is not grammatically complete and uses this hold to search his list for an appropriate verb/action for his task question as in (3.16b) and (3.16c). Upon finding a verb, he re-marks the re-start of the task launch with 'okay' (line 88) and utters the complete task question which is responded to by Reinaldo (line 90).

The excerpts presented in the previous section illustrated a context for talk-in-interaction that is likely to be unique to a classroom setting: consecutive sequences of face-to-face interaction in which students are to perform the same task with a different student. This context provides an interesting site for the investigation of an individual learner within the classroom community of practice showing the details of talk-in-interaction used at a point where both face-to-face interaction and task interaction must be accomplished. Jorge's opening moves for his interactions from week 40 in the serial dyadic interaction task are outlined below in Table 3.4.

Table 3.4 shows that the sequences of talk used in opening the interactions in week 40 were more complex than in week 2 suggesting evidence for Jorge's change in his degree of participation in the classroom community of practice. In his second week of ESL classes, in a series of four interactions with different peers, Jorge uses postural orientation, discourse markers and his interlocutors' names as address terms and summonses to establish an opening frame with his interlocutor for the start of the teacher assigned task. In the fourth interaction of that series, due to physical location, he engaged in a greeting sequence with his peer. While those first

Table 3.4 Summary of moves in Jorge's week 40 openings

	Task prefatory moves					Launch
	Posture shift	Discourse marker	Address term	Inquiry into readiness	Discourse marker	Launch
3.16a	—	—	—	—	—	Launch
3.16b	—	—	—	Physical alignment	Address term	Launch: Pause at non-TRP
3.16c	—	—	Physical alignment	Address term	Discourse marker	Launch: Pause at non-TRP
3.16d	—	—	Physical alignment	Address term	Inquiry to readiness	Launch
3.16e	—	Physical alignment	Address term	Use of Spanish	Discourse marker	Launch: Pause at non-TRP

Opening Dyadic Task Interactions 81

term interactions of Jorge's were successful task interactions, the time he took between his consecutive interactions suggests a bit of hesitation or need for more time to start the interactions.

Forty weeks later, in a similarly designed serial dyadic interaction task, Jorge uses similar practices to frame the task interaction. However, along with postural orientation, discourse markers, and peers' names, other practices appear as part of Jorge's and his peers' shared repertoire for opening dyadic tasks in his week forty (level 'B') classroom community of practice. In two of the interactions, Jorge uses language that does the work of explicitly assessing his peers' potential recipiency for the upcoming task. In the first excerpt from the series, he orients to his deskmate, Julia, writing in her notebook and inquires as to whether she is ready for the start of the task: 'are you ready?' In a later interaction of the same serial task, orienting to his peer writing on her worksheet and recently disengaged from interaction with a classmate, asks if she has finished: 'you finish?' In Jorge's task openings in week forty the differences noted in the comparison of openings at different proficiency levels are apparent. Overall, in the interactions from week 40, a greater degree of participation in English talk-in-interaction is displayed in the number and types of verbal moves used to open his interactions.

These details for interaction in Jorge's openings of serial dyadic task interactions forty weeks apart show the micro-level language work which entails different degrees of participation and indexes the negotiation through language that is characteristic of different classroom communities of practice. We will see Jorge's work again in Chapter 5 working in the same interactions with the same interlocutors when the focus of the analysis shifts to how learners disengage from their face-to-face task interactions.

Conclusion

While previous research on interactions in everyday conversation and institutional settings has noted the phenomenon of transitional topics at the start of these interactions (Maynard & Zimmerman, 1984; Sacks, 1992 [1970 winter lecture 5]; Stokoe, 2000), in serial dyadic interaction tasks in a language learning classroom, for the most part, we do not see full topics emerging as 'false firsts' (Sacks, 1992). The prefatory framing work is greatly reduced because of the goal-oriented nature of the interactions and the limited time for the interactions set by the teachers. Though the time frame for the interactions is limited, the examples presented in this chapter show that adult language learners of different levels of proficiency co-construct different ways to frame and launch their task interactions.

These examples also show the starts of tasks to be sites where the negotiation of reified language for teacher-assigned tasks and local participation intersect in the practices for accomplishing the opening action of the tasks, practices that become the language of a classroom community of practice.

A uniformity of practices in different classroom communities of practice is seen in the findings that all students, regardless of proficiency level, open their dyadic task interactions in the language learning classroom with a physical orientation to frame the interaction as a dyadic task interaction. At beginning levels of language proficiency, students with fewer language resources are more likely to directly launch the start of the task after the physical orientation. For these novice users of English, however, we saw that the teacher-designed dyadic interactions provide opportunities for them to use teacher-provided language (role assignment) as a way to organize the starts of their task interactions by assigning roles for the task. With that role assignment they are also allocating turns for the task – who will take the first and who will take the second turn. When teachers did not explicitly model the task as involving role assignment at a later time, students were still able to use the teacher's language of role assignment from previous tasks to get their interactions underway.

In classes in which students have greater proficiency in the language, the result of this proficiency is that participation in the classroom community of practice includes more talk before the starts of dyadic task interactions. The students observed in more advanced proficiency classroom communities of practice were more likely to start their interactions by orienting to a shift in participation structures using discourse markers, by explicitly allocating turns for the task and by clarifying and confirming aspects of the upcoming task. This introductory space for the framing of the upcoming task, however, was also a site for students to display camaraderie and mutual appreciation through humorous exchanges. Any work of this type in the beginning level communities of practice was more likely to be done non-verbally.

Chapter 4
Story Tellings in Dyadic Task Interactions

Introduction

Once their dyadic task interactions are underway, student interaction is, to no surprise, most often oriented directly to the task assigned by the teacher. As the previous chapter showed, the talk-in-interaction students use to start these tasks is not directly taught and (in most cases) not part of the teachers' instructions for carrying out tasks. Similarly, while the task is underway, students face micro-contexts when a particular social action may be relevant but for which (as in the case of opening the interaction) the teacher-assigned task has not provided language. The social action of focus here are non-elicited story tellings. As with opening interactions, the fact that story tellings are not taught by the teacher should not be seen as a fault of task design; well-designed classroom tasks provide space for students' creativity with the language. What is apparent is that in doing task-focused dyadic interaction, even in classes for students at a beginning proficiency level, students use the linguistic and interactive resources available to them to engage in the basic mechanisms of turn taking regardless of what the teacher-assigned task is. Such mechanisms include the preference for one speaker to speak at a time, repairing areas of trouble in their talk (Hellermann, forthcoming) and, as this chapter illustrates, undertaking story tellings. The forthcoming analyses will show that the mechanisms that adult learners of English use for their story tellings and their purposes for their undertaking are similar to those methods used by expert speakers of the language reported in the literature on conversational story tellings in US American English (Jefferson, 1978; Ochs, 1997; Sacks, 1974, 1992). These unsolicited story tellings from student-student dyadic task interaction show more evidence for the uninstructed micro-interactive practices that (re)constitute the adult language learning classroom community of practice.

Research on Formats for Conversational Story Telling

Conversational story tellings are reports of one-time events in the past that occur in conversation interactions in unobtrusive, unmarked ways. Such story tellings are co-constructed by participants in a way so that the perspective teller of the story signals that he/she is about to launch a story. When the recipient orients to this potential launch of a story telling, the teller tells the story and the unmarked turn taking system (alternating turns between, e.g. two people A-B-A-B...) is suspended briefly while teller relays the story in a more monologic format.

One of the first discoveries or understandings about conversation as a social system was the systematic ways that conversationalists take turns. At the time of the development of conversation analysis (mid-1960s), Harvey Sacks and colleagues began to formulate the 'mechanisms' by which speakers of US American English order their turn-taking in conversations (this research resulted in the seminal 'turn-taking' paper by Sacks *et al.*, 1974). With the understanding that participants in conversations take turns, alternating, in an orderly fashion (A-B-A-B...), and that the participants themselves orient to conversational turn taking in this way, Sacks (1972, 1992) wondered how it is that participants sometimes are able to hold the floor for longer periods of time, beyond a single turn without it being treated as some kind of breach of talk-in-interaction. 'How do you deal with a situation where you want to talk for more than a sentence-length utterance?' (Sacks, 1992: 225). In the research and lectures of Sacks and in the research in the years following (Jefferson, 1978; Lerner, 1992; Mandelbaum, 1993; Norrick, 1998; Polyani, 1985; and others), the answer to this question was explored in more detail. This work illustrated the members' methods for broaching, launching and maintaining these longer story projects within the context of a conversation where the majority of the talk proceeds as a sequence of turns, taken every other one by one participant. Excerpt (4.1), from a conversation among three friends in the United States having dinner (Jim, Judy, Karl), shows the start of a typical conversational story telling.

(4.1)
    Jim-Judy [6:24]

1	**Jim:**	no, but I say banahna because that's the right
2		⌈way to say it.
3	**Karl:**	⌊hih heh heh heh
4	**Judy:**	mm hm
5	**Karl:**	heh
6		(1.5)

```
7   Judy:=>    did you hear about this guy calling up the
8              queen?
9   Jim:       I did actually.=it was quite funny.
10  Judy:      hm hhm.
11  Karl:      no. who called the queen.
12             (.5)
13  Judy:      a Canadian dee jay? ((DJ))
14  Karl:      me(h)ehah!
15  Jim:       pretended to be the Premier of
16  Karl:      eohoh! ↑he ⌈ohh
17  Judy:                 ⌊of Canada
18  Karl:      rea:lly,
19  Judy:      ye⌈ah and they had a private conversation for
20  Karl:        ⌊great
21  Judy:      about seventeen minutes.=disc⌈ussing the
22  Karl:                                   ⌊mm
23  Judy:      future of Quebec and stuff.
```

Just before the story telling is launched by Judy, the three friends had been talking about Jim's leaky roof when Jim (who is from Scotland) commented on the way he pronounced the word 'tympani' (describing the sound of water dripping into his apartment). He ended that spate of talk with an ironic remark about his dialect being the 'right' way to speak English. After some laughter and a short pause, Judy broaches a possible story telling with a pre-question (line 7). The story telling is done collaboratively between Jim and Judy at first before Judy takes over in line 19.

Stories are launched successfully when the teller has judged the position within the sequence of talk in the interaction to be appropriate. The story is launched because it is deemed to be relevant in the context of the ongoing talk and appropriate for the particular reciepient(s) (Sacks, 1992, v. II: 229). Stories get underway when the potential teller makes it clear to the recipient that a story is forthcoming and recipient(s) allow the trajectory of the talk to move into a story. Often, a teller marks a forthcoming story with some discourse marker ('oh') and embedded repetition (Jefferson, 1978) – the recycling of some previous talk to make the forthcoming story cohesive with the previous talk. Such recyclings are familiar in the typical format 'speaking of X' (Jefferson, 1972).[16] In this way, stories are sequentially implicative in that they are launched in a way that shows they are accounting to the sequence of the interaction so far. In (4.1), Judy does not start with a discourse marker or a recycling of previous talk, but makes a more subtle topical link. Jim's commenting on his dialect of English (from the United Kingdom) allows Judy's story about the Queen of England to be heard as relevant at this point in the conversation.

When the story is launched, recipients for the story cooperate by allowing teller to proceed by not taking full turns alternating with teller. Recipients orient to stories as underway by offering minimal and supportive receipt tokens ('mm hm', 'yeah' and the like). At the end of a story telling, participants implicate the story's place in the overall sequence of talk in interaction when they orient to the story as a story ('formulating') (Garfinkel & Sacks, 1970), that is, doing talk that orients to the fact that a story was just accomplished. This may be done by recipient assessing the story or by recipient offering a 'second' story (Sacks, 1992) that is topically coherent to the just completed 'first' story. Sacks presented this example as a case of a story following a story:

(4.2)

```
1   A:  Say did you see anything in the paper last night or
2       hear anything on the local radio, Ruth Henderson and
3       I drove down to Ventura yesterday, and on the way
4       home we saw the most gosh awful wreck.
5   B:  You know, I looked and looked in the paper-I think I
6       told you f-for the uh f-fall over at the Bowl that
7       night. And I never saw a thing about it, and I
8       ⌈looked in the
9   A:  ⌊mm hm
10  B:  next couple of evenings
11      (1.0)
12  B:  never saw a th- a mention of it.
```

In lines 5–12, B's 'second' story is given as a response to A's first story (lines 1–4).

Story Tellings in the Adult Language Learning Classroom Community of Practice

In the adult language learning classrooms of focus, the physical arrangement of students (seated next to one another) and the classroom participation structures for instruction (students frequently working on language learning tasks in dyads) provide a site for potential story tellings between peer learners. Almost all the non-elicited story tellings in the collection for this study were done during interaction that was part of language learning tasks (one occurred between student and teacher at the start of the class period). By definition, felicitous story tellings cannot be considered 'off task': they are done because of and as part of the trajectory of the talk-in-interaction. When a story telling is attempted and its timing is inappropriate or its topic is not relevant, participants will orient to that attempted story telling as inappropriate and the non-felicitous telling does not continue. In the classroom, this means when stories are attempted, oriented to and get underway during dyadic task interaction, they have been done felicitously, they will have topical coherence and a recognized reason for being told.

The presence of story tellings in the adult language learning classroom show how dyadic language learning task interactions are important sites for fostering unplanned talk-in-interaction between students. They also display another part of the micro-linguistic make up of the classroom community of practice. Students' use of story tellings in their dyadic tasks shows another type of social action through talk, another language competency, that teachers cannot plan for in the design of their language learning dyadic tasks. Besides the opportunities for language development, students' use of story tellings in their dyadic interaction also allows them to do interpersonal relationship work which is important in building an effective learning community. Moreover, while resulting in language development and interpersonal relationship work, learners launch stories in these contexts for a story telling in these contexts is for the purpose of accomplishing the particular language-learning task interaction.

Unfortunately, my collection of story tellings is not large enough to show a longitudinal perspective on any individual learner's language development. The story tellings in the collection are all not elicited by a teacher as part of the instructions for a teacher-assigned language-learning task. The collection includes 17 story tellings in total, 12 from intermediate level classes and 5 from beginning level classes. While the analysis will not show any individual's development through story tellings in a longitudinal way, the analysis will show differences between the way stories are implemented by learners in these two class levels as evidence for how story tellings are social practices done through talk as part of the make up of different classroom communities of practice and are sites for seeing language development.

Similarities of These Tellings to Previous Reports of Conversation

Markers for story openings and story prefaces

One aspect of story tellings in conversational interaction which was remarkable to Sacks in his first discussions of this issue was subtle way in which the interaction moved from the standard turn taking mechanism to a situation when one person had the floor. In the examples from the classroom, upcoming story tellings have opening markers (discourse markers, temporal locators, topical connections). As with the openings of task interactions, there is not a great deal of story prefacing or 'entrance talk' (Polyani, 1985), however.[17] Excerpts (4.3–4.5) show typical examples of the linguistic marking used to start the stories in the classrooms.

(4.3) Intermediate proficiency level: Temporal locator
5-28-04, 206, D, [1:28:27]

S: **when I was study** English before?
   ((story underway))

(4.4) Intermediate proficiency level: Discourse marker
5-4-04, 204, C, [27:30], Richard and Katrina

R: .hh **you know**, ahh: I send my camera to Portland location repair. to repair. ((While D uses a present tense verb, 'send', this is the launch of a one time event in the past.))

(4.5) Beginning proficiency level: pre-question and address term
5-10-02, 206, B, [2:37:30], Raisa and teacher

R: **you know what? Daniella?** heh hah hah hah
   ((story starts))

Locally occasioned

Another aspect of the story tellings in the classroom dyadic interaction that is similar to those reported on in the literature on conversational interaction are the fact that they are locally occasioned and topically relevant. Topic familiarity resulting in topic cohesion has been shown to be an important factor for language learners to produce fluent talk (Smith, 1989; Zuengler, 1989) and novice learners have been shown to exhibit a lack of topic coherence due to their lack of grammatical control (Kramsch, 1983; Long, 1980). However, other studies show that learners can negotiate change in topics in a gradual way, though they may speak about more topics than native speakers would (Fernandez Aguero, 2003). In (4.6) from an intermediate class, students (Masha and Lan) are working on a dyadic task in which they are to ask one another about what they did on the

Story Tellings in Dyadic Task Interactions

weekend, remember that information, and then use that information to write a paragraph about that peer. Early in the task, Lan reports that she had been looking for a job over the past weekend (lines 1–3). Seven minutes later in the task, students are assessing the difficulty of looking for a job when there is something like a closing sequence to that assessment talk (lines 5–7). After the closing, Masha starts a turn with a temporal clause (line 8) focusing on the past followed by a story telling sequence.

(4.6) Intermediate proficiency level
4-27-04, 204, C, [17:42; 24:50-25:24], Masha & Lan
http://www.labschool.pdx.edu/Viewer/viewer.php?pl= JKHCP&cl=4.6

```
1    L:      you were looking for a job
2    M:      yes I was looking for a job.
3    L:      mm what did you find (.) find (.) find out.
4    M:      I didn't find ((shaking head))
             ((seven minutes pass))
5    L:      it's (.) hard
6    M:      very hard. very hard.
7            (2)
8    M:=>    when I came here I was looking for a job.
9    L:      ((nods))
10           (1)
11   M:      after one week abo- I was two months
12   L:      two months?
13   M:      yes but I couldn't find a job.
14           (6)
15   M:      (but) I spent a lot of money
```

Masha's start of the story telling in line 8 uses a temporal locator and the multi-clause turn ends pragmatically incomplete (Ford & Thompson, 1996); the progressive aspect suggests a duration during which something else may have happened. Lan orients to a story getting underway and offers a minimal receipt token (non-verbal nodding in line 9).

In (4.7), students (Hae and Mei) have been assigned to talk about characteristics of their home towns and home countries. The two students had been engaged in the task activity for six minutes at the point where the story telling starts. Just before the start of the story telling, students have been speaking about the levels of crime in their respective countries. Before her telling, Hae assesses her country as having little crime (line 5). In lines 6–10 there is a clarification and closing sequence to the talk about crime in Hae's country. Mei orients to the task-focus for this talk by pointing to her worksheet (line 8). This talk about crime in each country makes the story that Hae launches (line 9) about crime in the United States relevant.

(4.7) Intermediate proficiency level
2-15-05, 206, C, [39:13-39:41], Hae and Mei
http://www.labschool.pdx.edu/Viewer/viewer.php?pl=JKHCP&cl=4.7

```
1    H:      it just the small n ⌈o big no kill people just (.) took
2    M:                          ⌊the small?
3                    something? you kno:w, (.) just this.
4                    (2)
5    H:      yeah so ((smacks lips)) my country there in a fe:w
6    M:      a few?=
7    H:      =yeah
8    M:      okay little ((points to worksheet))
9    H:=>    nhoh
10   M:      little
11   H:      I'm- work I'm worker in- in here?
12   M:      mm h ⌈m
13   H:            ⌊I'm worker in a: in the clothes?
14   M:      unh huh
15   H:      store?
16   M:      unh huh
17   H:      yesterday:y,
18   M:      unh huh
19   H:      just on- only me in the work.
20   M:      unh huh
18   H:      the the: two: black skin people womans the come in
19   M:      mm hm
20   H:      I- I saw in a (.) young people.
21                    (2)
22   H:      sh- I think mn she (very um) (.) in the bad action,
23   M:      pay ah (pa ⌈y) ah huh okay uh huh
24   H:                 ⌊(    ) I'm from I saw in the hall,
25   M:      uhuh
26   H:      >(saw in the   ). HHHHHH HHHHHHHH ⌈he he
27   M:                                        ⌊s- stole
                                                  something
```

Story Tellings in Dyadic Task Interactions

In (4.7), the students' engagement in task-oriented talk about a particular topic category (crime) made a subcomponent example of that topic category (in Hae's story) relevant.

Assessments by story recipient

Assessments by story recipients are one common response to stories that have also been noted in reports on conversational interaction. An assessment following a story shows first that recipient is orienting to the story as complete and secondly, that recipient has understood the just-completed story. Excerpts (4.8) and (4.9) show recipients assessing just completed stories.

(4.8)
 2-15-05, 206, C, [41:04-41:13], Hae and Mei
 http://www.labschool.pdx.edu/Viewer/viewer.php?pl=JKHCP&cl=4.8

11	H:	((points to self)) so, I ((gestures with fingers))
12		⌈(sell)
13	M:	⌊stolen.
14	H:	yeah she going in outsi:de.
15	M:=>	↑**wo:w** ((looks to front of room))
16	H:	hhawh ((adjusts posture toward front of room))

(4.9)
 5-4-04, 206, D, [2:39:09-2:39:31], Huan and Eunyoung
 http://www.labschool.pdx.edu/Viewer/viewer.php?pl=JKHCP&cl=4.9

20	H:	be↑cause. they don't know ↑life. (1) they very good
21		student, very good college er everything study good
22		good perfect. .hh but (.) he don't know li:fe.= so,
23	E:	so, ⌈so ye:ah
24	H:	⌊it's a big pr<u>o</u>blem.
25	E:=>	**but that case is just a little.** all most student do not
26		kill.

In (4.8), after speaking of an incident of shoplifting, Mei assesses Hae's story in line 15 with a high pitched and stretched emotive token. A different, slightly critical assessment is given by recipient (Eunyoung) in Excerpt (4.9). After Huan tells her about a case of a student suicide, Eunyoung assesses the story as something of an exaggeration in line 25.

Differences Between These Tellings and Previous Reports of Conversation

Negotiation for meaning of a lexical item

The learners' status as novice members of the 'fluent English users' community of practice is also seen in the story telling examples. While the story tellings in the classroom dyadic task interactions have many of the defining characteristics of conversational story telling, there are overt examples of language proficiency issues that appear in these stories that has not been noted in previous research on story tellings in conversation. For example, in (4.10), we see the possible start of a telling (lines 1 and 3) get delayed after Perla's repair initiation (line 7) and following side sequence to clarify the word 'rent'.

(4.10) Beginning proficiency level
　　5-7-02, 206, B, [16:20-17:18], Raisa and Perla
　　http://www.labschool.pdx.edu/Viewer/viewer.php?pl= JKHCP&cl=4.10

> Lines 1 & 3: Possible prefaces to a story telling

```
1   R:  ((laughs)) I'm all time work.
2   P:  ((laughs))
3   R:  because my house it's dirty,
4       (3.0)
5   R:  mm (1) my house it's rent somebody?
6       (.5)
7   P:  rent?
8   R:  umm=
9   P:  =apartment?
10      (.5)
11  R:  no. (.5) okay. I have a house,
12  P:  ((nods))
13  R:  okay but I want to: (.) ((gestures))
12      not sell (.) um (3) um (.) >okay< ((puts hand on P's leg))
        somebody come in my house, and uh okay
13      I want sit sit here, and give me (.) one month
14      rent. okay?
15  P:  mm hm
16      (2.0)
17  R:  first (.) first month give me rent. and next month
18      give me rent. and next (.) rent.
```

> Lines 7–15: Side sequence negotiating the meaning of the word 'rent'

Repair sequences and word searches happen ubiquitously in the conversations of fluent speakers of a language for various reasons. Excerpt (4.10) shows, however, that their novice status with the language (working out the meaning of a fairly basic word such as 'rent'), makes such sequences likely in the story tellings of these learners. Negotiation sequences over lexical items or grammatical form, however, do not derail the learners' ongoing course of action. The adult learners from this database observed for this and other research (Harris, 2004) shows the persistence of learners in the completion of their work as learners. This is seen in (4.8) as well when Raisa's preface to her story continues in line 17.

Absence of 'second stories'

Several other structural infelicities in the performance of story tellings by the learners also emerged. The first is that, while the story tellings themselves are always oriented to as such by recipients, there were no examples of recipients proffering stories in response to a just-completed story. Such 'second stories' have been noted to be common ways that recipients display that they understood the just-completed story and that they found it relevant to the ongoing talk (Sacks, 1992). While novice proficiency in the language might be one reason for the lack of these second stories, the nature of the context of the classroom is also a likely reason for their absence. Story tellings occur when students are engaged in dyadic task interaction. Such interactions are always limited in time with the teacher usually specifying at the start of the task that students have some period of time (from two to ten minutes usually) to complete the task. For this reason, potential second story tellers in classroom dyadic task interaction may forego this more lengthy response to a first story.

Story misinterpretation

Two other examples of stories needing repair work occurred in one story told to the entire class by a student in an intermediate level classroom. In (4.11), after her story is underway, Huan tells of a situation when a student she used to work with used to hit people (lines 5–6). Her classmates assess this report as something laughable (line 7). Huan takes her classmates laughter as their interpretation that her report in line 5 was a punch line or main point of the story and that the story is over. She tells her classmates to 'hold on', that the story is 'not finished'. Huan's orientation to other students' laughter has been noted to occur in US English conversational story telling (Jefferson, 1978). As the laughter subsides, Huan continues the story.

(4.11)
5-7-04, 206, D, [1:00:15-1:03-28], Huan
http://www.labschool.pdx.edu/Viewer/viewer.php?pl=JKHCP&cl=4.11

```
1    H:         I remember one example (there is) really uh really
2               interesting. I think the the high school uh teacher is
3               very very important for the social. Why. I ha(ve) a one
4               student in my university. He mean for everybody. This
5    =>         class is ten person, he bock bock bock ((pantomimes
6    =>         boxing)) every ⌈one    no hold on not finished.
7    Ss:=>                      ⌊((laughter))
8                         ⌈(.5)
9    Ss:                  ⌊((laughter))
10   H:         the the g- the department my department the the (.) the
11              the uh: the ((looks to teacher)) ( ⌈ )
12   Te:                                          ⌊director
13   H:         the director. Uh Huan, can you take care of he?
14              try, so, he come my class, so, I I told- because he
15              believe me. I'm good artist, I'm dah dah dah, he believe
16              me. the first.
17   Te:        mm hm ⌈trust
18   H:               ⌊I- yeah tru⌈st me     (so I say)
19   Te:                          ⌊trust is the most important thing
20   H:         (with) him, show me your artwork. he show me. (.) the all
21              work, for example the paper, the paper? he make things
22              here.
23              (.)
24   H: =>      if the paper bigger this, he make things he ⌈re or
25   Ss:=>                                                  ⌊((laugh))
26   H: =>      here >no no no< <don't laugh> he ha(s) a problem.
27   A:         why.
28   H:         ↑wh⌈:y the paper (.) bigger, he made here.
29   A:            ⌊what kind of problem.
30   H:         cause he always
31   Te:        oh: bec⌈ause he was
32   H:                ⌊(it's his)
33   Ss:        ah::
34   Te:        ah::
35   H:         he have this problem because in the high school.
```

When Huan gets to another report of that same student's behavior (line 24) (that he drew very small figures on large pieces of paper), students laugh again (line 25) and Huan reprimands her classmates for interpreting her report of the behavior as intended for laughter (line 26) and gives an account for her reprimand ('he has a problem', line 28). After the reprimand, Ain asks Huan why the behavior of the student in her story was problematic showing to Huan that Ain's and the other classmates' laughter, given the information in and the telling of the story, was a valid-at-that-time interpretation of the story. Huan goes on to give an account (with the help of the teacher) for why the student's behavior should not be treated as laughable.

While Huan orients to her interlocutors' misinterpretation of the story and the trouble involved in its production, we see that Huan was able to successfully get the point of her story across after some repair work. Its original design and trajectory, however, show that relaying and interpreting subtle points in a story telling may be more easily done with a larger repertoire of linguistic and communicative resources.

Classroom context and teachers' rights

The excerpts in (4.10) and (4.11) showed how language-related issues play a role in how story tellings are done in the language learning classroom. The classroom and learning context for the unsolicited story tellings in the collection (classroom dyadic interaction) are also oriented to as relevant by the participants in several other ways. Research on classrooms has often focused on the ways that teachers and students exhibit their orientation to the greater rights that teachers have for turn allocation in the classroom (McHoul, 1978; Mehan, 1979). During a teacher-fronted activity such as a full-class discussion, students may launch into a story telling but when they do, they orient to it as possibly imposing on the teacher's plan and ask permission from the teacher for doing so. Excerpt (4.12) shows such an example:

(4.12) Intermediate proficiency level:
   5-7-04, 206, D, [1:00:15-1:00:44], Huan
   http://www.labschool.pdx.edu/Viewer/viewer.php?pl=JKHCP&cl=4.12

```
1   Te:    you've got a very good point. very good point.
2   H:=>   yeah. I know I have a (.6) do you have time?
3   Te:    ⌈weyah I don't know=
4   Ss:    ⌊(( laughter    ))
5   Te:    =does everybody else have ti(huh)me? well you are
6          expressing an opinion and this is what we're working
```

```
7                on and I'm paying attention to what you're saying
8                th- what you're using. and you said I think that so
9       =>       keep on going.=it is good it is good
10               ⌈for the other students.
11      H:=>     ⌊I have one one experience (it's uh) really uh
12               really interesting. ((story continues))
```

In (4.12), the class has been discussing problems in U.S. high schools. In line 1, the teacher assesses a comment made by Huan who follows up with an agreement of that assessment and a pre-question to a longer telling – a request to tell a story. It appears (line 3) that the teacher is a bit surprised by the request as she makes a little joke and thinks through the justification for allowing the story at this point in the class (lines 5–10) deciding that it fits in with the trajectory of the lesson.

Other orientation to teachers' greater rights for turn allocation in the classroom is seen at the end of story tellings. As with disengagements from dyadic interaction in general (discussed in Chapter 5), when students are engaged in a story telling sequence, stories may end quickly due to the teacher's call for a shift in the participation structure of the classroom from a peer-dyad focus back to a teacher-cohort focus. At these points students orient to the teacher as having greater rights in the turn allocation system of the classroom and end their story tellings soon after the teacher's call. In (4.12), Raisa has been telling Perla a story about a delinquent renter living in one of her rental properties. Students had been working in pairs for about seven minutes at this point in their interaction and the teacher moves to the front, utters a discourse marker 'okay' (line 25) which Raisa orients to immediately as the teacher's signal for the end of their time for their dyadic task (line 26). By saying 'two minutes' in line 26, Raisa is commenting on the teacher's instructions that students would speak for 'two minutes'. In line 28, she adds an increment to her time noun phrase, making the two-part turn into a question which also shows her orientation to the teacher ending the task – 'two minutes it's enough?'

(4.13) beginning proficiency level
5-7-02, 206, B, [22:11-22:34], Raisa and Perla
http://www.labschool.pdx.edu/Viewer/viewer.php?pl= JKHCP&cl=4.13

```
21    R:    I give you the a:ll paper, we we write I write with
22           you with ⌈him okay. and he's okay don't worry (.5)
23    P:            ⌊mm hm
24    R:    I : ⌈: ((looks at Te))
25    Te:       ⌊okay.
```

```
26  R:   two minu ⌈tes
27  Te:          ⌊finished?
28  R:   ((slaps hands together)) it's enough?
29  Te:  yeah two minutes did you talk the whole time?=did she
30       talk?
31  R:   yeah yeah. she she's (.) she's two days week, she is
32       sick.
```

We see in (4.13) how the teacher's role and her greater rights to turn allocation and to starting shifts in participation structure is oriented to by students. Story tellings between students in classroom interaction are subject to ending when the teacher, as in (4.13), addresses the entire class and moves to a new participation structure.

Evidence of Language Development in the Story Telling Practices

Just in numbers of story tellings uncovered, there appears to be a difference in the story tellings of different classroom communities of practice. There were more than twice as many story tellings in the intermediate level classes compared to the beginning level classes (12 versus 5). More telling of differences in the practices for doing story tellings in the two different classroom communities of practice, however, are several aspects of their production formats. As outlined in Table 4.1, story framing using time locators ('yesterday', 'when I...', 'one day', 'I have one experience') occurred commonly in the intermediate classroom communities of practice but we see only one such instance in the beginning level community of practice ('**before** I talk with my friend'). Other pre-sequence markers ('for example', 'look'), and past tense verbs ('I was', 'was working', 'they said') used in the intermediate level communities of practice also suggest evidence of language code proficiency manifest in the story tellings. Only one of the story tellings from the beginning level communities of practice used grammatical markers (past tense) to frame the telling as a past time event.

Table 4.1 summarizes some of the lexical-grammatical and discourse aspects of the differences in how story tellings were performed by students working in different communities of practice. There were also larger, sequential differences. The instances of extended pretelling sequences also only occurred in the intermediate proficiency level classroom communities of practice. Each pretelling sequence started with a student's prequestion (Schegloff, 1980). In (4.14), an excerpt previously presented as (4.12), the teacher is engaged in a full-class discussion with

Table 4.1 Outline of some features of the production formats for story tellings in different classroom communities of practice

	Beginning proficiency	*Intermediate proficiency*
1	mm husband #uh:# **call** my uncle.	I'm worker in the clothes store? **yesterday** womans **come** in
2	mm my house it**'s** rent somebody? ... yeah. I I **tell** (for) him	when I study , **when I was** study
3	I **need** bus I **go** to the trimet	the **first time live** in Portland I **have** two bus twenty
4	eh she she **told** me she **told** me what is the art okay, I **said** okay. I I **looked** here.	in the drama, some guys wife is a lesbian so they **divorced**
5	people **say**, ... **before** I **talk** with my friend	**I have** one experience ... **I have** one student
6		**you know**, I **send** my camera to Portland location but the repairer **told** me
7		**yesterday** I **have** a customer ask me, how are you. I **said** I'm fine.
8		**one day** my daughter uh she with her friend, **go** to a restaurant,
9		**you see** my um my my children uh they uh they **is born** uh they **are borned**,
10		yeah **I was working** ... **I was working** three to twelve,
11		when **I came** here **I was looking** for a job
12		look for example I know somebody ... they got

students when a student (Huan) asks the teacher if there is time for her to tell her story to the class. This question is characterized as a pre-question because, while it makes an answer conditionally relevant, the question itself projects a more substantial main course of action to come after the answer to that question. In this case, after Huan's question in line 2 'do you have time' and the teacher's rather lengthy answer, (an affirmative 'keep on going' in line 9), Huan launches a story telling about a student she had when she was a high school teacher in China.

Story Tellings in Dyadic Task Interactions

(4.14)
  5-7-04, 206, D, [1:00:15-1:00:44], Huan
  http://www.labschool.pdx.edu/Viewer/viewer.php?pl= JKHCP&cl=4.14

```
1    Te:      you've got a very good point. very good point.
2    H:=>     yeah. I know I have a (.6) do you have time?
3    Te:      ⎡weyah I don't know=
4    Ss:      ⎣(( laughter    ))
5    Te:      =does everybody else have ti(huh)me? well you are
6             expressing an opinion and this is what we're working
7             on and I'm paying attention to what you're saying
8             th- what you're using. and you said I think that so
9      =>     keep on going.=it is good it is good
10            ⎡for the other students.
11   H:=>     ⎣I have one one experience (it's uh) really uh
12            really interesting. ((story continues))
```

As discussed previously, Huan orients to the teacher's special status for turn allocation when, after acknowledging a compliment from the teacher, she asks if the teacher has time for something. The teacher responds equivocally, orienting to Huan's question as a prequestion projecting a longer project. The teacher is equivocal because in this context (full class discussion) an extended project by one student may not be something pedagogically appropriate nor something the rest of the class would like to be part of.

A more extended pre-telling sequence also occurred in an intermediate-level class (4.15) in a peer-peer dyadic interaction context during a task in which students were to share their opinions about controversial subjects in the news. The students have reached same sex marriage as their topic for discussion when, in lines 6–7, each gives an abbreviated opinion of the issue. The task topic makes relevant a particular story telling by Sang Mi who asks a question in line 11 which leads to her story telling about an example of same sex marriage in a popular U.S. television program called 'Friends'. When Sang Mi establishes that Ain has seen the television program (line 16) she launches the story in line 19 naming a character 'that guy's Ross'.

(4.15)
  5-11-04, 206, D, [1:00:40-1:01:29], Sang Mi and Ain
  http://www.labschool.pdx.edu/Viewer/viewer.php?pl= JKHCP&cl=4.15

```
6    A:    I I I don't agree with this.
7    S:    uh me ↑too(h) huh
```

```
 8                  (1)
 9    S:      °huh heh heh° uh d- diuh
10    A:      huh
11    S:=>    do you see the: uh drama #uh# friends?
12    A:      ((puzzled look))
13    S:      friends?
14    A:      friends=                    [pre-question]
15    S:      =yeah friends. the drama=
16    A:      ↑friends yes=
17    S:      =yah
18    A:      ye(h)s
19    S:=>    the oh : : that guy's eh Ross ((pointing)) d-
20            do you know Ross?
21    A:      eh no um I I ((gestures)) saw the ((gestures)) final ah:
22    S:      ⌈AHHH
23    A:      ⌊ah: yeah
24    S:      just the ⌈final AHHHH      ⌈AHHHH
25    A:               ⌊just a little just a ⌊little bit
26    A:      I don't know um ⌈many things about ⌈this uh ⌈:
27    S:                      ⌊#ah#              ⌊#yi#   ⌊#i:#n the
28            drama, i- in the the drama, uh the some guy's, uh
29            some ⌈guy's
30    A:           ⌊married
31    S:      wife is a lesbian.    [recipient design for the telling]
32    A:      mm=
33    S:      =so they divorced, and uh the wife is uh married to
34            woman.
35    A:      wow
```

While a teller can assume that the use of a name at the start of the story is, by implication, a character in the just-named drama, the use of the membership categorization device (a name) assumes that Ain knows and can distinguish the different characters in the drama. After Sang Mi uses such a membership categorization device in line 19, she quickly self repairs, moving back one step in the establishment of appropriate recipient design (Sacks, 1992) for her story and asks a second pre-question (line 20) 'do you know Ross'. When it is established that Ain does not know the program well enough to know the characters (see Sang Mi's news marker receipts in lines 22 and 24), Sang Mi re-launches the story telling using an indefinite determiner noun combination ('some guy'), changing the membership categorization device from a very specific 'Ross' to 'a male character'.

Story Tellings in the Classroom Communities of Practice

In summary: story tellings occur less frequently and are generally shorter in the beginning level communities of practice. Along with their relative scarcity and shorter durations, story tellings in the beginning level communities of practice lacked the story prefacing work that occurred in higher proficiency level communities of practice. This evidence suggests that the practices involved in the social action of story tellings are an epiphenomenon of language proficiency. While stories can be told without story prefacing, the prefatory work is important for contextualizing and framing one's talk grammatically, topically and interactionally as an extended telling or story. While I did not look for aborted story tellings, my hunch is that without such framing, potential stories may not get underway.

When the story tellings occur in the beginning level communities of practice, students do not have as many linguistic or sequential resources available for telling the stories that students with higher proficiency in the language have. While adult learners with less experience with the language who are in beginning proficiency level classes may not have the lexical-grammatical resources used by learners in the more intermediate level classes as shown earlier in Table 4.1, they manage to engage in story telling sequences. Such tellings get underway not simply because of luck. Story tellings are recognized as such and achieved in beginning proficiency levels as part of the work of doing talk-in-interaction even when participants do not have a large repertoire of lexical-grammatical resources. The social practice of conversational story telling is likely, to some degree, a universal practice for human social interaction (Beach & Lindstrom, 1992; Lee, 1998) and language classrooms are able to take advantage of this incidental language learning opportunity when learners to speak to one another in the language being learned. In the dyadic interactions in adult language learning classrooms, such story tellings occur without being directly elicited by the teacher or by other students. When engaged in face-to-face interaction, the interaction itself affords places for these tellings to occur. Again, here is evidence for face-to-face interaction in a language learning classroom and language classroom communities of practice themselves as having social actions and practices overlap with the social action and practices of talk in everyday communication.

The negotiation of reified and participatory language that is a key characteristic of a community of practice is illustrated persuasively in the way that learners do story telling in their dyadic interaction. In these instances, a past-time event, a reified object, is made relevant for a current retelling due to local interactional circumstances of participants, topic, location and the like. In the lead up to and in the telling itself, the past time event is activated as a current process of interaction in the production and in the way it is formatted for production. Although learners are interacting in a classroom, the type of practices for topical and grammatical contextualization work necessary to bring off a story telling are not explicitly taught. Rather, they emerge because of interaction taking place within the community of practice.

Chapter 5
Disengagements from Dyadic Task Interactions

Introduction

After showing the micro-level interactive practices for co-constructing classroom communities of practice in the way adult language learners open classroom language-learning tasks (Chapter 3) and explicate understanding in those tasks through story tellings (Chapter 4), the focus of analysis in chapter five moves to another 'boundary' interaction that students negotiate: moving out of, or, disengaging from face-to-face task interactions.

Previous research: 'Closing' talk and 'disengaging' from interaction

The context for the research reported on in this chapter is like that in Chapter 3 – a boundary zone between dyadic task engagement and independent or teacher-oriented engagement in the classroom. The analysis shows how learner dyads working on teacher-assigned language-learning tasks move from interaction mediated by a teacher-assigned language-learning task to the following context for interaction that does not include explicit mediation from the teacher. These are members' methods for disengaging (Szymanski, 1999) from this dyadic task interaction. As with opening dyadic interactions, the talk in disengagement sequences is oriented to the task, to the interlocutor, and the discursive practices of the particular classroom community of practice. While similar sequences have been investigated in previous research on other contexts (Antaki, 2002; Goldberg, 2004; Hartford & Bardovi-Harlig, 1992; House, 1982; Jefferson, 1973; Schegloff & Sacks, 1973; Szymanski, 1999), studies have not focused on the language-learning classroom context to understand these practices of students. After observing the collection of dyadic task interactions, categories for disengagement from these interactions emerged reflecting the orderly practices for talk that members of the classroom community of practice use for these particular contexts.

Conversation analytic investigations of the sequential practices for ending telephone calls called 'closings' started with Schegloff and Sacks' (1973) seminal paper 'Opening up closing' which was motivated by their noting the orderliness of conversations in general and in their endings in particular. Absence of talk occurs quite regularly as part of conversations or other talk-in-interaction. Yet, most of these points are not recognized by the participants as the end of the interaction. Schegloff and Sacks sought to answer the fundamental question of how it is that the 'ending' of some stretch of talk-in-interaction is not heard and oriented to by other participants as simply a 'normal' silence within the interaction.

Their research showed the practices for closing conversational interactions in a locally-achieved and co-constructed manner through sequences of talk-in-interaction. During an interaction, shorter, information-poor turns at talk which do not add to or develop a current topic in an interaction (discourse markers, receipt tokens, aphoristic phrases) may be oriented to as possible preclosing moves. At points when a marker of possible closing is uttered by one participant in an interaction, participants have a possibly-last chance to bring up any item or topic for talk that is appropriate or necessary to the current (and perhaps only the current) context. Such 'urgent' topics are characterized as 'mentionables' (Schegloff & Sacks, 1973). If, after a first possible pre-closing move is uttered, no move is made by other participants to extend the current topic or introduce a new topic (a 'mentionable'), other participants will also give minimal responses to orient to the previous turn as a possible pre-closing or move into the terminal exchange of farewells. A typical closing sequence (from a telephone conversation) is shown in lines 6–10 of Excerpt (5.1).

(5.1)
   P&J 1

```
 1  Cl:  may I speak to Chris please?
 2  Ca:  he's not here. he's over at Paul's.
 3       (1.0)
 4  Cl:  oh alright. C- ⌈could you just tell him I called,
 5  Ca:                 ⌊hmm?
 6  Cl:  yeah I will
 7  Ca:  okay thank you.
 8  Cl:  sure.
 9  Ca:  b ⌈ye.
10  Cl:   ⌊bye.
```

In (5.1), the caller calls to speak to a friend who happens not to be home. The recognition that no more information is necessary to be exchanged in this conversation is oriented to gradually in the stepwise movement out of the conversation that follows the callers request. After the caller makes the request to the recipient of the call to tell his friend that he has called (line 4), that request is accepted. Though the 'called' party accepts the request (line 6), 'called' could have made a request of her own, asked for clarification or proffered a topic to begin a conversation of their own. The two-part response of affirmation and promise (line 6) is oriented to by the caller as not topic initiating and he responds with a receipt token and an appreciation as a possible preclosing move. 'Called' accepts the thanks which is oriented to by both 'caller' and 'called' as the endpoint of the conversation as they overlap in their final moves of the terminal exchange (lines 9–10).

What is important to note here is that in retrospect, with respect to relaying information, either 'caller' or 'called' could have hung up the telephone after line 6 without losing any information that was exchanged. At the time of its production, however, neither party knows what the other 'has in mind' with respect to the extent of information to be exchanged. Realizing that all the information that either member wished to share has been shared is done through this fairly familiar sequence of talk. It is also important to mention, however, that though this sequence of talk is familiar to members of the language-culture, the words, moves and sequences of turns are not a script that needs to be followed verbatim. Each move is produced and interpreted as part of the ongoing sequence of turns in the unfolding action of closing the conversation.

CA's conceptual understanding of 'closings' has been used by research in a variety of face-to-face contexts investigating how endings are accomplished in academic advising sessions (Bardovi-Harlig et al., 1991; Hartford & Bardovi-Harlig, 1992; Jeon, 2003) doctor-patient interaction (Heath, 1986; Robinson, 2001), grade school work groups (Szymanski, 1999), and acquaintances (LeBaron & Jones, 2002). All of these studies show how, in face-to-face interactions, contextual factors involving visual cues and physical co-presence around a dyadic interaction provide for different trajectories in disengagements and give the participants a number of different resources for the disengagements than are available over the telephone. As earlier, more speculative research on face-to-face interaction suggested (Goffman, 1967, 1971; Knapp et al., 1973), the subsequent empirical investigations of naturalistic behavior in face-to-face interaction (mentioned above) showed how physical co-presence influences the way that disengagements are managed.

LeBaron and Jones (2002) show that as a chance meeting between two old friends at a beauty salon nears an end, the participants' disengagement is accomplished through an orientation to verbal and non-verbal information from others present (but not involved in the interaction). The encounter is co-constructed at its outset as a 'reunion' by the participants and others present in the beauty salon. This projects the closing to be done as the close of a reunion. Contextual materials and physical behavior of the participants also play an important role in the way the interaction is closed. Postural disalignment (accomplished in a stepwise manner) and touching become relevant as a moves oriented to signaling a closing as does other contextual materials available to participants; one participant returns to the hairdresser's chair where she was occupied at the outset of the reunion while the participant who engaged in a reunion with the woman in the hairdresser's chair re-engages with her purse.

In their study of a more service oriented encounter (advising sessions), Hartford and Bardovi-Harlig (1992) discuss the nature of closing institutional encounters. In such interactions, topics are somewhat limited to the service which is the goal of the encounter and closings get underway when that business is perceived to be over. They note that appreciations are almost always offered as part of the closing and that while talk may continue beyond the close of the service task, there are topics and closing trajectories which are oriented to as inappropriate for at these moments. Once the goal of the meeting (advising) is accomplished, unlike conversational interactions where 'mentionables' (Schegloff & Sacks, 1973) are appropriate to bring up before the conversation comes to a close, except for a few topics, once the goal of the meeting is oriented to as accomplished, other topics are not proffered in the advising sessions. The goal-oriented nature of these encounters and the limit on raising 'mentionables' at the end of such interactions are evidence of the institutional nature of advising sessions.

Szymanski's (1999) research on disengaging from face-to-face interactions in third grade classroom work groups is particularly relevant for the research in this chapter. It shows how non-verbal and textual resources are relevant for the sequences that are produced by students to disengaging from spates of talk-in-interaction within tasks. The activity focus of the participants in these interactions also influences the organization of disengagement sequences as these activity-oriented sequences of talk have possibly-projectable endings available to their participants from their very start of the interaction.

This chapter first discusses disengagements as an interesting site for understanding interaction, the classroom as community of practice and language development. Following this discussion, various local contexts and disengagement types in the adult language learning classroom are illustrated. The third section of the chapter describes the common sequences used by students to accomplish disengagements and the relationship of disengagement types to different classroom communities of practice. The last analytic section of the chapter returns to Jorge, the student from Chapter 3, focusing on the disengagement sequences in the serial dyadic interaction tasks that we saw him opening. The focus on series' of disengagements 40 weeks apart gives a longitudinal perspective to understanding the practices involved in disengaging from face-to-face interaction as a site for observing changes in participation and learning within a classroom community of practice.

What a study of disengagements in classroom communities of practice can show

As discussed in Chapter 3, boundaries of students' face-to-face interactions are rich sites for studying members' methods of implementing their moment-to-moment interaction with various degrees of language support in classroom communities of practice. In observing classroom interaction, the sequence of talk and interaction at the completion of teacher-assigned language tasks are notable for several reasons. While instructors give clear instructions for carrying out these tasks, even the best instructions do not include how learners should disengage from and end their task interaction. That is, teachers do not instruct learners how the they might use talk to signal to one another that they believe the task has ended or that they would like to either continue or end their face-to-face interaction. Given this situation, in disengaging from their teacher-assigned language-learning task interaction, the student participants find themselves moving from interaction heavily mediated by task-supplied language and interactional ordering into relatively un-mediated face-to-face interaction.

When teachers devise dyadic language-learning tasks, it is understood that a precise period of time cannot be allotted for such tasks. Given that uncertainty, student dyads often find themselves faced with the question of what to do in the window of time after they have completed the task assigned by the teacher but before the teacher has called for the class' attention to shift participation structures and begin some new course of action. It is rare for student dyads to disengage from all interaction at these points. There may be momentary disengagement after the teacher-assigned task is co-constructed as complete but if the teacher has not yet called for the attention of the class, the student dyads will, normally, engage in some other kind of interaction until the teacher calls for their attention.

The rarity of disengagement from all interaction may be due, in part to norms of physical positioning and human interaction. Like adults who are strangers but happen to be in close proximity in public (Goffman, 1963), as competent social adults we expect that learner peers seated next to one another at small tables in a language classroom will feel the right if not the obligation to engage in some form of communication with one another. Students are not explicitly told by their instructors that they should interact with one another. Yet the students observed studying at the data collection site in the four years of data collection display their mutual orientation to the joint enterprise of English language learning and engaged civilly as social adults working together in classroom communities of practice.

At the end of their teacher-assigned dyadic task interaction, members of each student dyad either returned to or remained seated at their desk next to their deskmate. The seating arrangement left participants with the challenge of how and to what degree to disengage from a face-to-face interaction when they reached the end of their teacher-assigned task while remaining in close physical proximity to their peer. These points were sites where the reified patterns for participation in teacher-assigned language-learning tasks had ended and where students co-constructed the participation patterns that, in part, emerged as practices for their classroom community of practice.

In the movement from teacher-mediated interaction to less mediated interaction and from dyadic to other participation structures, points of disengagement from task interaction are important sites for witnessing how the rights and responsibilities of social interaction facilitate language use. These are also sites where the dialectic of members' orientation to the historical-cultural-institutional nature of task interaction and the local, situated needs for conducting face-to-face interaction through talk can be highlighted. This dialectic is a nexus where we can see the way that communities of practice are instantiated through situated language practices for talk-in-interaction (Wenger, 1998) and see language learners negotiating their participation in shifting participation structures through their use of language (Mondada & Pekarek Doehler, 2004).

Local Contexts For and Possible Next Actions After Students' Disengagement from Classroom Dyadic Interaction

Disengagement prompted by teacher's shift in participation structure

As mentioned earlier, given the turn allocation system which is the context of classrooms, in many cases, the disengagement from a student–student

Disengagements from Dyadic Task Interactions

task interaction is not initiated by students. This occurs when a shift in participation structure to a teacher-fronted activity is prompted by the teacher soliciting the attention of the entire student cohort. This teacher call for attention has the effect of both ending the current dyadic participation structure and concomitant activity and starting some new course of teacher-led action. While there may be more talk by the student dyads following the teacher's call to attention, and in a few cases the teacher needed to explicitly suggest to students that they attend to her, only rarely did the post-solicitation talk by student dyads amount to a full disengagement sequence. Rather, when there was more talk by the student dyads after a teacher's call for attention, it was the second pair part in an adjacency pair or some last turn of a then aborted sequence of talk. This type of end to the task interaction recurs massively in the data for at least two reasons. First, teachers cannot know when each student dyad has completed its task. Also, students, generally, orient to the teacher as a leader of the classroom and allow such abrupt shifts in participation structures to occur as unremarkable.

Excerpt (5.2) shows one example of the teacher solicitation ending a student dyadic interaction and the shift in participation structure in an intermediate classroom community of practice.

(5.2)
   9-26-03, 204, C, [1:36:25-1:36:46], Sambath and Julia
   http://www.labschool.pdx.edu/Viewer/viewer.php?pl=JKHCP&cl=5.2
   (Students are asking one another about activities to activate the adverbs of frequency)

1 S: do you ever go swim
2 J: go swimming?
3 S: ((nods))
4 J: ⌈go swimming sometimes.
5 Te: ⌊((raises and keeps her hand raised))
6   (1) ((S looks up at teacher))
7 J: some⌈times
8 S: ⌊((points at teacher))
9 J: ((turns around)) oh.
10 Q: ((looks up))
11 I: ((turns around))
12 Te: ladies and gentlemen g- heh hah hah hah okay,
13   let's take a break,
14 I: oh okay
15 Te: let's take a break it's ten thirty-five,

In (5.2), the student dyad had been working on a task designed to elicit adverbs of frequency. Julia is working with Sambath who is seated behind her. As a result, Julia has her back to the front of the class where the teacher is positioned. At the same time as Julia's response (lines 4–5) to Sambath's question about swimming, the teacher raises her hand, a sign she used throughout the term to get the students attention. Sambath notices the teacher's action (line 6) and immediately after Julia confirms her answer, in line 8, non-verbally indicates to Julia that the teacher is soliciting the attention of the class. Julia orients her posture to the front of the classroom uttering the news marker 'oh' and there is no further task talk by either student. Excerpt (5.3) shows a similar example of students ending their face-to-face interaction without the use of a closing sequence of talk, this in a beginning level classroom community of practice.

(5.3)
2-28-02, 204, A, [1:24:27-1:24:38], Jin and Deng
http://www.labschool.pdx.edu/Viewer/viewer.php?pl=JKHCP&cl=5.3

(Jin and Deng are doing an activity in which one student tells the other a time and the other student moves the clock to that time)

1 **D:** seventeen
2 **J:** ((moves her clock))
3 **D:** fifteen. ((commenting on another group))
4 **Te:** okay. now remember before
5   ((J and D look toward Te))
6 **D:** °fifteen°
7 **Te:** on Monday. we talked about stress?

In (5.3), students are practicing a speaking and listening task focusing on time phrases. In line 4, the teacher, standing in front of the classroom and facing the students, opens a new participation structure in which she talks to the whole class about contrastive word stress. In line 5, after the teacher addresses the class, Deng and Jin orient to this as an end to their time for dyadic task interaction and align their posture to the teacher without any other verbal or non-verbal moves – the disengagement from their task interaction. In both Excerpts (5.2) and (5.3), we see this shift in participation structure is not facilitated by sequences of talk between the student dyad showing the normative orientation by students to the teacher's interruption of their task activity with the call for their attention. This lack of sequences of talk-in-interaction to disengage from a task interaction is further empirical evidence for the specialized turn allocation system in the classroom (Hellermann, 2005a; Mehan, 1979) and the nature of student–student communication within the classroom community of practice.

Task disengagement and repeating the task

Another possible context for the ending of a dyadic interaction and its following action occurs provided the teacher does not call for the attention of the student group. In these cases, as a student dyad progresses through their teacher-assigned dyadic task to a place that seems like, to one or both members, the end of that task, students may co-construct a sequence of talk for disengaging from their task-oriented interaction and move into a restart of the task, to go through the task another time 'for practice'. This is seen in Excerpt (5.4) from an intermediate level classroom community of practice.

(5.4)
   1-13-04, 204, C, [2:23:42-2:24:22], Julia and Jung
   http://www.labschool.pdx.edu/Viewer/viewer.php?pl=JKHCP&cl=5.4
   (Julia and Jung are asking and answering yes/no questions about ability provided by the teacher on the board)

```
1  Jn:  do they speak English?
2       (.)
3  Jl:  yes they do but not very ell.
4       ((both students laugh))
5  Jl:  .hh okay. ((writing)) i:s he ey a student, is he
6       (.) ey a stude:nt, a student.
7  Jn:  ( ) (.) (better not better   ) ⌈(laughs))
8  Jl:                                  ⌊(laughs))
9       (.)
10 Jl:  ye:s
11 Jn:  are you a student?
12 Jl:  yes I am.
13 Jn:  can you speak English?
```

After completing the question-answer task with the last question on the list of teacher-provided questions and Julia's answer in line 3, Julia and Jung share laughter (line 4). While laughter has been noted to occur often as part of a closing sequence (Glenn, 1991/1992), here, it seems to be the only verbal move for closure of the language learning task routine. Julia moves out of the laughter with a discourse marker (line 5) bridging the close of the previous task interaction and the opening of something new (Beach, 1993) – an individual task. She writes down a note about the formation of the answer (line 5, 'he is a student'). There is some talk by Jung and response by Julia (lines 7 and 10) which is not oriented to as a formal disengagement from their interaction as Jung restarts the sequence of teacher-provided questions (line 11) which Julia responds to without comment. This repeat of the task question-answer sequence shows that after 'doing the task' one time, students may perform some type of disengagement from that 'first round' and continue the task-focused interaction by re-doing the task, orienting to this as part of classroom task procedure.

Focusing on points of possible or actual disengagements from peer dyadic task interaction in Excerpts (5.2)–(5.4) we see how students from different proficiency levels orient to and accomplish the action of disengagement through practices for talk-in-interaction for the entire classroom community of practice. While the teacher is oriented to as the final arbiter of participation structures and turn allocation in the classroom, students also orient to the talk-in-interaction of dyadic peer interaction in the adult language-learning community of practice as an opportunity for language learning through language use.

Task disengagement and opening a new topic

Often, there is very little gap between the end of a teacher-assigned dyadic task interaction and the call for attention by the teacher to shift to a new activity. This shows the synchronicity between teachers' and students' actions in the classroom, a synchronicity which is a product of experienced planning by the teacher as well as students' and teachers' mutual monitoring of each others' behavior. When there is time at the endpoint of a teacher-assigned task interaction and before the teacher solicits student attention, however, students orient to dyadic interaction as a time for language use when they co-construct a disengagement sequence from the teacher-assigned dyadic task but continue their face-to-face interaction taking up another topic. In such cases, the topic students engage in is one not explicitly assigned by the teacher but often, peripherally related to the topic of the teacher-assigned task. This extended face-to-face interaction may, in turn, have a disengagement sequence of its own or be aborted without an explicit disengagement if the teacher calls for the attention of the class [as shown in (5.2) and (5.3)]. In the following Excerpt (5.5) from an intermediate level classroom community of practice, we see students disengaging from their task interaction and then re-engaging in a new topic of their own selection.

(5.5)
    10-3-03, 204, C, [29:53-30:27], Reinaldo and Jingli
    http://www.labschool.pdx.edu/Viewer/viewer.php?pl=JKHCP&cl=5.5
    (Students are asking and answering questions given by Teacher: *When did you come to the US?, Do you have children?, When is your birthday?, What are their birthdays?, When do you normally pay your rent?, Do you have siblings?, What are their birthdays?, Are you married?, When is your anniversary date?*)

```
1   R:   what is your anniversary date?
2   J:   uh my (.) uh anniversary? (.) is ah: un: (.)
3        September? September:: Septem(h) huokay
4        September (.) twelfth.
5   R:   twel ⌈ve?
6   J:        ⌊( ) yeah huh heh
7   R:   September twelfth ⌈((shifts posture))°oh heh
8   J:                     ⌊((averts gaze))
9   R:   huh°
10  J:   thank you °huh huh°
11       (1)
12  J:   uh what=>are you from Mexico<?
13  R:   yes I'm from Mexico. Are you from China?
14  J:   yeah you you okay. eh (.) .hh wi- y- with you
15       family, come here?
16  R:   no ((shakes head))
```

In (5.5), Reinaldo and Jingli complete the sequence of question prompts and subsequent responses and clarification which make up the language of this task (lines 1–6). In lines 7–10, a subtle disengagement sequence is accomplished starting with Reinaldo's second repetition of Jingli's answer for her anniversary date. This second repetition adds no new information to move the topic forward and immediately following, Reinaldo shifts his posture while Jingli averts her gaze from Reinaldo. Reinaldo then softly utters some non lexical tokens, perhaps laughter which is followed by Jingli's appreciation (Button, 1987) and slight laughter (line 10). These verbal and non-verbal markers in lines 7–10 form a sequence for disengaging from face-to-face and task interaction. After this co-constructed sequence for disengagement, following a very slight pause, Jingli restarts the dyadic face-to-face interaction with a question to Reinaldo (line 12) about his country of origin, a question not assigned as part of the task.

Task disengagement followed by independent work

The excerpt in (5.5) shows the importance of students working together in dyadic interaction for the development of interpersonal relationships within a classroom community of practice. In this case, students use time at the end of a teacher-assigned task to continue their language practice by asking one another personal questions. While students most often continue their talk-in-interaction until a change in participation structure occurs, students may disengage from their task interaction and remain disengaged. This can occur either after an interaction associated with the teacher-assigned task or after a conversational interaction like the one launched just previously by Reinaldo and Jingli in (5.5). After either type of disengagement, students may work independently (writing, reading) or wait (without overtly 'working') for the teacher to announce the next activity. These types of action trajectory are relatively rare in the data. The more likely is the latter when a teacher-assigned language task stresses a written result for the interaction and students are concerned to produce the required written product. Such an example is shown in (5.6) from an intermediate level classroom community of practice.

(5.6)
2-15-05, 206, C, [39:11-39:39], Jin and Phong
http://www.labschool.pdx.edu/Viewer/viewer.php?pl=JKHCP&cl=5.6
(Jin and Phong are asking and answering questions about one another's home town activating 'there is' and 'there are')

```
1  J:  you know lake
2  P:  is the same (as) river ( ⌈ )
3  J:                         ⌊yeah (same for)
4      river uhhhh
5  P:  ( ⌈ )
6  J:    ⌊sea
7      (.)
8  J:  the wa ⌈ter.
9  P:         ⌊( )
10 J:  huh
11 P:  no
12 J:  no? (.) °↑yeah°
13 P:  ((writing))
14 J:  you eh guys they you guys uh there is right?
15     ((taps P on the shoulder)) is.
16 P:  ((turns head slightly )) no, ((keeps writing))
```

17 J: lake ⌈is ((to self))
18 P: ⌊(are)
19 J: are? they are

In (5.6), J asks P if there is a lake in his hometown. P needs to look up the word 'lake' in his dictionary and after he is finished looking in his dictionary, J asks him, in line 1, if he knows the word. After some negotiation of the meaning of 'lake', P is clearly displaying that the task interaction should be over focusing on his writing (indicated in lines 13 and 16 of the transcript). J continues asking P questions, in line 14, for confirmation of a grammatical structure. But the writing continues to occupy P who only turns his head to answer J in line 16 and J disengages from interaction with P as she repeats the first troublesome noun, 'lake', and it's copula (line 17) which she repairs and repeats in line 19.

Sequence Types for Talk-in-Interaction for Disengagement from Task Interaction

As research has shown in collections of various action sequences in everyday conversational interaction, for classroom learners, there are no specific scripts or formulae which learner dyads follow to end their interactions in classroom interaction. There are, rather, constellations of different practices which, when accomplished in sequence, co-construct disengagement. In this section of the chapter, some of those interactional practices used by the learners and the disengagement sequences which develop out of those practices are outlined. At the end of the section, the functions of these practices and sequences with respect to the action they are moving out of and into are presented.

Non-verbal moves

Posture and body torque

The only type of move for disengagement in the collection that can be claimed as all-pervasive is some degree of postural disalignment by students from one another. Depending on the degree of physical closeness and body torque during their task engagement, the postural disalignment which indexes disengagement from face-to-face interaction may be quite overt or subtle. Postural disalignment is sometimes the only cue for disengagement from interactions but is often accompanied by verbal moves of some kind. The postural disalignment is coordinated more or less together between the members of the dyad, but there were instances in which one student disaligned without the other expecting it. Such a move leaves the still-aligned participant looking somewhat vulnerable, and in its deviance, shows a preference or regularity in mutual postural disalignment. There were a few cases when students never fully align posturally for their interactions. Such a lack of alignment (and subsequent disalignment) occur when the task interaction is heavily mediated by text written on the board and students rely on reading this information to engage in the task.

Postural disalignment has been noted to be an important interactional event in situations outside the classroom (Erickson & Schultz, 1982; Schegloff, 1998) and the enactment of this type of non-verbal behavior shows the orientation of students to practices basic to human face-to-face communication in general. While postural shift can clearly demarcate the end of a task or conversational interaction in the students' seated interactions, as the students are seated in fairly close proximity to one another, these moves for postural disalignment are often very subtle. However subtle, they are, in some cases (especially in interactions from level 'A' communities of practice), the only discernable marker of the end of a student dyadic interaction. This is illustrated in the disengagement in (5.7).

In (5.7), students have been doing a post-task expansion activity started by Jin reciting the alphabet (line 9). Zoya joins the recitation when Jin gets to letter 'e'. As the joint recitation ends in line 14, Zoya nods. Jin nods in return, repeats the last letter two more times (line 15) and there is mutual postural disalignment as the students each start paging through their books.

(5.7)
    4-1-02, 204, A, [44:36-45:12], Zoya and Jin
    http://www.labschool.pdx.edu/Viewer/viewer.php?pl=JKHCP&cl=5.7
(The students finish their 'show me' task for the letters of the alphabet by reciting the alphabet)

```
8           ((mutual postural disalignment))
9    J:     ((recites alphabet, pointing to letters in book))
10   Z:     ((joins J in recitation around 'e' and orients
11          posture to her))
12          (13) ((students reciting letters))
13   J:    ⌈ex, why, zee. ((names of letters))
14   Z:    ⌊ex, why, zee. ((nods))
15   J:     zee ((looks at Z)) uh ((nods)) zee.
16          ((mutual postural disalignment))
17   Z:    ⌈((pages through book))
18   J:    ⌊((pages through book))
```

Disengagements from Dyadic Task Interactions 117

After Jin repeats the last letter of the recitation (line 15), nods, and repeats the letter again, the two students shift their posture away from one another and each looks through their books independently.

Posture, gesture, gaze, material manipulation
Together with posture realignment, other subtle non-verbal moves that facilitate disengagement from dyadic interaction include slight shifts of the position of the head, hands or the materials the students are working with as we see in (5.8) from a beginning level classroom community of practice.

(5.8)
2-25-02, 204, A, [2:43:46-2:44:27], Jin and Maricel
http://www.labschool.pdx.edu/Viewer/viewer.php?pl=JKHCP&cl=5.8
(Jin and Maricel have been carrying out the teacher-assigned task of reading a story together)

1 **M:** shesnt- she's not married
2 **J:** married
3 **M:** she's single.
4 **J:** single.
5 **M:** yes.
6 **J:** single
7 **J:** she go she go
8 **():** she's going to school?
9 **M:** she's going to school.
10 **J:** single.
11 **M:** single.
12 **J:** single. single.
13 **():** she's going to school? teacher and oos
14 **Te:** to school. to school
15 **J:** to school
16 **M:** to school
17 **J:** to school. school. ⌜school. school.
18 **M:**   ⌞school.
19 **J:** (mm) ((turns page and moves it into her space))
20 **M:** ((takes her page out of mutual orientation space))
21   ((mutual posture disalignment))
22 **T:** if you look, on page two, here is the story.

In (5.8), students are talking about a story and sharing their understanding of that story together in lines 1–12. There is a question-answer sequence between an unknown student and the teacher (lines 13–14) and Maricel and Jin repeat the teacher's answer in lines 15–18 after which Jin turns the page in her book and moves it out of the common workspace between the two students. Maricel reciprocates this move for disengagement in line 20 and mutual postural disalignment follows in line 21. In (5.8), the postural disalignment is the terminal exchange but was facilitated, likely, by the sequence of repetition of the teacher's response (lines 15–16) and Jin's moving the written focus of the language-learning task out of the students' mutual work space.

Previous research on closings for face-to-face interactions does not report the co-construction of disengagements without verbal support like those in (5.7) and (5.8). Although such disengagements rarely occurred in the collection, the question arises as to why these types of disengagement do occur. One answer is that because this collection of disengagements sequences are done by language learners, disengagement using verbal sequences of talk may not occur because the learners lack the linguistic resources to accomplish them. Yet, sequences using verbal moves for disengagement occur often even at the lowest levels of proficiency, so these learners at all levels of proficiency can use some verbal resources but sometimes choose not to.

Another reason for the possibility for disengagement from face-to-face interactions without verbal sequences is the structured, goal-oriented nature of the language-learning task talk interactions. In the interactions of students involved in teacher-assigned language-learning tasks, mediation for the task given by the teacher may make explicit verbal moves for disengagement seem optional for learners. Teacher-assigned language-learning tasks are clearly defined by sequential steps which suggest a start and ending point to the task (Szymanski, 1999). These sequential steps are often written lists of questions or statements which are used as prompts for the pair interaction. When the student pair has 'used' all the given prompts, the task can be considered complete and the interaction considered closed with no more than mutual shift in posture.

While the postural shifts and other non-verbal behavior used to index disengagement may be quite subtle, they may occur as part of a multi-move sequence which includes other minimal verbal moves such as the utterance of a discourse marker or other receipt token. This is displayed in Excerpt (5.9) from an intermediate level classroom community of practice.

(5.9)
    11-21-03, 204, C, [1:14:45-1:15:08], Reinaldo and Ain
    http://www.labschool.pdx.edu/Viewer/viewer.php?pl=JKHCP&cl=5.9
    (Reinaldo and Ain are practicing asking and answering questions using the structure 'going to' to express the future)

Disengagements from Dyadic Task Interactions 119

```
1   A:   are you going to take a trip?
2   R:   mm::::
3   A:   no.
4   R:   I am no: quite sure.
5   A:   (okay)
6   R:   I don't have money. maybe in the future I have
7        mon(h)ey.
8   A:   insha'Allah
9   R:   heh heh ((looks around the room))
10  A:   ((looks around the room))
11       (4.0)
12  R:   ((orients to A)) ⌈how how long is stay here. (.)
13  A:                    ⌊((yawns))
14  R:   ((points at A))
15       (1.5)
16  A:   me?
17  R:   yeah.
```

In (5.9), we see how the participants end their task interaction with a short sequence in lines 4–8. The students had been asking and answering questions using the structure 'going to' when in line 4, Reinaldo gives an equivocal response to his peer, Ain's, question. When she produces a discourse marker, a possible boundary marker in line 5, Reinaldo offers an account for his equivocal response in line 4 and then speculates on the future ending that speculation with a slight laugh token on the word 'money' in line 7. This account and fanciful speculation is followed by Ain's wish in line 8 (using her first language), laughter and a posture shift by Reinaldo in line 9, and a posture shift by Ain. This particular posture shift by Reinaldo seems to have two possible interactive functions. First, as a slight movement of the body following an exchange of minimal receipt tokens and a pause, it can signal the finality of a disengagement sequence. The physical behavior also indexes a more specific move: that is, Reinaldo is looking at what other students are doing which may suggest that he is monitoring the task progress of other student dyads. Seeing that other students are still engaged, following a pause, in line 12, Reinaldo restarts the dyad's face-to-face engagement by asking Ain how long she has lived in the United States.

Assessments: Change in participation over time

As teachers assess student responses to their subject matter questions (Hellermann, forthcoming), students, likewise, may treat their peer's responses to their task prompts as assessable. Such assessments serve as a sign that the student has heard and understood the peer's response. In some cases, they also serve as part of the practice for doing a disengagement from a task interaction. We see examples of assessments used as part of task disengagement in both beginning and intermediate proficiency level communities of practice. The following series of four disengagements over the course of ten months involving one student show how disengagements, and the use of assessments for disengagements, can be seen as a site for language development.

In an interaction between two students in a level 'A' class (5.10a), Zoya and Jin have been engaged in the teacher-assigned task in which one student names a letter and the other is to point to the printed letter in her book. Jin and Zoya finish that teacher-assigned task with a short disengagement sequence as Zoya makes some kind of assessment for the task or for her interlocutor (line 5) and Jin shows appreciation for that assessment with laughter. A slight postural shift follows (line 8) in which students disalign from one another.

(5.10a)
4-1-02, 204, A, [44:36-45:12], Zoya and Jin
http://www.labschool.pdx.edu/Viewer/viewer.php?pl=JKHCP&cl=5.10a
(The students finish their 'show me' task for the letters of the alphabet by reciting the alphabet)

```
1  Z:  show me please, double you
2  J:  dahble you.
3  Z:  and uh 'y'.
4  J:  uh the 'y' ((points to 'y' in her book))
5  Z:  everybody nice
6  J:  ((laughs))
7      (.)
8      ((mutual postural disalignment))
9  J:  ((recites alphabet, pointing to letters in book))
```

Excerpt (5.10a) shows that while students in this beginning proficiency level classroom community of practice do not have a large repertoire of linguistic moves to use for their task interactions and the disengagements from their interactions, they manage to disengage from the task interaction using an interesting example of a verbal practice for disengagement. In this disengagement sequence, Zoya uses a pronoun-adjective combination (line 5: 'everybody nice') in a sequential position where an assessment may be relevant – a third position after her directive to Jin (line 3) and Jin's response (line 4). This is the eleventh directive-response of Zoya's part of the task and potentially, their last (Jin had given the task directives to Zoya). While the particular pronoun-adjective combination is not part of the target language repertoire, the grammatical categories used by Zoya fill the slots occupied by an assessment such as 'we're good', 'that's good' and may be a reduction of 'we did a good job'.

Such speculation about Zoya's turn in line 5 is not intended to interpret what Zoya 'wanted' to say or 'had in mind' to say. Rather, it is to highlight what she said, where she said it, and how it was interpreted by Jin. Given the utterance's grammatical form, its sequential position, and the recipient's response to the utterance (laughter), I am suggesting that Zoya's turn is making an assessment and through that assessment, making a possible preclosing move which is oriented to as such by Jin. Such a move can be considered part of a practice for doing a disengagement that is interactionally, if not grammatically, 'target-like'. In similar contexts from times later in the term and in future terms of study at the data collection site (Excerpts 5.10b–5.10d), we see Zoya using similar and expanded assessments as part of the disengagements from dyadic interaction.

In (5.10b), from three weeks later (in spring, 2002), Zoya is working with Jin again in the same level 'A' class. At the end of their task, Zoya is giving directives to Jin to point to the picture which best represents the noun she says. When Jin gestures over the whole book and says 'grandfather', Zoya assesses Jin's response with a discourse marker and adjective 'nice' (line 7) which Jin responds to with laughter and the task interaction ends at that point.

(5.10b)
 4-22-02, 204, A, [1:00:52-1:01:06], Zoya and Jin
 http://www.labschool.pdx.edu/Viewer/viewer.php?pl=JKHCP&cl=5.10b

1 Z: (daughter) family.
2 J: ((points))
3 Z: grinfather.
4 J: ((gestures over her book)) everybody
5 Z: grin- okay everybody family grandfather
6 J: grandfather
7 Z: ↑okay nice
8 J: h huh ⌈huh huh ((laughing))
9 Z: ⌊**grandfather nice**

In (5.10b), Zoya uses the same adjective for the assessment as she used three weeks previously this time in combination with the final noun of focus – 'nice grandfather nice'.

In (5.10c), from fall 2002, five and a half months after the previous excerpt, we see Zoya disengage from the task interaction with a repeat of WenLing's last response, discourse marker, and intensified assessment (line 4).

(5.10c)
10-14-02, 206, A, [2:24:17-2:24:30], Zoya and WenLing
http://www.labschool.pdx.edu/Viewer/viewer.php?pl=JKHCP&cl=5.10c

```
1  Z:  We- Wadnesday okay. I col- I calleand house on?
2      Friday.=
3  W:  =I do laundry (1) on Saturday.=
4  Z:  =Saturday okay very ni:ce! ((shifts posture))
```

Zoya's assessment in (5.10c) uses the same adjective ('nice') as the previous two examples, this time with the intensifying adverb ('very').

Finally, in (5.10d), from spring 2003, four months after the previous excerpt, we see Zoya disengage from the task interaction with an assessment and compliment to her peer (lines 7 and 9).

(5.10d)
2-13-03, 206, A, [1:22:37-1:22:54], Zoya and WenLing
http://www.labschool.pdx.edu/Viewer/viewer.php?pl=JKHCP&cl=5.10d

```
1  Z:   mm (3) get bre::::sah- um
2  W:   um
3  Z:   eat bre:: ⌈:
4  W:         ⌊breakfast uh
5  Z:   brea- eat bre- breakfast
6  W:   yes. I do eve ⌈ryday
7  Z:                ⌊very good uh you
8  W:   yes
9  Z:   student
10 W:   no no yes so so
```

In this final example of Zoya using an assessment as part of a sequence for disengaging from a task interaction, she uses the common adverb-adjective combination 'very good', followed by a compliment on her peer's qualities as a student which her peer, Wen Ling, downgrades to 'so so' (line 10).

This series of four excerpts in which Zoya used assessments as part the sequence of talk-in-interaction for the action of disengaging from task

Table 5.1 Zoya's change in participation seen in the language practices of assessments for disengagements

1 April 2002	'Everybody nice'
18 April 2002	'Nice grandfather nice'
14 October 2002	'Saturday okay very nice'
13 February 2003	'Very good uh you student'

interactions exhibits subtle differences that suggest a change in her level of participation in her community of practice. The context for each disengagement is a seated dyadic teacher-assigned task. When the students get to what may be the end of that teacher-assigned task, Zoya assesses her peer's work, a practice which then becomes part of the sequence of talk-in-interaction for ending the interaction in the teacher-assigned task. Within that practice of assessment in service of the action of disengaging from a task interaction, Zoya's language practice changes (illustrated in Table 5.1) from the use of the awkward sounding pronoun-adjective combination 'everybody nice' in her second week of class (1 April 2002) to the commonly occurring adverb-adjective combination 'very good' ten months later (13 February 2003).

Disengagement Moves for Serial Dyadic Interaction Tasks

As with the openings for dyadic task interactions in classroom interaction (Chapter 3), the language and interaction used by students to disengage from their interactions while seated at their tables is notably different from the talk-in-interaction used for disengaging from serial dyadic interaction tasks, tasks often accomplished while standing as part of the engagement with a series of interlocutors across the classroom. The two most notable differences in student disengagement from their serial interaction tasks are the different non-verbal work and the great frequency of appreciations.

Non-verbal work

In the serial dyadic interaction tasks, students are often standing and moving around the classroom. This physical setup accounts for some different embodied action during disengagements. As in seated tasks, we see an orientation to mutual postural disalignment at the end of interactions but this is in combination, most often, with one or both students physically departing the scene of the interaction. Bowing and smiling seem to be the two non verbal behaviors that are present in many of the serial dyadic interaction tasks but which are not common in seated interaction. Bowing is difficult to do from a seated position and for those students from cultures where bowing is prominent, would not be culturally appropriate from a seated position. The fact that smiles occur more frequently in the serial dyadic interaction task disengagements suggests that students are displaying moves for departure as well as for disengagement from a task interaction. These different types of moves will be illustrated in the following sections on verbal disengagement from serial dyadic interaction task interactions.

Appreciations

Appreciations were noted by Button (1987) as actions which index and are oriented to by participants as possible pre-closing moves. As noted above, we see very few examples in the data of students thanking one another to mark the end of their face-to-face interactions when they are seated side by side. However, when a disengagement from a task interaction aligns with physical leave taking as occurred in the serial dyadic interaction tasks, it is very common to use appreciations as part of the closing sequence of talk. This is illustrated in Excerpt (5.11) from a beginning level classroom community of practice. In (5.11), Inez has asked several classmates in various parts of the classroom the two questions assigned her for her task interactions. When she arrives in Mun's presence, she launches their task interaction in line 1.

(5.11)
10-17-02, A, 204 [1:07:14-1:07:34], Inez, Mun, and Zi
http://www.labschool.pdx.edu/Viewer/viewer.php?pl=JKHCP&cl=5.11
(Students have been assigned to ask one another their first name and one other question – different for each student)

```
1  I:   .hh do you works part time?
2       (.)
3  I:   do you ⌈work part time
4  M:         ⌊mm       (.) no I don't.
5  I:   no I don't?
6  M:   yeah=
7  I:   okay (.) thank you M- Mun
8  M:   ((laughs))
9  I:   ((turns)) hi
```

10 Z: hello. ⌈((laugh))
11 I: ⌊((laugh))

Inez asks her question (line 1 – she knows Mun's name so does not need to ask that one) and self repairs (line 3). There is some negotiation of the meaning of the response to the question (lines 5–6). Inez then utters the discourse marker 'okay' and the appreciation to Mun (line 7), who, responds with laughter. Inez turns, likely because the next student (Zi) is waiting to ask her task questions, and, in line 9, that interaction is launched immediately following the disengagement between Inez and Mun. The use of 'thank you' by one learner acts as an interpersonal appreciation for the interlocutor's contribution to the task as well as a signal that the information was received. This, in turn, implies the end of the task.

Change in Participation: Disengagement Sequences in Serial Dyadic Interaction Tasks

Jorge's disengagements from serial dyadic interaction tasks: Week 2

From the perspective of community of practice theory, learning is noted as one's change in participation in that community of practice. That change in participation is both a result of and catalyst for a learner's language development and can be seen in learners' participation as they negotiate interactive practices in the classroom such as disengaging from a face-to-face interaction. As is the case for teacher-assigned language-learning tasks in general, when serial dyadic interaction tasks are assigned, the teacher gives instructions for the task and models how she expects the task to be carried out. However, this instruction and modeling focuses on the language to be used in the task and not on the social or interactional aspects of the task. The members of the classroom community of practice co-construct the interactional aspects of these tasks through situated, commonsense practices that involve language forms incorporated from previous use and developed through repeated practice.

Such processes make students' disengagements from a dyadic interaction an interesting site for understanding language development within a community of practice. By focusing on one student in this final section of the chapter, the same student of focus from Chapter 3, we will trace the development of practices for negotiating the action of disengaging from pair dyadic interactions over time giving the study of details of negotiating a specific area of practice an important longitudinal perspective. The excerpts of focus that illustrate disengagements are the same serial dyadic interactions examined in the chapter on openings (Chapter 3). As in

Figure 5.1 Screen shot of student-made grid for task for the excerpts in (5.12)

Chapter 3, the student is Jorge. The first four excerpts (5.12a–d) come from his second week in ESL class; the last six (5.13a–f) from a class in his fortieth week of ESL classes.

In the task for the first four excerpts (5.12), students have been instructed to ask three other students about personality characteristics ('are you sad?' etc.) and fill in the grid that they have constructed for the task (see Figure 5.1). In the row across the top of the grid is 'name' indicating students are to fill in their peers' names in the column below. In the next boxes in the first row are the characteristics they are supposed to find out about: 'happy', 'tired', 'sad' and 'shy'.

In the first excerpt, (5.12a), Digna, seated in the desk to the left of Jorge, has been collecting the information on personality characteristics from Jorge. In eliciting this information, she has not been using the target English interrogative forms to make questions but rather, uses the declarative form with first person pronoun (as in line 26). In line 26, she is eliciting a response for the last question of the series from Jorge. Jorge takes this declarative as a question about him ('are you shy?'). He answers that he is sometimes shy (line 27) for which Digna confirms receipt and records the information on her worksheet (line 29).

(5.12a)
   7-1-02, A, 204, [1:22:09-1:22:26], Jorge and Digna
   http://www.labschool.pdx.edu/Viewer/viewer.php?pl=JKHCP&cl=5.12a

(Students have been instructed to ask four other students yes/no questions about personality characteristics)

```
26  D:   I am ss ⌈shy
27  Jo:          ⌊shy shy sometimes
28  D:   sometimes
29       (5.5) ((Digna writes, Jorge waits))
30  V:   ((pointing to Jorge's paper)) may be
31  Jo:  maybe
32  V:   °maybe°
33  Jo:  °tired°
34  V:   °tired°
35  D:   ((moves out of the postural alignment for
36       engagement with Jorge))
```

As Digna writes (line 29), Jorge maintains his postural orientation to her until Vladilen leans toward Jorge, points to his paper, and utters one of the adverbs students are to use in the task, possibly as a way to confirm the pronunciation. Digna has elicited the answers for all the questions in the teacher-assigned task and when she finishes recording Jorge's last response, Jorge is engaged (to some extent) with Vladilen and Digna leaves the interaction space she shared with Jorge. The disengagement from the task interaction occurs non-verbally when Digna is writing information for the task and Jorge becomes engaged in an interaction by his deskmate. Digna leaves the interactional space without final verbal moves to end their interaction.

As a result of Vladilen's engagement with Jorge, the two begin the task interaction. As the task comes toward a close in (5.12b), Vladilen is asking Jorge the task questions and collecting information from him. Jorge answers Vladilen's last prompt in line 101 which Vladilen repeats in line 102. Jorge helps Vladilen locate the word on his worksheet and when he is writing the information, Jorge disengages posturally from his interaction with Vladlilen as he looks around the room for another student from whom he can collect information (line 105).

(5.12b)
  7-1-02, 204, A [1:24:17-1:24:54] Jorge and Vladilen
  http://www.labschool.pdx.edu/Viewer/viewer.php?pl=JKHCP&cl=5.12b

```
100  V:   ah: ⌈shy  shy shy
101  Jo:      ⌊some- ah: sometimes some ⌈times times.
102  V:                                 ⌊<some times>
```

```
103  Jo:  yeah it's ((points to V's paper))
104  V:   some times ((V writes))
105  Jo:  ((looks toward other students)) Digna ((to self))
106       ((writes on paper))
107       (5)
108  V:   (meese) (.) times
109  Jo:  ((shifts posture to D)) Digna. does tu esta are
110       you happy?
```

The first two disengagements are done non-verbally when the students get to the final prompt of the task. In each case, Jorge moves to a new interaction when his interlocutor is recording his last response. In (5.12c), Jorge has been interacting with Digna again because he had not collected information from her in their first interaction (5.12a). In this interaction, Jorge asks the final task question to Digna in line 120. She responds in line 121 with a word that Jorge interprets as 'sometimes' with his repair initiation (line 122) and which Digna confirms in line 123 with her repetition of Jorge. Jorge does not write down the response yet, however. He may be thinking that he needs to write down 'yes' or 'no' as instructed by the teacher and in line 128, when Jorge does start to write down Digna's response, she shifts her posture out of their mutual workspace. At 135, when Jorge finishes the writing, he sees that Digna is engaged in the task with another student and begins looking around the classroom, shifting his posture toward Vladilen.

(5.12c)
    7-1-02, 204, A [1:25:08- 1:25:42], Jorge and Digna
    http://www.labschool.pdx.edu/Viewer/viewer.php?pl=JKHCP&cl=5.12c

```
120  Jo:  a:re you sh ⌈y
121  D:             ⌊(s  ) sumeekt
122  Jo:  sometimes,
123  D:   sometimes
124  Jo:  ((looks at paper, then back to D))
125  D:   ((nods)) sumekt ⌈((points to Jorge's paper))
126  Jo:                  ⌊some(times)
127  D:   sumek
128  Jo:  some ((begins writing))
129       (2) ((D orients her posture away from Jo))
130       some (4) ((Jorge writes))
131  Jo:  °sometimes°
132       (9)
```

133	Jo:	sometimes
134		(4)
135	Jo:	sometimes ((looks at paper)),
136		((looks toward D))
137		((looks around the class))
138		((shifts posture to orient to his deskmate))
139		((looks at deskmate and around the room))

When students finish the task instructions from the teacher in (5.12c), Digna gives her attention to another student (the nature of the participation structure of a serial dyadic interaction task) while Jorge is recording Digna's information. This leaves Jorge 'stranded' without an interlocutor. He repeats Digna's last response several times and begins his own search for a next interlocutor for the task.

After his first three interactions with Vladilen and Digna in the area at his desk, for his fourth interaction, Jorge moves a few desks away to engage in the task with Tina. When Tina and Jorge get to the last prompt for the task (about being shy), Tina starts her response to Jorge's question (line 158). When she gets to what could be the end of a one-word response ('sometimes'), Jorge's confirming turn overlaps Tina's turn (line 159). Tina offers Jorge support with print by pointing to Jorge's paper. After finishing recording Tina's last response, Jorge offers an appreciation (line 163) to which Tina replies to form a terminal exchange and Jorge returns to his desk.

(5.12d)
7-1-02, 204, A [1:27:41-1:28:00], Jorge and Tina
http://www.labschool.pdx.edu/Viewer/viewer.php?pl=JKHCP&cl=5.12d

157	Jo:	are you sh- shy?
158	T:	sometimes ⌈shy shy
159	Jo:	⌊sometimes shy. shy
160	T:	((points to Jorge's paper)) ⌈shy.
161	Jo:	⌊shy
162		(7) ((Jorge writes))
163	Jo:	thank you. ((leaves Tina's desk))
164	T:	you're welcome.
165	Jo:	((returns to desk))

As noted earlier, when appreciations occur as part of a task disengagement, they occur when students leave a peer's desk as is the case in the serial dyadic interaction type of tasks, when students are required to collect information from classmates other than their deskmates. These tasks involve entering and exiting a new interpersonal and work space and [as seen in (5.12d)] make an appreciation conditionally relevant when taking leave of an interlocutor. Here, after working with two peers on the task while he was seated at his desk, Jorge engaged in the task at a peer's desk and returned to his own desk afterward. This leave-taking provided, perhaps, a richer context for which Jorge found the use of an appreciation in coordination with the end of a task more appropriate than when seated. As we will see in the analysis of his disengagements from forty weeks later, the use of appreciations during task disengagements is later expanded to contexts in which he remains at his seat.

The series of four disengagements from Jorge's second week of classes shows that ending these serial dyadic interaction tasks need not be done verbally. The print support given by the teacher (the worksheet where students collect information on one another) offers a procedural template which guides the interaction of the student dyads, including indexing the ends of task engagement. When a learner asks the last question of his peer, that learner can record the answer and stop the interaction by simply not physically orienting to that peer and starting work with another peer. This is not oriented to by the students or the teacher as remarkable in any way. As with the findings on opening task interactions, the disengagements of students in the beginning level proficiency communities of practice display a reduced repertoire of verbal moves. In their use of a reduced shared repertoire of practices for accomplishing the disengagements, these learners are participating legitimately, if peripherally, in the community of practice of 'fluent English language users'.

Jorge's disengagements from a serial dyadic interaction task: Week 40

Forty weeks later in Jorge's tenure of classes at the data collection site, he took part in another serial dyadic interaction task [as we saw in Chapter 3, excerpts (3.13) and (3.14)]. The following six excerpts (5.13a–f) come from that serial dyadic interaction task forty weeks after those shown in (5.12) and present evidence for Jorge's increased participation, participation that is representative of the more advance proficiency classroom community of practice. His use of English at points of disengagement from these tasks also shows that there has been development toward more full participation in the community of 'fluent English language users'.

In these excerpts, students have been assigned to ask one another yes/no questions from a list about activities that they might have done the day before to elicit the short response 'yes I did' or 'no I didn't'. In (5.13a),

Disengagements from Dyadic Task Interactions

Jorge and Julia are seated together and engage in the 'first round' of the serial task. Jorge has asked all the questions to Julia who then reciprocates. After she asks the last question (line 215) and Jorge responds affirmatively (line 216), the disengagement sequence gets underway with Julia's nodding, confirmation of receipt of Jorge's response (line 217) and recording of Jorge's response and name. After assisting Julia by showing her his printed name, Jorge also records Julia's name before their interaction is complete. After being able to see Julia's name, Jorge offers an appreciation (line 221) which, as we have seen in many cases, could be oriented to as a transitional move or move for disengagement. Julia remains seated, however, as Jorge writes her name. When Jorge confirms that her name has been recorded (line 223) and Julia remains seated at their table, Jorge explicitly invokes the task procedure, making a directive to Julia to take the next step of the activity and ask the task questions to other students. Jorge then models this action by getting out of his chair to seek another peer interlocutor.

(5.13a)
    4-18-03, 206, B, [35:39-36:04], Jorge and Julia
    http://www.labschool.pdx.edu/Viewer/viewer.php?pl=JKHCP&cl=5.13a
(Students are to ask one another yes/no questions about possible activities from the previous day. Jorge has asked the question to Julia)

```
215  Ju:  do you: eh::: did you: cook ywesterday
216  Jo:  mm:: jes I did
217  Ju:  ((nods)) °yes°
218       (1) ((Julia writes down the information))
219  Jo:  ((turns his name card so Julia can see it))
220       (2.5)
221  Jo:  Julia let me see your name oh Julia. thank you.
222       (2) ((Jo writes))
223  Jo:  Julia. ((gestures)) you aks ( ) different (.)
224       students ((leaves chair and moves to another
225       student))
```

The disengagement sequence in this excerpt shows how the task orientation facilitates the disengagement in several ways. First, after completing the task's sequence of questions, the students record one another's names as part of the organization of information collected in the task. When, after names are recorded, a disengagement has not been achieved, Jorge makes a directive to Julia that glosses the procedures for serial dyadic interaction tasks and the students take leave of one another.

After moving from his seat and engaging in the task interaction with Eduardo (5.13b), Eduardo asks his last question to Jorge 'did you watch t.v.' (line 255) to which Jorge responds affirmatively. The disengagement from their task, however, is interrupted by Eduardo's question to the teacher (line 258) which initiates a long side sequence, a discussion about whether in English one 'eats' or 'drinks' chocolate. During this side sequence between Eduardo and the teacher, Jorge remains standing near Eduardo orienting to their lack of disengagement. But just after Eduardo closes his sequence with the teacher (line 272), another student, Jing, asks a task prompt question to Jorge (line 275) and they start an interaction without a formal disengagement occurring between Jorge and Eduardo.

Excerpt (5.13b) includes more than the point of possible task disengagement to preview a task expansion initiated by Jing (lines 282–287). This task expansion is presented here because a similar expansion is incorporated by Jorge in the later task disengagement with Jing, an action that will be discussed more fully later.

(5.13b)
 4-18-03, 206, B, [37:41-38:44], Jorge and Eduardo
 http://www.labschool.pdx.edu/Viewer/viewer.php?pl=JKHCP&cl=5.13b

```
255  E:   ah did you: (3) yesterday watch tee vee,
256  Jo:  ah jes I did,
257       (5) ((E prepares to write))
258  E:   ((gestures to Te for help)) ah one question.
259       what is the
260  Te:  eat
261  E:   eh chocolate.
262  Te:  chocol ⌈ate
263  E:         ⌊n- no I drinking?
264  Jo:  no e ⌈s eat
265  Te:       ⌊no: ((shakes head)) eat
266  E:   eat?
267  Te:  eat eat chocolate. like little (.) candy.=
268  E:   =OH candy.
269  Te:  yeah I know in Mexico you drink chocolate but in
270  E:   yeah
271  Te:  here we eat (.) chocolate
272  E:   yeah ((laugh)) okay (.) thank you ((to teacher))
273  Ji:  Jorge ((initiating another interaction))
274  E:   Jorge ((writing Jorge's name))
```

```
275  Ji:    did you? (.) did you (.) drink coffee?
276  Jo:    jeste ⌈rday?
277  Ji:         ⌊yesterday?
278  Jo:    no I didn't.
279  Ji:    ⌈(no I didn't)
280  Jo:    ⌊no I didn't
281         (1.5)
282  Ji:=>  do you (.) do you drink
283  Jo:    no I s did
284  Ji:    do you dr⌈ink coffee
285  Jo:             ⌊°(do you drink)°
286  Ji:    everyday?
287  Jo:    everyday?=no never. heh heh ne(h)ver
288         ((lines missing -- Jorge tells Eduardo he is
289         going to work with other students))
```

In this task assigned by the teacher, students are to ask one another yes-no questions about what they might have done the previous day to elicit the past tense short answers. After the question–answer sequence is initiated by Jing (lines 275–280), Jing asks a post-expansion (Schegloff, 1998) question which expands the interaction beyond the task instructions – to the use of simple present tense for describing habits. In lines 282, 284 and 286 Jing asks the question 'do you drink coffee everyday', using the adverb of frequency 'everyday' paired with the simple present tense question form. After an initial attempt at repair where it appears Jorge hears Jing's question to be the same as his first question (line 283), Jorge repeats part of Jing's question with the tense shift (line 285) and in line 287 gives a negative answer which he elaborates on with a corresponding adverb of frequency.

The task between Jorge and Jing continues as Jorge moves away from Eduardo's desk and the disengagement from the task between Jorge and Jing is seen in Excerpt (5.13c). After Jorge asks his task question (line 290) and Jing responds, Jorge repeats the response as a confirmation of receipt and follows that with an affirmative discourse marker ('okay').

(5.13c)
   4-18-03, 206, B, [38:56-39:19], Jorge and Jing
   http://www.labschool.pdx.edu/Viewer/viewer.php?pl=JKHCP&cl=5.13c

```
290  Jo:    did you: (.) eat chocolate yesterday?
291  Ji:    n:::o I didn't.
```

```
292  Jo:=>   no I didn't. okay. (.) sometimes? ((starting to
293          write))
294  Ji:     (eh ih Jing  ) ↑oh ((showing Jo where to write))
295          no.
296  Jo:     no? (.) oh n(h)o huh hah
297          (.5)
298  Jo:     sorry
299          (.5)
300  Jo:     Jing okay thank you Jing.
```

Jorge's confirmation of receipt and discourse marker (line 292) are followed by his use of an adverb of frequency which appears to be an expansion of the task, a shortened follow-up question by Jorge to Jing (outlined in Figure 5.2).

The use of this adverb of frequency is an action similar to the task expansion that Jing initiated when he asked the questions of Jorge, shown in the immediately previous Excerpt (5.13b) (lines 282–287). After apologizing for writing the information in the incorrect place on his worksheet (line 298), he repeats Jing's name, uses a closing discourse marker and offers an appreciation (line 300) before leaving the area.

The task expansion by Jing at a possible point of disengagement from the task interaction shows how this boundary site may be used by students for trying out related grammatical structures through slight expansions of the task before moving on to engage in the task assignment with another student. The attempted task expansion using a similar grammatical expansion by Jorge during his turn for questioning and just following Jing's own task expansion shows how the task and a peer's modeling through dyadic interaction in the classroom community of practice together facilitate a micro-level change in participation in the classroom community of practice by Jorge in the way he disengages from a task interaction.

```
Jing:    do you dr⌈ink coffee
Jorge:           ⌊(do you drink)?
Jing:    everyday?
Jorge:   everyday?=no never.

Jorge:   did you: (.) eat chocolate yesterday?
Jing:    n:::o I didn't.
Jorge:   no I didn't. okay. (.) sometimes?
```

Figure 5.2 Jorge's attempted task expansion modeled on Jing's

Disengagements from Dyadic Task Interactions 135

For his next interaction, (5.13d), Jorge has moved across the classroom and is interacting with Abebe. Jorge asks a question of Abebe (about calling a friend) who reciprocates and receives a negative response from Jorge. Abebe is writing down Jorge's name (mispronouncing it – line 301) and confirming Jorge's negative answer. Jorge, however, is not sure he heard the question correctly and asks Abebe to repeat it. After clearing up the question and answer, Abebe re-starts the disengagement sequence by asking Jorge his name (line 313) even though he had been writing it down at the start of the excerpt. When Abebe sees Jorge's printed name, he pronounces it as he sees it written (line 315) and the mispronunciation is confirmed by Jorge (line 316). As in a previous example, another student, Chris, overlaps this part of the closing with a task prompt for Jorge (line 317) and they begin an interaction.

(5.13d)
4-18-03, 206, B, [40:26-40:52], Jorge and Abebe
http://www.labschool.pdx.edu/Viewer/viewer.php?pl=JKHCP&cl=5.13d

```
301  A:  Geor ⌈gay  I didn't? ((checks Jorge's answer))
302  J:       ⌊what yeah   what did you (.) ask me? ( )
303          (.) (the) question?
304          (.5)
305  J:  can you repeat the: (.) your question?
306  A:  question yeah I'm (.) ask you the questions.=
307  J:  =yeah what is your question.
308  A:  eh::: did you drink coffee?
309  J:  oh. yesterday? n ⌈o I-   no I didn't
310  A:                  ⌊esterday
311       (    ) ⌈no I didn't
312  J:          ⌊no I didn't
313  A:  what's ya name
314  J:  ah Jorge ((points to his name on his paper))
315  A:  Georgay
316  J:  Georgay
317  C:  Georgay did you go to the market yesterday?
```

This excerpt shows the importance of recording the peer's name as part of the task and as a marker of disengagement from the task. When the name recording sequence is interrupted in line 302 and a re-peat of the question-answer sequence is undertaken, Abebe goes back to recording Jorge's name as the ending for their face-to-face interaction (line 313).

Excerpt (5.13d) also shows Jorge's orientation to the task when, in line 302, after Abebe's confirmation of Jorge's last response and his name, he requests a clarification of Abebe's last question before a disengagement can get underway. Such a move is reminiscent of the research on closings in telephone conversations in which participants orient to the end of the conversation approaching by getting in any important information ('mentionables') before the closing sequence can get underway (Schegloff & Sacks, 1973). This example provides evidence of Jorge's ability to project the trajectory of the sequences of talk in the serial dyadic interaction tasks as well as his concern for the integrity of his response to his peer.

As Jorge finished with Abebe, Chris launched the task interaction with Jorge. Following their interaction and then an interaction with Duc (not presented here), Jorge interacts with Jin and we see him completing that interaction in (5.13e). After responding to Jin's last question, she asks for his name and they negotiate the pronunciation (lines 354–362). After that negotiation, Jorge utters a discourse marker ('okay') and offers an appreciation to Jin (line 362) as a marker of the disengagement.

(5.13e)
4-18-03, 206, B, [44:08-44:41], Jorge and Jin
http://www.labschool.pdx.edu/Viewer/viewer.php?pl=JKHCP&cl=5.13e

```
350  Ji:  do you (call) uh: (2) re:- (.) relatives.
351  Jo:  do you call?
352  Ji:  (relatives)
353  Jo:  no I didn't.
354  Ji:  what's name.
355  Jo:  Georgay
356       (2) ((looks at name on Jorge's paper))
357  Ji:  jay. oh, are? ((spelling the name))
358  Jo:  ee
359       (2)
360  Ji:  Jorge
361  E:   (     )
362  Jo:  Jorge Georgay ((to E)) okay thanks ((to Ji))
363  Ji:  ((laughs))
364  Jo:  ((laughs))
365  Ji:  ↑Jorge
366  Jo:  Jorge yeah. Georgay.
```

Disengagements from Dyadic Task Interactions 137

In the last interaction from the series, Jorge has returned to his desk area where Reinaldo has been interacting with another student (5.13f). After starting the interaction with Reinaldo and answering his question, Jorge reciprocates with a task question in line 378. After Reinaldo responds affirmatively, Jorge expands the task prompt question by asking about the specific time Reinaldo woke up (line 380). After clarifying the time given by Reinaldo in his response, Jorge offers an appreciation (line 387) as a part of a disengagement from the interaction.

(5.13f)
4-18-03, 206, B [46:53-47:16], Jorge and Reinaldo
http://www.labschool.pdx.edu/Viewer/viewer.php?pl=JKHCP&cl=5.13f

```
378  Jo:  did you wake up early? yesterday?
379  R:   yes I did
380  Jo:  what time (.) d'jou wake up ((J sits at his desk))
381       (1)
382       mm: ((J is writing))
383       (2)
384  R:   s:: six in the morning
385  Jo:  ((stops writing)) six (.) six in the morning?
386  R:   ((nods))
387  Jo:  ((looking at board)) ((nods)) okay tank you
388       ((looks at paper))
389       (2)
390  R:   mm Jorge ((restarts task in Spanish))
```

Just before uttering the discourse marker and appreciation, Jorge moves his gaze away from Reinaldo and toward the front of the room and then after the appreciation, to his paper. Though Reinaldo remains standing near Jorge's desk, it appears that Jorge has disengaged from the interaction with Reinaldo. However, after a two-second pause, Reinaldo restarts the interaction in Spanish.

While we saw, even in his second week of classes (5.12d), that Jorge oriented to leave taking as implicative of offering an appreciation for the disengagement sequence, in this series of interactions from week 40, we see four examples of appreciations offered as part of the disengagement from dyadic task interactions in a more advanced classroom community of practice. In the first interaction of the task (5.13a), Jorge offered an appreciation which was not oriented to by his peer (Julia) as a possible pre-closing move and Jorge made a more explicit directive to his peer to work with another student. In (5.13c), after recording his peer's name, Jorge marked the end of the interaction with a discourse marker ('okay') and an appreciation before moving across the room to work with another peer. In (5.13e), after working out the spelling and pronunciation of his name, Jorge marks the disengagement with the discourse marker 'okay' and an appreciation. Also, in (5.13f), after expanding the task slightly with a more specific question, Jorge uses a discourse marker and appreciation to close the task interaction with Reinaldo.

Excerpt (5.13f), the last task interaction in the series, shows another example of a post-expansion sequence in which Jorge expanded the task beyond what was required in the teacher's instructions. This post-expansion question (line 380) is directly topically-linked to and works as a follow-up to the just-asked task question from Jorge to Reinaldo in line 378. The post-expansion question is a clear example of how teacher-assigned language-learning tasks provide incidental sites for language use and language learning. In this case, we see Jorge's ability to integrate interpersonal interaction with task interaction, creating a liminal space where he displays his increasing competence as a 'member' of his classroom community of practice as well as the community of practice of 'fluent English language users'.

This task expansion and the one previously discussed from (5.13c) are examples of what might be considered the microgenesis of language development taking place within the interactive context of the classroom community of practice. In the first case (5.13c), while Jorge was engaged in a dyadic interaction, at the point of possible disengagement (after the last task-question prompt is asked and responded to), the asker of the question, Jing, asked another question, expanding the grammatical field of the task from simple past tense to simple present tense and marking that expansion with an adverb of frequency. When the interaction called for a role change (Jorge asking questions of Jing), Jorge used the opportunity to make his role assignment parallel to Jing's. When he asked the follow-up question fragment in line 292 (using an adverb of frequency 'sometimes') and we ask, 'why that now?', the sequential context suggests that the interaction between Jing and Jorge (particularly Jing's task expansion) modeled and fostered the use of an adverb of frequency by Jorge to attempt a grammatical and interactional expansion of the task to expand the task similarly, as a reduced follow-up query to his partner about how often he might eat chocolate. Jorge's task expansion from his last dyadic interaction in the series (5.13f) is a full follow-up question that was not modeled previously by a peer. The question remains in the same grammatical field (past tense) as the original and is topically-related and a more specific

Disengagements from Dyadic Task Interactions 139

question to the first. These micro-level moments of developments or additions to the repertoire of practices are some of the foundational structures of a learner's move from 'legitimate peripheral' toward more 'core' participation in a classroom community of practice as well as the community of practice of 'fluent English language users'.

Summarizing the moves for disengagement from serial interaction tasks by that Jorge was involved in during his second and fortieth weeks of ESL classes will allow us to compare across time points for more longitudinal evidence of language development.

Table 5.2 shows that while in week two, the disengagements were done, for the most part, non-verbally, the practices used to accomplish disengagements in week 40 were quite different. In the series of interactions from a serial interaction task in Jorge's fortieth week of classes, we see a fairly consistent set of moves and sequences of moves that are used to invoke and accomplish disengagement from the task interactions.

Table 5.2 Summary of moves in Jorge's disengagement sequences in week 2 and week 40 interactions

	Week 2	Week 40
(5.12a) (5.13a)	• Launch/interruption by other	• Recording name • Appreciation • Invoke task instructions
(5.12b) (5.13b)	• Postural disengagement while writing	• Recording name • Side sequence with teacher • Launch by other
(5.12c) (5.13c)	• Postural disengagement while writing	• Task expansion • Recording name • Discourse marker • Appreciation
(5.12d) (5.13d)	• Recording answer in writing • Appreciation	• Recording name • Clarification request • Launch by other
(5.13e)	—	• Recording name • Discourse marker • Appreciation
(5.13f)	—	• Task expansion • (Recording name) • Discourse marker • Appreciation

In week 40, in all the sequences (except the last) students ask one another their names or to see a printed version of their names to aid in spelling them. In the first interaction, Jorge does not ask for Julia's name until she has asked for his name. In the subsequent interactions, Jorge asks for and records his peer interlocutor's name after asking his question prompt. In the last interaction of the series without the request for the name, it is likely that because Jorge's interlocutor ('Reinaldo') is a compatriot from Mexico, that he does not need to have the name spelled.

In the serial interaction task from week 2, the recording of names occurred at the start of the task as an artifact of the task design. Students used a grid layout provided by the teacher to record their information and because 'name' was the first box in the written grid layout, that was the first question asked in the task interaction. In week 40, students were not given such a template for recording their answers and needed to organize the information they collected by assigning a name to the particular information. This independently motivated name gathering as part of the task shows a difference in the practices for the 'week 40' classroom community of practice. The lack of written mediation for where and when in the interaction a name should be gathered is one reason that getting a peer's name was an important part of the disengagements from tasks in week 40 interactions.

Appreciations are also recurrent in the week 40 interactions while in week 2 there was only one instance of an appreciation, offered when Jorge was leaving the desk of his peer. In week 40, two of the four appreciations are offered when Jorge is at his own desk. Three of the appreciations in week 40 are also bounded by the transitional discourse marker 'okay' showing Jorge's ability to use verbal markers for the boundary of actions in the classroom. The use of discourse markers has been shown to emerge in the inventory of learners' language practices the longer they live in the target language culture (Hellermann & Vergun, 2007; Nakahama et al., 2001). While 'okay' was used by Jorge more often in task openings, in the disengagements, Jorge's use of the discourse marker 'okay' for marking shifts in participation structures appears later in his course of study showing how teacher-assigned language-learning tasks provide contexts in which discourse marker use is appropriate and a conduit for discourse marker use into the shared repertoire of language practices in this classroom community of practice.

While the uncovering of the turn-by-turn shifts in interaction show the micro-genetic development of different degrees of participation in a classroom community of practice, the differences in practices for disengaging from dyadic task interactions noted in Figure 5.2 for the two time periods can be seen as evidence of the practices which distinguish participation in two different classroom communities of practice. One (week 2) is the community of practice of a level 'A' class where many, if not most, of the students are in their first English language class. The other, from week 40, is the community of practice of a level 'B' class (upper beginning).

Conclusion

As with the other two examples of social actions embedded within teacher-assigned tasks (Chapters 3 and 4), the investigation of the disengagements from task interaction show similarities and differences to previous research on the organization of social interaction through language. Disengagements from task interactions in the language-learning classroom occur in a gradual, sequential way. Their production, however, is influenced by the language proficiency or competencies of the learner-members and by different contingencies in the task itself. In many cases, especially for students in the beginning level classroom communities of practice, many, if not all, of the sequential moves that make up a particular disengagement are non-verbal.

While the non-verbal disengagements are due, in part, to the novice proficiency level the learners, the contexts in which they occur also influence their production. The disengagements are situated, that is, their co-construction is influenced by students' orientations to their tasks, their interlocutors, and their classmates and the participation structures of the classroom as a whole. The interaction between Reinaldo and Ain (5.9) given here again as (5.14) is a good example of this. When Reinaldo and Ain get to the end of their task interaction, and engage in a possible closing sequence of talk (lines 8–9), each makes a visual survey the classroom (lines 9–10).

(5.14)
   11-21-03, 204, C, [1:14:45-1:15:08], Reinaldo and Ain
   http://www.labschool.pdx.edu/Viewer/viewer.php?pl=JKHCP&cl=5.9
   (Reinaldo and Ain are practicing asking and answering questions using the structure 'going to' to express the future)

1 **A:** are you going to take a trip?
2 **R:** mm:::::
3 **A:** no.
4 **R:** I am no: quite sure.
5 **A:** (okay)
6 **R:** I don't have money. maybe in the future I have

```
7           mon(h)ey.
8   A:      insha'Allah
9   R:      heh heh ((looks around the room))
10  A:      ((looks around the room))
11          (4.0)
12  R:      ((orients to A))  ⌈how how long is stay here. (.)
13  A:                        ⌊((yawns))
14  R:      ((points at A))
15          (1.5)
16  A:      me?
17  R:      yeah.
```

As I suggested earlier, as Ain and Reinaldo look around the classroom, the other students continue to talk to one another. This orientation to the actions of the other members of the classroom community of practice is similar to the work a teacher does in such situations. By understanding, through explicit observation of their activity, what their peers in the community of practice are doing, Reinaldo and Ain can see that disengaging from interpersonal interaction was not necessary and not warranted at that particular point. This is likely part of the reasoning behind Reinaldo's opening another topic for interaction (line 12).

When working in peer dyads on teacher-assigned language-learning tasks, the task itself provides a script that, in turn, provides a mutual orientation to a 'natural' end for an interaction. Although this does not happen frequently, when students finish the teacher-assigned task, they may disengage from interaction with one another without using verbal resources and this is not noted as remarkable by the student participants. As in the openings for task interaction discussed in Chapter 3, in the disengagements out of task interaction we see this boundary area highlighted with the use of discourse markers (most notably, 'okay'). While 'okay' can be used as a token of agreement, in the context of task ending and disengagement from interaction, the marker is used in the adult language-learning classroom as teachers often use it in classroom interaction (Hellermann, 2005a; Sinclair & Coulthard, 1975): to frame a course of action, either as starting or ending. The use of discourse markers in the context of disengagements is evidence for situated nature of disengagements, of learners' orientation to task and the institution of school – their classroom community of practice.

Chapter 6
Conclusions

Introduction

The research in this volume has advocated focusing on classroom language learning as a contextualized and situated process through action-oriented investigations of language, language learning and language-learning classrooms. In the previous three chapters, I have set the analytic lens for a rather powerful focus on details for micro-level social actions that adult language learners accomplished in their dyadic task interactions in their language learning classrooms. In concluding, I will step back with a much broader focus in discussing classrooms as communities of practice before coming back, at the end, to the details of face-to-face interaction in these communities to show the existence of the macro features within the micro practices (Steve Reder, pers. comm.).

How Language Learning is 'Situated'

The investigations in this volume focused on learners, their talk-in-interaction, and their co-construction of social practices for ordering their interactions in language-learning classrooms using theoretical perspectives on social organization and research findings from conversation analysis and situated learning. CA research has focused on describing how talk-in-interaction itself is a social organization worthy of investigation. That program's focus on indigenous methods for social order making through talk-in-interaction led to my attempt to uncover similar indigenous methods of organization through language that occur in the language learning classroom accomplished by adults with various competencies in the use of English. By describing these practices at different points in time, I attempted to show evidence of language development in micro-level language practices. The social practices uncovered and analyzed here were accomplished by adult language learners in their peer classroom dyadic interaction without instruction from the teacher and have not been the focus of the bulk of research on additional language learning (Kasper, 2006).

This is a notable gap in the research program of classroom language learning researchers. While the pedagogical task is, without question, an important source and catalyst for language learning in the classroom, understanding language development as it occurs in teacher-designed tasks presents problems for the assessment of learning. First is the issue of to what degree the language elicited and produced in a language learning task can transfer to out of task contexts (Foster, 1998; Morris & Tarone, 2003). A great deal of empirical research has shown that particular tasks facilitate the learning of language forms in experimental and quasi-experimental research design. We do not, however, have a good idea to what degree the language forms elicited in a particular experimental task are then used productively in other contexts. Research has shown that researcher-designed or teacher-designed tasks themselves are situated and locally contextualized (Cole, 1996). Even when performed in the same context (Coughlin & Duff, 1994; Kumaravadivelu, 1991), different learners do not carry out the task in the same way. This understanding tells us that when trying to understand the causal factors for learning in language learning tasks by comparing learner performance across similar tasks, contextual factors will confound the results.

I will not claim that the particular social actions of focus in this study occur 'independently' of task or other contextual influences. These actions and practices for their implementation were chosen because understanding language that occurs around teacher-designed tasks, the language of learner–learner interaction, can help us understand the social organization of the classrooms (Heap, 1985) and more specifically, the interactional contexts in which these dyadic tasks take place (Kasper, 2004; Seedhouse, 2005; van Lier, 2000; van Lier & Matsuo, 2000). These actions were also chosen as the focus of research because they must occur (openings and disengagements) or can occur (story tellings) in almost every language learning classroom interaction and must be part of a description of learner–learner interaction, the context for the processes involved in doing any language-learning task.

The object of analysis for language learning was re-focused from SLA's traditional focus on purely linguistic objects to show how learners orient to and use language practices to accomplish social action. Rather than conceptualizing learning as a decontextualization process (Lave, 1993) (learning in one context and generalizing that knowledge to other contexts) I understand learning in a process-oriented way and have tried to show evidence for that. Learners of a language use and participate in language practices in one context and then adapt such practices for participation in another context not because they are particularly flexible, adaptable learners, but because they must. They must be because they are interacting with different people or the same person at a different time, a person who plays a role in how a particular interaction is accomplished. Unlike what much experimental and quasi-experimental research on language learning suggests, there are no identically contextualized situations.

There is, however, a reflexive and indexical relationship between learners' past experience with language and present contextualized practices (Brown *et al.*, 1989; Wortham, 2001). This means we may not be able to effectively assess learning when we (researchers) provide what we consider to be controlled tasks as data elicitation devices because those 'controlled' task structures will be altered in unpredictable ways in subsequent instantiations. What learners have experienced through past language practices is relevant for a current context to the degree that a current context implicates its relevance. Put more concretely, a learner's 'time 1' experience or understanding of a concept at 'time 1' will be made available to that learner and his/her interlocutors and to researchers at some later 'time 2', only to the degree that the context of 'time 2' affords it.

The Contexts of Classroom Communities of Practice and Their Influence on Language Use

For this study, the particular 'current' contexts, the places for investigating examples of this indexing and language development, were classroom communities of practice. Several contexts for classroom interaction are important to highlight in understanding what constitutes a classroom community of practice.

Task and task design

As was illustrated most directly in Chapter 3, the teacher's task design is an important resource for structuring dyadic interaction in the classroom community of practice. In a classroom in which the teacher designed tasks to include two distinct roles for the dyad ('teacher' giving directives, and 'student' following directives), in opening their task interactions, students were able to use the assignment of those roles ('you teacher') as a way to do turn allocation for the task: the student assigned the role of 'teacher' takes the first turn. In intermediate proficiency classroom communities of practice, without language support from the task in the form of role assignment, students used language practices not derived from the language of the task to accomplish a similar action – turn allocation ('you first').

Literacy practices that were part of the teacher-assigned tasks were also seen to play a role in the spoken interaction. Students may have been required as part of their task interactions to record information in writing that they received in their face-to-face task interactions for later use by themselves or by the teacher. We saw how Jorge's dyadic task interactions, especially the disengagements from those interactions, were mediated by recording task information on a grid (Excerpts 5.12a, 5.12b). While writing for the task was seen to influence dyadic interactions in beginning level communities of practice, students in intermediate level communities of practice recorded information more often not as a direct result of the teacher's instructions but in a more independent manner, taking notes for themselves (Excerpt 5.6).

While it is not clear to what degree this was related to the task design, overall, we saw more task prefatory talk in the intermediate than in the beginning level classroom communities of practice. The task prefatory talk did task clarification, turn allocation, and, in some cases, seemed to work to do general alignment or confirmation work (3.12). For students in beginning level classroom communities of practice, the task itself was the talk as they frequently directly launched their task interaction after the teacher gave instructions for the task.

Participation structures/turn allocation systems

The orientation of students and teacher in the classroom to the different participation structures that are part of the curriculum and pedagogy offer several different contexts for language use. The classrooms I observed were traditional in the sense that each had one teacher and a number of students. The teacher often spoke to all students together (teacher–cohort participation structure). About 15% of the time (Reder *et al.*, forthcoming), students were working together in pairs or small groups (student–student participation structure). Within this classroom organizational pattern, students were faced with the unplanned task of managing the shift from teacher–cohort structure to a student–student structure and vice versa. We saw in the chapter on openings how the shift from teacher-fronted to student–student interaction was a boundary site where language practices were used to negotiate that action (an opening) for the a shift in participation structure. When the peer dyadic task interactions ended, students needed to shift from that participation structure back to the teacher–cohort order. Again, language practices were used to implement this action – the disengagement. Organizational shifts in the classroom communities of practice then become tasks for personnel management that students in the language learning class take on as part of doing teacher-assigned, language-learning dyadic tasks.

From a CA perspective, this change in participation structure can be seen in a shift in turn allocation systems (Sacks *et al.*, 1974) in the classroom. Classroom discourse research has shown the predominance of the three-turn sequence as a turn allocation system for traditional, teacher-fronted classrooms – the teacher initiation, the student response, and the teacher feedback to that response (Hall, 1997b; Hellermann, 2005a; Lee, 2006; Mehan, 1979; Sinclair & Coulthard, 1975). When students are working in dyads or small groups, this type of turn allocation system may still operate as we saw when a student assesses a peer in the third turn slot. However, the shift in participation structure from teacher–cohort to student–student coincides with a shift in turn allocation system in which the talk, even when task oriented, is more conversational in that each student alternates turns.

Student–student, person–person

The interpersonal aspect of teacher-assigned dyadic task interaction is seen in several aspects of the social actions observed. The interpersonal nature of the interactions is a chance for students to use self-deprecatory (3.11) or ironic (3.3) humor as they get their interactions started.

In many of the dyadic interactions, the interpersonal nature of the interaction afforded students the opportunity to engage in interpersonal interaction, conversation, after their task work ended. In Chapter 5, however, we saw several examples of student language practice affiliated with the task. We saw a change in the practices used by Zoya for assessing her peers' work at the end of their task interactions. For Zoya, an assessment was part of the disengagement sequence from the task interaction and a site for the development of new language practices to assess a peer's performance.

Two other examples of students using aspects of the task and the interpersonal nature of the dyadic task interaction to expand the task itself in the task interaction beyond what was planned by the teacher. In Jorge's interaction with Jing (Excerpts 5.13b and 5.13c) and later in the same class period with Reinaldo (5.13f). These examples show the difficulty of separating what has been called previously 'on-task' and 'off task' language. In the first of these three examples (5.13b), Jorge is the recipient of a task expansion by Jing. In the very next opportunity, Jorge attempts the same type of task expansion with Jing (5.13c) and then several minutes later, in the last interaction of the task, expands his task interaction in a different way with Reinaldo. In each case, the task expansion is a personal question related to the previous teacher-assigned task question. The personal nature of each expansion shows the importance of interpersonal communication as a catalyst for language use and language learning. These (and other) task expansions also show how dyadic language learning tasks are sites where creativity with the language occurs in unpredictable ways.

Teacher-student

In classroom communities of practice, students and teachers display an orientation to the teacher as having more rights and responsibilities for directing interaction. This orientation can be seen in the way students need to divide their attention between the different participation structures and different members of the community. Learners' orientation to two different potential participation structures is observable in video of classroom interaction during tasks and as a task interaction approaches its end.

While working in pairs to accomplish a teacher-assigned language learning task, students must actively be involved with their peer to accomplish that task while at the same time continually monitoring what the teacher is doing in other parts of the classroom. While the level of involvement with the peer might be seen as primary, the students seem to be strongly aware of what the teacher is doing during their peer interaction to the point where the teacher's movements around the room effect the sequence of turns of the students' pair interactions. Such effects by teacher movement in the classroom suggest students might consider their involvement with the teacher as 'dominant' to their involvement with their peer (Goffman, 1963).

This is illustrated in a task interaction from a beginning level classroom community of practice. In this Excerpt (6.1), we see Reinaldo and Abebe doing a task in which one member of the dyad asks the other questions about 'yesterday' to elicit the use of past tense verbs from interlocutor. Here, we see that Abebe notices what is going on outside of his immediate interaction with Reinaldo. He sees the teacher coming into their area (line 21) and displays that orientation to the teacher's presence by altering his task interaction (line 22).

(6.1)
4/18/03 206 B, [1:16:54-1:17:43] Reinaldo and Abebe[18]
1   R: did you:: (2) lear- learn Eng- learn English yesterday?
2   (1.5)
3   A: no I didn't.

Conclusions

```
4       (0.5)
5   R:  ↑no? no learn?
6       (1.5)
7   A:  what what?
8       (0.5)((Abebe turns to Reinaldo))
9   R:  learned. learned.
10  A:  uh learned he:h. yes I did.
11  A:  (2)((writes))
12  R:  you understand (the) learn?
13  A:  yeah understand? ye ⌈s.
14  R:                     ⌊mm
15      (3)
16  R:  did you::::::::::
17      (2)((both turn gazes to the left of them))
18  A:  ehh (.) ehehhee (.) ehhe
19      (6)((A and R shift posture with worksheets in hands))
20  R:  did you::::
21  A:  tomorrow she will (2) ((shifts posture))
22  A:  hwadido yesterday ((directs speech to teacher))
23      (0.5)
24  Te: what did I do yesterday? ((Te points to self))
25  A:  eah
26  Te: me? ((Te points to self))
27  A:  yeah
28  Te: like this? ((Te points at Abebe's worksheet))
29  A:  yeah. me. whatdido yesterday
30  Te: I didn't cook (.) I didn't watch tee vee, (.) I didn't
31      exercise,
```

The learner dyadic participation structures make contexts other than the task and immediate peer available as resources for language learning within the classroom community of practice. In their dyadic task interactions, we saw how student peers located beyond the immediate small group setting as well as the teacher were resources for language learning in the classroom community of practice. Learner–learner dyads, however, are themselves situated within a group of simultaneously interacting learner–learner dyads (displayed graphically in Figure 2.1 in Chapter 2). During these simultaneously occurring task interactions, the participants in one dyad can take advantage of their classmates' simultaneous interactions by directly questioning them regarding task procedures, using them as models (Excerpt 1.1) but also indirectly by observing their behavior at the starts and ends of their dyadic task interactions. These indirect observations are especially important for beginning level classroom communities of practice where community other students model how and when to start a peer–peer interaction after the shift from teacher–cohort participation structure. Interaction at the ends of task activity was also shown to be influenced by other peer dyads in the example of Reinaldo and Ain from an intermediate level classroom community of practice (Chapter 5) when after seeing their classmates' continued engagement, they continued their interaction on a new topic.

These boundary areas (openings and disengagements) and the students' story telling in the students' dyadic task interaction provide particularly rich contexts for observing adult learners' negotiation and changes in participation locally and over time. The negotiation of talk-in-interaction for organizing classroom dyadic interaction that is evident in these three actions involves the dialectic of reification and participation (Wenger, 1998). The negotiation involves adult learners using language and interactional structures in the teacher-assigned task and language structures inherent in the system of the language itself and in their own experiences with the language as the reified structures for face-to-face interaction. These reified aspects of their interactions meet the local, real-time needs of participation in interaction with peers. This intersection is negotiated in the boundary areas of openings and disengagements in the way that task interactions are framed and contextualized within the larger interactional context of human face-to-face social interaction and the negotiation is accomplished through uninstructed language mediated by task provided language.

In the story telling sequences during dyadic task interactions (Chapter 4), students used singular, reified past time events from their lives as a resource for explicating their task interactions. The reified object of the past-time event becomes a locally co-constructed action of participation in dyadic face-to-face interaction. The use of story tellings during task interactions is another piece of evidence of the lack of a clear distinction between interpersonal and task activity in the language learning classroom. Students' use of story telling during their English language learning tasks suggests that this is a cross-cultural or universal social action (Beach & Lindstrom, 1992) that adult learners use as a resource for language learning.

Language Learning in Classroom Communities of Practice

Several (and overlapping) communities of practice

Based on surveys of students at the data collection site (some reported on in Hellermann & Brillanceau, 2007), it is apparent that the adult language

Conclusions

learners of focus in this study have interactional competence as a primary goal for learning English. From the situated learning and conversation analytic perspectives, this goal of the learners is to be competent members of the community of practice I have been glossing as 'fluent English language users'. That particular community of practice is widespread, covering in class and out of class communities and, as with any community of practice, includes members who participate fully and members who participate peripherally. Students in different proficiency level classes at the data collection site are also members of that community of practice to varying degrees and display that membership through their talk-in-interaction in English in their classrooms.

In every classroom, the teacher and students interact in ways that co-construct what are considered appropriate forms of language and behavior for that classroom community of practice using English. In this way, students display their own degrees of participation in the 'classroom' and 'fluent English language user' communities of practice. In a beginning level classroom community of practice, students are not expected to be able to use the same repertoire of practices for language that the teacher uses. The use of 'too much' language or 'overly advanced' language forms is oriented to by the teacher and classmates and marks the student who uses those forms as a marginal member of the community of practice. A marginal status means that member's participation is not part of a 'peripheral' to 'full' trajectory. Other students treat marginal member students in overly-deferential ways and because of that marginal status an observant teacher will attempt to move that student to a more appropriate class.

In each classroom community of practice, there are members who cannot participate fully within that community of practice because of their status as newcomers or (in the language learning classroom) because they do not have the language proficiency to allow them to participate fully. They can, however, participate 'peripherally' in the practices of that community of practice (through observation and more heavily-mediated activity). In the ideal classroom community of practice, each type of participation (full and peripheral) will be considered 'legitimate' by the community. In this way, 'newcomers' to the classroom community of practice can learn with the help of 'oldtimers' and those 'oldtimers' can benefit from acting as peer mentors.

While each community of practice includes members who can participate to varying degrees in the practices of the community, there are consistencies in routines (Kanagy, 1999; Ohta, 2001a; Peters & Boggs, 1986) and practices for talk-in-interaction that help define each community of practice. The collections of instances of openings, story tellings, and disengagements show evidence for a consistency of repertoires of practices for social actions displayed by students in different proficiency levels. The repertoires of practices used in a particular class are the micro-level practices for talk-in-interaction that are part of the constitution of that particular classroom community of practice. In different class levels at the data collection site ('A', 'B', 'C' or 'D'), different classroom communities of practice formed through practices for talk-in-interaction. Progress toward fluent proficiency in the language is seen in the members of classroom communities of practice who have, as part of their membership in that community of practice, a larger repertoire for language practices and begin to have more access to practices that overlap with members of the community of 'fluent English language users'.

'Legitimate peripheral' participation in the classroom community of practice

A characteristic of learning within a community of practice is the ability to be able to participate 'legitimately' though 'peripherally': legitimate peripheral participation (Lave & Wenger, 1991). While Chapter 3 focused on the analyses of openings for face-to-face interactions, observations of the task openings of the focal learner of the chapter, Jorge, allowed me to see participation in his week 2 and week 40 classes that illustrates the concept of 'legitimate peripheral' participation. In week 2, in the interaction around Excerpts (3.15), the time he spent observing his peers was notable. After completing the task with peers who are seated near him (after Excerpt 3.15c), Jorge remains in his seat and observes Changying interacting with Vladilen and using an electronic dictionary.[19] After leaving his desk and engaging in the task with a third peer, Tina, Jorge returned to his seat and observed Vladilen and Changying for the last 2 minutes of the task.[20] In this instance, he helps Vladilen and Changying work out the letter to sound correspondences with her name, he reformulates Vladilen's questions to Changying in more complete grammatical form, and he practices pronunciation by repeating words for the task. In each of these cases, Jorge embodies the role of a legitimate peripheral participant in the classroom community of practice. In each instance, Jorge is not an originating member in the peer dyadic interaction, but sitting in the vicinity, both observes and assists others in doing their task as well as working independently repeating words softly to himself.

Another example of peripheral participation was seen in the task from week 40 in Excerpt (3.16b) before Jorge's interaction with Eduardo. In that interaction from a higher proficiency level classroom community of practice, by moving to another area of the classroom as part of the serial dyadic interaction task, he is able to observe the teacher's interaction with Eduardo and to participate peripherally, copying and collaborating with the teacher's modeling of the task language with Eduardo (see Chapter 3).

We also see evidence for learners' legitimate peripheral participation in the practices for the particular actions of focus (opening, story tellings and disengagements) – especially by beginning proficiency level students. The non-verbal practices for accomplishing these actions (postural shift and launch of the task, pointing for task clarification), the restricted linguistic repertoire ('you teacher' to indicate turn allocation) display these learners' statuses as peripheral members of the 'fluent English language users' community of practice. While these practices indicate a peripheral status with respect to other members of that community, their participation in adult language learning classes gives their peripheral participation legitimacy. There is an expectation that these learners will use the language and that the language they use will be 'peripheral' with respect to fluent speakers. The expectation is also that through that use that their increasing participation within the classroom community of practice will coincide with their increasing participation in the community of practice of proficient English language users.

Within a particular classroom community of practice, newcomers or novices become more competent and more full participants through repeated task interaction. This was evident in the serial dyadic interaction tasks (Chapters 3 and 5). There, we saw how Jorge developed new practices to perform the actions of opening and disengaging through the repeated task interactions both in his week 2 and week 40 classroom communities of practice. We have seen other examples of newcomers to the classroom being coached by a peer in doing serial dyadic interaction task (Hellermann & Cole, forthcoming) and after repeated participation, developing new practices for disengaging from tasks. Previous research from the same classrooms (Hellermann, 2006) showed how a student participated at the periphery of the classroom community of practice in literacy events and through observation, practice, and direct requests for help from teacher and students, displayed, one term later, more core participatory status in the community of practice.

Micro-level organization of talk defining classroom communities of practice: Dyadic interaction

Earlier, I presented a definition for learning from Lave that I have used for this research: 'the construction of present versions of past experiences for several persons acting together' (Lave, 1993: 8). Inherent in this definition of learning is at least one interlocutor. In a language learning classroom, this perspective on learning necessitated a focus on learner-learner interactions. I wanted to investigate the orderly language practices that adult learners of English use for social interaction in the classroom in how learners co-construct openings for their task interactions, how they explicate the talk within a task through story tellings and how they disengage from task and face-to-face interactions.

The summaries of the practices used by students for carrying out social actions in different proficiency level classroom communities of practice in Chapters 3–5 are descriptions of the foundational, micro-level practices of talk which build those classroom communities of practice. Evidence of these actions as sites for learning, considered as the change in participation in each of the three actions, was shown in a cross sectional way by comparing how the practices for each action were different in different proficiency classroom communities of practice. Specific instances of language development seen at the turn-by-turn (microgenetic) level were also shown for openings (Chapter 3) and disengagements (Chapter 5). In these cases, a student (Jorge) was observed adjusting practices for participation in subsequent engagements in the particular action based on what was required and provided by the local context for the engagement.

Closing Comments on Implications for Teaching and Learning

Teaching, learning and the nature of the classroom community of practice

As experienced teachers know, any given classroom will be made up of students with different levels of expertise in the subject matter of the class. In language learning classrooms, this heterogeneity in proficiency levels is usually considered a hurdle for teachers whose curriculum and pedagogy define uniform points of mastery for every member of their classroom. This heterogeneity in level of proficiency was seen in the classrooms observed for this research. In fact, in adult language learning classrooms, the heterogeneity among members of a particular classroom go beyond degrees of language proficiency. We see members of each classroom community of practice with varying degrees of experience with formal education (ranging between 0 and 22 years), varying degrees of life experience (18–82 years old), and varying degrees of experience within the particular classroom community of focus – old-timers and new-comers

(Lave & Wenger, 1991; Toohey, 1996). For many teachers, the prospect of providing quality instruction for such a diverse class is daunting. But given the research findings presented in the previous chapters, I would like to suggest that for teachers of adult learners of an additional language, understanding the classroom as a community of practice and understanding learning from a community of practice approach, this heterogeneity can be considered advantageous for learning.

When adult learners enroll in a language learning class, they are committing to engagement in a joint enterprise to learn a language. The commitment and persistence of the adult learners observed for this project illustrate their orientation to the classroom community of practice as a joint enterprise. This orientation facilitates that persistence which, in turn, fosters engagement in language use and language learning ventures in the areas around teacher-assigned language learning tasks where teachers may not expect language learning opportunities to be.

Adult language learners working in a classroom community of practice that is in a 'second language' learning situation (that is, they are living in the environment where the language they are learning is dominant), who find themselves in a classroom with speakers of a number of other languages will be mutually engaged just by the fact of their being together, that is, if the teacher assumes and plans for that to be the case. In the data for this study, it was teachers' expectations that their students – even absolute beginners – would be mutually engaged by communicating in English that encouraged the majority of students to be mutually engaged in English language use and English language learning. By using small group and dyadic participation structures in the classroom, mutual engagement is fostered and students quickly learned that they could, with the help of task and teacher-provided language, communicate in English. When this mutual engagement in interaction was fostered, dyadic or small group configurations offer students the many contexts for language use and language learning that were investigated for the research reported here that are not considered in pedagogical task planning.

As the focus on learners working in dyads has shown, the use of small group or dyadic interaction allows for language learning tasks to be mediated by peers' understandings of the task. This can be the result of a number of situations in which there is a different level of knowledge for a particular task. Mediation by a peer can be the result of having more experience in the particular class (an 'oldtimer' interacting with a relative 'newcomer'); students with more experience in the language classroom are able to use their expertise (in cooperation with the teacher and mediation of teacher-assigned language tasks) to facilitate the newcomers' learning in apprenticing (Rogoff, 1990) the newcomers to the practices for carrying out the tasks and using the language. As the data showed, this apprenticing can be done explicitly or tacitly, through negotiated practice. Working through teacher-assigned language learning tasks, we see how less proficient learners and newcomers participate from the start, legitimately, but peripherally and increasingly learn to participate more fully in the classroom community of practice, demonstrating and embodying increasing language proficiency.

It is certainly wise pedagogical practice for an instructor to have plenty of activity planned for a particular lesson, and research has advocated planning for extra tasks to ensure that students are engaged in language learning during their time in class (Markee, 2005). However, in the immigrant adult language learning context, especially for beginning learners, it is often very difficult to see the divisions between learning opportunities in what is often considered 'off' and 'on' task talk. In such contexts, the extracurricular language learning opportunities afforded by learner–learner face-to-face interactions, we have advocated assuring that students have enough time to work through teacher assigned tasks to make sure that they can take advantage of these practices (Harris, 2004).

Assessing a shared repertoire

Researchers focusing on the language production by individual learners noticed that the non-target like features produced by that particular learner (the errors) are often systematic suggesting that learners do not just make random errors with language form but that their developmental language is, like the language of a fluent speaker/user, also systematic. This learner system is located somewhere between the target ideal and the learner's first language, an 'interlanguage' (Selinker, 1972). From a community of practice perspective approach to language learning, we might consider 'inter-language' in terms of to what degree there are systematic practices for learners using contextualized language to communicate with a variety of interlocutors. The goal for understanding this type of interlanguage would be to discover the systematic features of the language practices of a group of language learners in a classroom community of practice: the nature of their 'shared repertoire'.

An important question that the research in this volume only begins to address is how we might systematically assess language learning within the community of practice. An individual's level of proficiency and subsequent progress in language learning, even in traditional code-focused ways, is not an easy task. It is understood that even the most highly rated standardized language assessments do not always accurately predict one's ability to use the language being assessed. Individualized and communicative assessments of language learning have begun to address contextualized perspectives of language and language learning (McNamara, 1997; McNamara & Roever, 2006). Research on talk-in-interaction used by language learners is needed to inform such assessments to show what might be considered felicitous communicative practices for particular contexts. The research outlined in this book suggests reconsidering how we might think of a language learner's competence and how we might consider assessing that learner's language proficiency and competence as it occurs in contexts that are mediated by linguistic, social and interpersonal interactional resources.

Appendix: Transcription Conventions

Transcript Conventions in Conversation Analysis (Adapted from Schegloff, 2000)

I. Temporal and sequential relationships

    [hey   Bracketing indicates overlapping talk
    [that

=   'latched utterances' no break or pause between utterances
(0.5)   Numbers in parentheses indicate silence, represented in tenths of a second
(.)   A dot in parentheses indicates a 'micropause'

II. Aspects of speech delivery, including aspects of intonation

A. The punctuation marks are not used grammatically, but to indicate intonation.

- .   period indicates a falling intonation contour, not necessarily the end of a sentence.
- ?   question mark indicates rising intonation.
- ,   a comma indicates 'continuing' intonation.
- ;   a semicolon is used to indicate a rise greater than a comma but less than a question mark.
- :: Colons are used to indicate the prolongation or stretching of the sound just preceding them. The more colons, the longer the stretching.
- -   A hyphen after a word or part of a word indicates a cut-off or self-interruption
- w<u>o</u>rd Underlining is used to indicate some form of stress or emphasis, either by increased loudness or higher pitch.

Appendix: Transcription Conventions

WOrd	Especially loud talk may be indicated by upper case; again, the louder, the more letters in upper case. And in extreme cases, upper case may be underlined.
°	The degree sign indicates that the talk following it was markedly quiet or soft.
↑↓	The up and down arrows mark sharper rises or falls in pitch.
><	The combination of 'more than' and 'less than' symbols indicates that the talk between them is compressed or rushed.
<>	Used in the reverse order, they can indicate that a stretch of talk is markedly slowed or drawn out.
hhh	Outbreath
.hh	Inbreath
(( ))	Descriptions of events: ((cough)), ((sniff)), ((telephone rings)), ((footsteps))
(word)	All or part of an utterance is in parentheses indicates transcriber uncertainty.
#	Creaky voice.
$	Smile voice.

Notes

1. Markee is one researcher who does not mind including situated research on language learning within the realm of SLA, using the phrase 'CA-for-SLA' (2000, 2005, forthcoming) to refer to research on language acquisition that uses methods from conversation analysis.
2. Many readers will see this terminological distinction going back to Krashen's (1982) explicit distinction between learning and acquisition for second language contexts. While the argument is more complex, he proposed that the term 'learning' should refer to the active, conscious aspect of language development while 'acquisition' refers to the subconscious changes that occur in a student's system of interlanguage.
3. These constructs from community of practice theory will be discussed in the next section.
4. Words like 'this' and other deictic expressions have as their primary role a pointing function and are heavily reliant on context for their meaning, but even concrete objects in our everyday lives that we consider to have fairly stable and rigid meanings are dependent, in part, on the local context. In the directive 'bring me the chair', the meaning of 'chair' accommodates a local reference.
5. The National Labsite for the Student of Adult ESOL was supported, in part, by grant R309B6002 from the Institute for Education Science, U.S. Dept. of Education, to the National Center for the Study of Adult Learning and Literacy (NCSALL). The Lab School was a partnership between Portland State University and Portland Community College. The school and research facilities were housed at the university while the registration, curriculum, and teachers of the ESL students were from the community college.
6. There were four proficiency level classes at the data collection site. Level 'A' classes were for very beginning learners; level 'B' classes for 'upper beginners'; level 'C' classes for 'lower intermediate' students; and level 'D' classes for students at an 'intermediate' level of proficiency.
7. All data extracts discussed in this book are viewable over the internet via the web links provided for each extract. The excerpts are available using Class Action Viewer (© Portland State University), a free, downloadable browser plug-in for Microsoft Internet Explorer. The user is prompted to download the software when visiting the links.
8. For more complete descriptions of ethnomethodological conversation analysis, see (Clayman & Maynard, 1995; Hutchby & Woofit, 1998; Markee, 2000; Schegloff, 2007a; Seedhouse, 2004; ten Have, 1999).
9. This hyphenated term is used to show that analyses of naturally-occurring spates of language are undertaken with CA methods but are not necessarily conversations (911 emergency calls, classroom interaction, etc.).

10. Sacks' (1992) collected lectures were transcribed by Gail Jefferson and edited by Emanuel Schegloff. Some seminal papers in the field are by Schegloff (1968, 1980, 1987a, 1991, 1996) and Jefferson, (1972, 1973, 1974, 1978, 1984, 1988).
11. For a key to the most common transcription conventions used in conversation analysis, see the Appendix.
12. I would like to thank Bryan Crow for this recording and transcript.
13. Such a perspective is shared by interactional sociolinguists (Duranti & Goodwin, 1992; Gumperz & Levinson, 1996) and cognitive anthropology (Chaiklin & Lave, 1993; Goodwin, 1995; Hutchins, 1995) has also found it useful to examine text and context as mutually constitutive in practice.
14. I would like to thank Bryan Crow for this recording and transcript.
15. The instructors were chosen for the data collection site because of the superior evaluations they received from their superiors at their place of employment.
16. In this two line dialogue from a telephone conversation, 'B' uses such a 'speaking of X' format to introduce the related weather topic of tornados:

   A: We've had some awful weather
   B: yeah I heard, did you hear about the tornados in Wisconsin?

17. Examples of such story prefatory work are when a sequence of turns is used for teller to say 'I am going to tell you a story' and recipient acknowledges 'okay, I am ready'.
18. Johannes Wagner did the original transcript for this excerpt.
19. For a link to this interaction see: http://www.labschool.pdx.edu/Viewer/viewer.php?pl=JKHCP&cl=6.2.
20. For a link to this interaction see: http://www.labschool.pdx.edu/Viewer/viewer.php?pl=JKHCP&cl=6.3.

References

Anderson, J.R., Reder, L.M. and Simon, H.A. (1996) Situated learning and education. *Educational Researcher* 25 (4), 5–11.
Antaki, C. (2002) 'Lovely': Turn-initial high-grade assessments in telephone closings. *Discourse Studies* 4 (1), 5–23.
Au, K.H. (1980) Participation structures in a reading lesson with Hawaiian children: Analysis of a culturally appropriate instructional event. *Anthropology and Education Quarterly* 11 (2), 91–115.
Bardovi-Harlig, K., Hartford, B.A.S., Mahan-Taylor, R., Morgan, M.J. and Reynolds, D.W. (1991) Developing pragmatic awareness: Closing the conversation. *ELT Journal* 45 (1), 4–15.
Barton, D. and Tusting, K. (eds) (2005) *Beyond Communities of Practice*. Cambridge: Cambridge University Press.
Bateson, G. (1972) *Steps to an Ecology of Mind*. New York: Ballantine Books.
Bayley, R. and Preston, D.R. (eds) (1996) *Second Language Acquisition and Linguistic Variation*. Philadelphia: John Benjamins.
Bayley, R. and Schecter, S.R. (eds) (2003) *Language Socialization in Bilingual and Multilingual Societies*. Clevedon, UK: Multilingual Matters.
Beach, W.A. (1993) Transitional regularities for 'casual' 'Okay' usages. *Journal of Pragmatics* 19, 325–352.
Beach, W.A. and Lindstrom, A.K. (1992) Conversational universals and comparative theory: Turning to Swedish and American acknowledgment tokens in interaction. *Communication Theory* 2 (1), 24–49.
Berger, P. and Luckmann, T. (1967) *The Social Construction of Reality: A Treatise in the Sociology of Knowledge*. New York: Anchor Books.
Billig, M. (1999) 'Whose terms? Whose ordinariness? Rhetoric and ideology in conversation analysis'. *Discourse and Society* 10 (4), 543–558.
Breen, M. (1989) The evaluation cycle for language learning tasks. In R.K. Johnson (ed.) *The Second Language Curriculum* (pp. 187–206). Cambridge: Cambridge University Press.
Brillanceau, D. (2005) Spontaneous conversations: A window into learners' autonomy. *Focus On Basics* 8 (A), 22–25.
Brooks, F.P. and Donato, R. (1994) Vygotskian approaches to understanding foreign language learner discourse during communicative tasks. *Hispania* 77 (2), 262–274.
Brouwer, C.E. and Wagner, J. (2004) Developmental issues in second language conversation. *Journal of Applied Linguistics* 1 (1), 29–47.
Brown, A. and McNamara, T. (2004) 'The devil is in the detail': Researching gender issues in language assessment. *TESOL Quarterly* 38 (3), 524–538.
Brown, J.S., Collins, A. and Duguid, P. (1989) Situated cognition and the culture of learning. *Educational Researcher* 18 (1), 32–42.

Bucholtz, M. (1999) 'Why be normal?': Language and identity practices in a community of nerd girls. *Language in Society* 28 (2), 203–223.
Button, G. (1987) Moving out of closings. In G. Button and J.R.E. Lee (eds) *Talk and Social Organisation* (pp. 101–151). Clevedon: Multilingual Matters.
Cazden, C.B. (1988) *Classroom Discourse: The Language of Teaching and Learning*. Portsmouth, NH: Heinemann.
Cekaite, A. (2007) A child's development of interactional competence in a Swedish L2 classroom. *Modern Language Journal* 91 (1), 45–62.
Chafe, W.L. (1974) Language and consciousness. *Language* 50 (1), 111–133.
Chaiklin, S. (1993) Understanding the social scientific practice of Understanding Practice. In S. Chaiklin and J. Lave (eds) *Understanding Practice: Perspectives on Activity and Context* (pp. 377–401). Cambridge: Cambridge University Press.
Chaiklin, S. and Lave, J. (eds) (1993) *Understanding Practice: Perspectives on Activity and Context*. Cambridge: Cambridge University Press.
Chomsky, N. (1986) *Knowledge of Language: Its Nature, Origin, and Use*. New York: Praeger.
Cicourel, A.V. (1974) Some basic theoretical issues in the assessment of the child's performance in testing and classroom settings. In A.V. Cicourel, K.A. Jennings, S.H.M. Jennings, K.C.W. Leiter, R. McKay, H. Mehan and D.R. Roth (eds) *Language Use and School Performance* (pp. 300–351). New York: Academic Press.
Clayman, S.E. and Maynard, D.W. (1995) Ethnomethodology and conversation analysis. In P. ten Have and G. Psathas (eds) *Situated Order: Studies in the Social Organization of Talk and Embodied Activities* (pp. 1–30). Washington, DC: International Institute for Ethnomethodology and Conversation Analysis and University Press of America.
Cole, K. and Zuengler, J. (2003) Engaging in an authentic science project: Appropriating, resisting, and denying 'scientific' identities. In R. Bayley and S.R. Schecter (eds) *Language Socialization in Bilingual and Multilingual Societies* (pp. 98–113). Clevedon: Multilingual Matters.
Cole, K. and Zuengler, J. (eds) (2007) *Research Processes in Classroom Discourse Analysis: Current Perspectives*. Mahwah, NJ: Lawrence Erlbaum Associates.
Cole, M. (1996) *Cultural Psychology: A Once and Future Discipline*. Cambridge, MA: Belknap Press of Harvard University.
Cole, M., Dore, J., Hall, W.S. and Dowley, G. (1978) Situational variability in the speech of preschool children. *Annals of the New York Academy of Science* 318, 65–105.
Coughlin, P. and Duff, P. (1994) Same task, different activities: Analysis of SLA task from an activity theory perspective. In J.P. Lantolf and G. Appel (eds) *Vygotskian Approaches to Second Language Research* (pp. 173–193). Norwood, NJ: Ablex.
Couper-Kuhlen, E. (1992) Contextualizing discourse: The prosody of interactive repair. In P. Auer and A. Di Luzio (eds) *The Contextualization of Language* (pp. 337–364). Amsterdam: John Benjamins.
Couper-Kuhlen, E. (2001) Interactional prosody: High onsets in reason-for-the-call turns. *Language in Society* 30 (1), 29–53.
Creese, A. (2005) Mediating allegations of racism in a multiethnic London school. In D. Barton and K. Tusting (eds) *Beyond Communities of Practice* (pp. 55–76). Cambridge: Cambridge University Press.
Davila, E. (2005) Communicative resources in ESL student interaction: Gaze, gesture, text and speech. Unpublished MA thesis, Portland State University, Portland, Oregon.

Dewey, J. (1938). *Education and Experience*. New York: Touchstone.
Donato, R. (1994) Collective scaffolding in second language learning. In J.P. Lantolf and G. Appel (eds) *Vygotskian Approaches to Second Language Research* (pp. 33–56). Norwood, NJ: Ablex.
Donato, R. (2000) Sociocultural contributions to understanding the foreign and second language classroom. In J.P. Lantolf (ed.) *Sociocultural Theory and Second Language Learning* (pp. 27–50). Oxford: Oxford University Press.
Donato, R. (2004) Collaboration in pedagogical discourse. *Annual Review of Applied Linguistics* 24, 284–302.
Doughty, C.J. and Long, M.H. (eds) (2003) *The Handbook of Second Language Acquisition*. Oxford: Blackwell.
Duranti, A. and Goodwin, C. (1992) *Rethinking Context: Language as an Interactive Phenomenon*. Cambridge: Cambridge University Press.
Ellis, R. (2000) Task-based research and language pedagogy. *Language Teaching Research* 4 (3), 193–220.
Ellis, R. (2003) *Task Based Language Learning and Teaching*. New York: Oxford University Press.
Erickson, F. (1982) Classroom discourse as improvisation: Relationships between academic task structure and social participation structure in lessons. In L.C. Wilkinson (ed.) *Communicating in the Classroom* (pp. 153–181). New York: Academic Press.
Erickson, F. (1996) Going for the zone: The social and cognitive ecology of teacher-student interaction in classroom conversations. In D. Hicks (ed.) *Discourse, Learning, and Schooling* (pp. 29–62). Cambridge: Cambridge University Press.
Erickson, F. and Mohatt, G. (1982) Cultural organization of participation structures in two classrooms of Indian students. In G. Spindler (ed.) *Doing the Ethnography of Schooling: Educational Anthropology in Action* (pp. 132–175). New York: Holt, Rinehart, and Winston.
Erickson, F. and Schultz, J. (1981) When is a context? Some issues and methods in the analysis of social competence. In J. Green and C. Wallat (eds) *Ethnography and Language in Educational Settings* (pp. 229–252). Norwood, NJ: Ablex.
Erickson, F. and Schultz, J. (1982) *The Counselor as Gatekeeper*. New York: Academic Press.
Eskildsen, S.W. and Wagner, J. (2007) *What Counts as Evidence for Language Learning in Longitudinal Studies?* Paper presented at the American Association for Applied Linguistics, Costa Mesa, CA.
Fernandez Aguero, M. (2003) Analysis of topicality in classroom discourse: Topic switch and topic drift in conversations in EFL contexts. *Estudios ingleses de la Universidad Complutense* 11, 73–89.
Firth, A. (1996) On the discursive accomplishment of 'normality': On lingua franca English and conversation analysis. *Journal of Pragmatics* 26, 237–259.
Firth, A. (2007) On the methodological and theoretical implications of 'CA for SLA'. Paper presented at the 17th Pragmatics and Language Learning Conference, Honolulu, Hawai'i.
Firth, A. and Wagner, J. (1997) On discourse, communication, and (some) fundamental concepts in SLA research. *Modern Language Journal* 81 (3), 285–300.
Firth, A. and Wagner, J. (2007, forthcoming) S/FL learning as a social accomplishment: Elaborations on a 'reconceptualized' SLA. *Modern Language Journal*.

Fisher, E. (1993) Distinctive features of pupil-pupil classroom talk and their relationship to learning: How discursive exploration might be encouraged. *Language and Education* 7 (4), 239–257.
Fisher, E. (1994) Joint composition at the computer: Learning to talk about writing. *Computers and Composition* 11 (3), 251–262.
Flynn, S. and O'Neill, W. (eds) (1988) *Linguistic Theory in Second Language Acquisition*. Dordrecht: Kluwer Academic Publishers.
Ford, C.E. (1999) Collaborative construction of task activity: Coordinating multiple resources in a high school physics lab. *Research on Language and Social Interaction* 32 (4), 369–408.
Ford, C.E. and Fox, B.A. (1996) Interactional motivations for reference formulation: He had. this guy had, a beautiful, thirty-two Olds. In B.A. Fox (ed.) *Studies in Anaphora* (pp. 145–168). Amsterdam: John Benjamins.
Ford, C.E., Fox, B.A. and Thompson, S.A. (1996) Practices in the construction of turns: The 'TCU' revisited. *Pragmatics* 6 (3), 427–454.
Ford, C.E., Fox, B.A. and Hellermann, J. (2004) Getting past 'no': Sequence, action and sound production in the projection of no-initiated turns. In E. Couper-Kuhlen and C.E. Ford (eds) *Sound Production in Interaction* (pp. 233–269). Amsterdam: John Benjamins.
Ford, C.E., Fox, B.A. and Thompson, S.A. (eds) (2002) *The Language of Turn and Sequence*. Oxford: Oxford University Press.
Ford, C.E. and Thompson, S.A. (1996) Interactional units in conversation: Syntactic, intonational and pragmatic resources for the management of turns. In E. Ochs, E.A. Schegloff and S.A. Thompson (eds) *Interaction and Grammar* (pp. 134–184). Cambridge: Cambridge University Press.
Forrester, M.A. and Reason, D. (2006) Competency and participation in acquiring a mastery of language: A reconsideration of the idea of membership. *The Sociological Review* 54 (3), 446–466.
Foster, P. (1998) A classroom perspective on the negotiation of meaning. *Applied Linguistics* 19 (1), 1–23.
Frawley, W. and Lantolf, J.P. (1985) Second language discourse: A Vygotskyan perspective. *Applied Linguistics* 6 (1), 19–44.
French, P. and Local, J. (1983) Turn-competitive incomings. *Journal of Pragmatics* 7 (1), 17–38.
Garfinkel, H. (1967) *Studies in Ethnomethodology*. Englewood Cliffs, NJ: Prentice Hall.
Garfinkel, H. (2002) *Ethnomethodology's Program. Working out Durkheim's Aphorism*. Lantham: Rowman and Littlefield Publishers.
Garfinkel, H. and Sacks, H. (1970) On formal structures of practical actions. In J.C. McKinney and E.A. Tiryakin (eds) *Theoretical Sociology: Perspectives and Developments* (pp. 338–366). New York: Appleton Century Crofts.
Garland, J.N. (2002) Co-construction of language and activity in low-level ESL pair interactions. Masters thesis, Portland State University.
Gass, S. (1998) Apples and oranges: Or, why apples are not orange and don't need to be. A response to Firth and Wagner. *Modern Language Journal* 82 (1), 83–90.
Gass, S. and Schachter, J. (eds) (1989) *Linguistic Perspectives on Second Language Acquisition*. Cambridge: Cambridge University Press.
Gass, S. and Varonis, E. (1985) Variation in native speaker speech modification to non-native speakers. *Studies in Second Language Acquisition* 7 (1), 37–57.

Gee, J.P. (1996) *Social Linguistics and Literacies: Ideology in Discourses* (2nd edn). London: Taylor and Francis.
Gee, J.P. (2003) *What Video Games Can Tell Us about Learning and Literacy*. New York: Palgrave/Macmillan.
Gee, J.P. (2005) Semiotic social spaces and affinity spaces: From the age of mythology to today's schools. In D. Barton and K. Tusting (eds) *Beyond Communities of Practice* (pp. 214–232). Cambridge: Cambridge University Press.
Glenn, P. (1991/1992) Current speaker initiation of two-party shared laughter. *Research on Language and Social Interaction* 25, 139–162.
Glenn, P. (2003) *Laughter in Interaction*. New York: Cambridge University Press.
Goffman, E. (1959) *The Presentation of Self in Everyday Life*. New York: Anchor Books: Doubleday.
Goffman, E. (1961) *Encounters: Two Studies in the Sociology of Interaction*. Indianapolis, IN: Bobbs-Merrill.
Goffman, E. (1963) *Behavior in Public Places: Notes on the Social Organization of Gatherings*. New York: Free Press.
Goffman, E. (1967) *Interaction Ritual: Essays in Face to Face Behavior*. Chicago: Aldine.
Goffman, E. (1971) *Relations in Public*. New York: Harper Colophone Books.
Goffman, E. (1981) *Forms of Talk*. Philadelphia: University of Pennsylvania Press.
Goffman, E. (1983) The interaction order. *American Sociological Review* 48 (1), 1–17.
Goldberg, J.A. (2004) The amplitude shift mechanism in conversational closing sequences. In G. Lerner (ed.) *Conversation Analysis: Studies from the First Generation* (pp. 257–297). Amsterdam: John Benjamins.
Goodwin, C. (1979) The interactive construction of a sentence in natural conversation. In G. Psathas (ed.) *Everyday Language: Studies in Ethnomethodology* (pp. 97–121). New York: Irvington.
Goodwin, C. (1981) *Conversational Organization: Interaction Between Speakers and Hearers*. New York: Academic Press.
Goodwin, C. (1986) Gesture as a resource for the organization of mutual orientation. *Semiotica* 62 (1/2), 29–49.
Goodwin, C. (1994) Professional vision. *American Anthropologist* 96 (3), 606–633.
Goodwin, C. (1995) Seeing in depth. *Social Studies of Science* 25 (2), 237–274.
Goodwin, C. (1996) Transparent vision. In E. Ochs, E.A. Schegloff and S. Thompson (eds) *Interaction and Grammar* (pp. 370–404). Cambridge: Cambridge University Press.
Goodwin, C. and Heritage, J. (1990) Conversation analysis. *Annual Review of Anthropology* 19, 283–307.
Green, J. and Wallat, C. (eds) (1981) *Ethnography and Language in Educational Settings*. Norwood, NJ: Ablex.
Greeno, J. (1997) On claims that answer the wrong question. *Educational Researcher* 26 (1), 5–17.
Greeno, J.G., Smith, D.L. and Moore, J.L. (1993) Transfer of situated learning. In D.K. Detterman and R.J. Sternberg (eds) *Transfer on Trial: Intelligence, Cognition, and Instruction* (pp. 99–167). Norwood, NJ: Ablex.
Gregg, K.R. (1990) The variable competence model of second language acquisition, and why it isn't. *Applied Linguistics* 11 (4), 364–383.
Gregg, K.R., Long, M.H., Jordan, G. and Beretta, A. (1997) Rationality and its discontents in SLA. *Applied Linguistics* 18 (4), 538–558.

Grice, H.P. (1975) Logic and conversation. In P. Cole and J. Morgan (eds) *Syntax and Semantics. Vol. 3: Speech Acts* (pp. 41–58). New York: Academic Press.
Gumperz, J.J. (1982) *Discourse Strategies*. Cambridge: Cambridge University Press.
Gumperz, J.J. and Levinson, S. (eds) (1996) *Rethinking Linguistic Relativity*. Cambridge: Cambridge University Press.
Hall, J.K. (1993) The role of oral practices in the accomplishment of our everyday lives: The sociocultural dimension of interaction with implications for the learning of another language. *Applied Linguistics* 14 (2), 145–166.
Hall, J.K. (1995) 'Aw man, where you goin'?': Classroom interaction and the development of L2 interactional competence. *Issues in Applied Linguistics* 6 (2), 37–62.
Hall, J.K. (1997a) A consideration of SLA as a theory of practice: A response to Firth and Wagner. *Modern Language Journal* 81 (3), 301–307.
Hall, J.K. (1997b). Differential teacher attention to student utterances: The construction of different opportunities for learning in the IRF. *Linguistics and Education* 9 (3), 287–311.
Hall, J.K. (2004) Language learning as an interactional achievement. *Modern Language Journal* 88 (4), 607–612.
Hanks, W.F. (1996) *Language and Communicative Practices*. Boulder, CO: Westview Press.
Hardy, I.M. and Moore, J.L. (2004) Foreign language students' conversational negotiations in different task environments. *Applied Linguistics* 25 (3), 340–370.
Harris, K. (2004) *Pair Activities in Beginning Adult ESL Classes*. Paper presented at the Meeting of the Minds Research Symposium, 9–11 December, Sacramento, CA.
Harris, K.A. (2005) Same activity, different focus. *Focus On Basics* 8 (A), 7–10.
Hartford, B.S. and Bardovi-Harlig, K. (1992) Closing the conversation: Evidence from the academic advising session. *Discourse Processes* 15 (1), 93–116.
He, A.W. (2004) CA for SLA: Arguments from the Chinese language classroom. *Modern Language Journal* 88 (4), 568–582.
Heap, J. (1985) Discourse in the production of classroom knowledge: Reading lessons. *Curriculum Inquiry* 15 (3), 245–279.
Heath, C. (1984) Talk and recipiency: Sequential organization in speech and body movement. In J.M. Atkinson and J. Heritage (eds) *Structures of Social Action* (pp. 247–265). Cambridge: Cambridge University Press.
Heath, C. (1986) *Body Movement and Speech in Medical Interaction*. Cambridge: Cambridge University Press.
Hellermann, J.K., Cole, K. and Zuengler, J. (2001) Developing thinking communities through talk: Two case studies from science classes. *CELA Research Report Series*, 3.
Hellermann, J. (2005a) Syntactic and prosodic practices for cohesion in series of three-part sequences in classroom talk. *Research on Language and Social Interaction* 36 (1), 105–130.
Hellermann, J. (2005b) Turn taking in adult ESOL classroom interaction: Practices for interaction in another language. *Focus on Basics* 8 (A), 25–28.
Hellermann, J. (2006) Classroom interactive practices for literacy: A microethnographic study of two beginning adult learners of English. *Applied Linguistics* 27 (3), 377–404.
Hellermann, J. (2007a) The development of practices for action in classroom dyadic interaction: Focus on task openings. *Modern Language Journal* 91 (1), 83–96.

Hellermann, J. (2007b) The contextualization of participation in the asthma project: Response sequences in classroom talk. In J. Zuengler and K. Cole (eds) *The Research Process in Classroom Discourse Analysis: Current Perspectives*. Mahwah, NJ: Lawrence Erlbaum Associates.

Hellermann, J. (forthcoming) Language learning seen in practices for repair. *Scandinavian Journal of Research in Education*.

Hellermann, J. and Brillanceau, D. (2007) Adult immigrant-learner identity and language learning: Learner Portraits. On WWW at http://www.labschool.pdx.edu/learner_portraits/. Accessed 15.8.07.

Hellermann, J. and Vergun, A. (2007) Language which is not taught: The discourse marker use of beginning adult learners of English. *Journal of Pragmatics* 39 (1), 157–179.

Hellermann, J. and Cole, E. (forthcoming) Disengagements from task interactions as a site for language learning. *Applied Linguistics*.

Heritage, J. (1984a) *Garfinkel and Ethnomethodology*. London: Polity Press.

Heritage, J. (1984b) A change of state token and aspects of its sequential placement. In J.M. Atkinson and J. Heritage (eds) *Structures of Social Action: Studies in Conversation Analysis* (pp. 299–345). Cambridge: Cambridge University Press.

Hester, S. and Eglin, P. (eds) (1997) *Culture in Action: Studies in Membership Categorization Analysis*. Washington, DC: International Institute for Ethnomethodology and Conversation Analysis and University Press of America.

Hester, S. and Francis, D. (eds) (2000). *Local Educational Order: Ethnomethodological Studies of Knowledge in Action*. Amsterdam: John Benjamins.

Hopper, R. (1989) Sequential ambiguity in telephone openings: 'What are you doin'. *Communication Monographs* 56 (2), 240–252.

Hosoda, Y. (2001) Conditions for other-repair in NS/NNS conversation. *The Language Teacher* 25 (11), 29–31.

House, J. (1982) Opening and closing phases in English and German dialogues. *Grazer Linguistische Studien* 16, 52–83.

Hutchby, I. and Wooffitt, R. (1998) *Conversation Analysis*. Cambridge: Polity Press.

Hutchins, E. (1995) *Cognition in the Wild*. Cambridge, MA: MIT Press.

Huth, T. (2006) Negotiating structure and culture: L2 learners' realization of L2 compliment-response sequences in talk-in-interaction. *Journal of Pragmatics* 38 (12), 2025–2050.

Jacoby, S. and McNamara, T. (1999) Locating competence. *English for Specific Purposes* 18 (3), 213–241.

Jayyusi, L. (1984) *Categorization and the Moral Order*. London: Routledge and Kegan Paul.

Jefferson, G. (1972) Side sequences. In D. Sudnow (ed.) *Studies in Social Interaction* (pp. 294–338). New York: The Free Press.

Jefferson, G. (1973) A case of precision timing in ordinary conversation: Overlapped tag-positioned address terms in closing sequences. *Semiotica* 9 (1), 47–96.

Jefferson, G. (1974) Error correction as an interactional resource. *Language in Society* 3 (2), 181–199.

Jefferson, G. (1978) Sequential aspects of storytelling in conversation. In J. Schenkein (ed.) *Studies in the Organization of Conversational Interaction* (pp. 219–248). New York: Free Press.

Jefferson, G. (1984) On the organization of laughter in talk about troubles. In J.M. Atkinson and J. Heritage (eds) *Structures of Social Action: Studies in Conversation Analysis* (pp. 346–369). Cambridge: Cambridge University Press.

Jefferson, G. (1988) On the sequential organization of troubles talk in ordinary conversation. *Social Problems* 35 (4), 418–441.

Jefferson, G. (2002) 'No' an acknowledgment token? Comparing American and British uses of (+)/(–) tokens. *Journal of Pragmatics* 34 (10–11), 1345–1383.

Jefferson, G. (2004) A note on laughter in 'male-female' interaction. *Discourse Studies* 6 (1), 117–133.

Jeon, M. (2003) Closing the advising session. *Working Papers in Educational Linguistics* 18 (2), 89–106.

Kanagy, R. (1999) Interactional routines as a mechanism for L2 acquisition and socialization in an immersion context. *Journal of Pragmatics* 31 (11), 1467–1492.

Kasper, G. (1979) Pragmatische Defizite im Englischen deutscher Lerner. *Linguistik und Didaktik* 10 (4), 370–379.

Kasper, G. (1997) 'A' stand for acquisition: A response to Firth and Wagner. *Modern Language Journal* 81 (3), 307–312.

Kasper, G. (2004) Participant orientations in German conversation-for-learning. *Modern Language Journal* 88 (4), 551–567.

Kasper, G. (2006) Beyond repair: Conversation analysis as an approach to SLA. *AILA Review* 19, 83–99.

Kidwell, M. and Zimmerman, D. (2007) Joint attention as action. *Journal of Pragmatics* 39 (3), 592–611.

Knapp, M.L., Hart, R.P., Friedrich, G.W. and Shulman, G.M. (1973) The rhetoric of goodbye: Verbal and nonverbal correlates of human leave-taking. *Speech Monographs* 40 (3), 182–198.

Koole, T. (2003) The interactive construction of heterogeneity in the classroom. *Linguistics and Education* 14 (1), 3–26.

Korobov, N. and Bamberg, M. (2004) Positioning a 'mature' self in interactive practices: How adolescent males negotiate 'physical attraction' in group talk. *British Journal of Developmental Psychology* 22 (4), 471–492.

Koschmann, T. and LeBaron, C. (2002) Learner articulation as interactional achievement: Studying the conversation of gesture. *Cognition and Instruction* 20 (2), 249–282.

Koschmann, T., Zemel, A., Conlee-Stevens, M., Young, N.P., Robbs, J.E. and Barnhart, A. (2005) How *do* people learn: Members' methods and communicative mediation. In R. Bromme, F.W. Hesse and H. Spada (eds) *Barriers and Biases in Computer-Mediated Knowledge Communication and How They May be Overcome* (pp. 265–294). New York: Springer.

Kramsch, C.J. (1983) Discourse function of grammar rules: Topic construction in German. *The Modern Language Journal* 67 (1), 13–22.

Kramsch, C. (1986) From language proficiency to interactional competence. *Modern Language Journal* 70 (4), 372–366.

Kramsch, C. (ed.) (2002) *Language Acquisition and Language Socialization*. London: Continuum.

Krashen, S. (1977) Some issues relating to the Monitor Model. In H. Brown, C. Yorio and R. Crymes (eds) *On TESOL '77* (pp. 144–158). Washington, DC: TESOL.

Krashen, S. (1982) *Principles and Practice in Second Language Acquisition*. London: Pergamon.

Kress, G., Ogborn, J. and Martins, I. (1998) A satellite view of language: Some lessons from science classrooms. *Language Awareness* 7 (2–3), 69–89.

Kumaravadivelu, B. (1991) Language-learning tasks: Teacher intention and learner interpretation. *English Language Teaching Journal* 45 (2), 98–107.

Lado, R. (1957) *Linguistics Across Cultures*. Ann Arbor, MI: University of Michigan Press.

Lantolf, J. (ed.) (2000a) *Sociolinguistic Theory and Second Language Learning*. New York: Oxford University Press.

Lantolf, J.P. (2000b) Introducing sociocultural theory. In J.P. Lantolf (ed.) *Sociocultural Theory and Second Language Learning* (pp. 1–26). Oxford: Oxford University Press.

Lantolf, J.P. and Appel, G. (eds) (1994) *Vygotskian Approaches to Second Language Research*. Norwood, NJ: Ablex.

Lantolf, J.P. and Thorne, S.L. (2006) *Sociocultural Theory and the Genesis of Second Language Development*. Oxford: Oxford University Press.

Lantolf, J.P. and Yanez, M. (2003) Talking yourself into Spanish: Intrapersonal communication and second language learning. *Hispania* 86 (1), 97–109.

Larsen-Freeman, D. (2004) CA for SLA? It all depends... *Modern Language Journal* 88 (4), 603–607.

Lave, J. (1988) *Cognition in Practice*. Cambridge: Cambridge University Press.

Lave, J. (1993) The practice of learning. In S. Chaiklin and J. Lave (eds) *Understanding Practice: Perspectives on Activity and Context* (pp. 3–32). Cambridge: Cambridge University Press.

Lave, J. (1996) Teaching, as learning, in practice. *Mind, Culture, and Activity* 3 (3), 149–164.

Lave, J. and Wenger, E. (1991) *Situated Learning: Legitimate Peripheral Participation*. Cambridge: Cambridge University Press.

Lazaraton, A. (2003) Evaluative criteria for qualitative research in Applied Linguistics: Whose criteria and whose research? *The Modern Language Journal* 87 (1), 1–12.

LeBaron, C.D. and Jones, S.E. (2002) Closing up closings: Showing the relevance of the social and material surround to the completion of interaction. *Journal of Communication* 52 (3), 542–565.

Lee, K.S. (1998) Text organisation in Japanese storytelling: A structural and cultural analysis of oral narrative. *Sophia Linguistica* 42–43, 87–104.

Lee, Y.A. (2004) The work of examples in classroom instruction. *Linguistics and Education* 15 (1–2), 99–120.

Lee, Y.A. (2007) Third turn position in teacher talk: Contingency and the work of teaching. *Journal of Pragmatics* 39, 108–206.

Leki, I. (2001) 'A narrow thinking system': Nonnative-English-speaking students in group projects across the curriculum. *TESOL Quarterly* 35 (1), 39–67.

Lerner, G. (1991) On the syntax of sentences-in-progress. *Language in Society* 20 (3), 441–458.

Lerner, G.H. (1992) Assisted storytelling: Deploying shared knowledge as a practical matter. *Qualitative Sociology* 15 (3), 247–271.

Lerner, G.H. (1995) Turn design and the organization of participation in instructional activities. *Discourse Processes* 19 (1), 111–131.

Long, M.H. (1980) Inside the 'black box': Methodological issues in classroom research on language learning. *Language Learning* 30 (1), 1–42.

Long, M.H. (1983) Linguistic and conversational adjustments to non-native speakers. *Studies in Second Language Acquisition* 5 (2), 177–193.
Long, M.H. (1993) Assessment strategies for second language acquisition theories. *Applied Linguistics* 14 (3), 225–249.
Long, M.H. (1996) The role of the linguistic environment in second language acquisition. In W.C. Ritchie and T.K. Bhatia (eds) *Handbook of Second Language Acquisition* (pp. 414–468). New York: Academic Press.
Lynch, M. (1993) *Scientific Practice and Ordinary Action: Ethnomethodology and Studies of Science*. Cambridge: Cambridge University Press.
Macbeth, D.H. (1990) Classroom order as practical action: The making and un-making of a quiet reproach. *British Journal of Sociology of Education* 11 (2), 189–214.
Macbeth, D. (1994) Classroom encounters with the unspeakable: "Do you see, Danelle?". *Discourse Processes* 17 (2), 311–335.
Macbeth, D. (2000) Classrooms as installations: Direct instruction in the early grades. In S. Hester and D. Francis (eds) *Local Educational Order: Ethnomethodological Studies of Knowledge in Action* (pp. 21–71). Amsterdam: John Benjamins.
Macbeth, D. (2003) Hugh Mehan's *Learning Lessons* reconsidered: On the differences between the naturalistic and critical analysis of classroom discourse. *American Educational Research Journal* 40 (1), 239–280.
Macbeth, D. (2004) The relevance of repair for classroom correction. *Language in Society* 33 (5), 703–736.
Mandelbaum, J. (1993) Assigning responsibility in conversational storytelling: the interactional construction of reality. *Text* 13 (2), 247–266.
Markee, N. (2000) *Conversation Analysis*. Mawah, NJ: Lawrence Erlbaum Associates.
Markee, N. (2005) The organization of off-task talk in second language classrooms. In K. Richards and P. Seedhouse (eds) *Applying Conversation Analysis* (pp. 197–213). London: Palgrave.
Markee, N. and Kasper, G. (2004) Classroom talks: Introduction to the special issue. *Modern Language Journal* 88 (4), 491–500.
Maynard, D.W. and Zimmerman, D.H. (1984) Topic talk, ritual and the social organization of relationships. *Social Psychology Quarterly* 47 (4), 301–316.
Maynard, D.W. and Clayman, S.E. (2003) Ethnomethodology and conversation analysis. In L.T. Reynolds and N.J. Herman-Kinney (eds) *The Handbook of Symbolic Interactionism* (pp. 173–202). Walnut Creek, CA: Altamira Press.
McDermott, R.P. (1993) The acquisition of a child by a learning disability. In S. Chaiklin and J. Lave (eds) *Understanding Practice: Perspectives on Activity and Context* (pp. 269–305). Cambridge: Cambridge University Press.
McHoul, A. (1978) The organization of turns at formal talk in the classroom. *Language and Society* 7 (2), 183–213.
McNamara, T. (1997) 'Interaction' in second language performance assessment: Whose performance? *Applied Linguistics* 18 (4), 446–466.
McNamara, T. and Roever, C. (2006) Language testing: The social dimension. *Language Learning* 56 (supplement 2), 1–291.
McNeill, D. (ed.) (2000) *Language and Gesture*. Cambridge: Cambridge University Press.
Mead, G.H. (1934) *Mind, Self, and Society*. Chicago: University of Chicago Press.
Mead, M. (1943) Our educational emphases in primitive perspective. *The American Journal of Sociology* 48 (6), 633–639.

Mehan, H. (1979) *Learning Lessons: Social Organization in the Classroom*. Cambridge, MA: Harvard University Press.
Moerman, M. (1988) *Talking Culture*. Cambridge: Cambridge University Press.
Mondada, L. and Pekarek Doehler, S. (2004) Second language acquisition as situated practice: Task accomplishment in the French second language classroom. *Modern Language Journal* 88 (4), 501–518.
Mori, J. (2002) Task design, plan, and development of talk-in-interaction: An analysis of a small group activity in a Japanese language classroom. *Applied Linguistics* 23 (2), 323–347.
Mori, J. (2004) Negotiating sequential boundaries and learning opportunities: A case from a Japanese language classroom. *Modern Language Journal* 88 (4), 536–550.
Mori, J. and Hayashi, M. (2006) The achievement of intersubjectivity through embodied completions: A study of interactions between first and second language speakers. *Applied Linguistics* 27 (2), 195–219.
Morita, N. (2004) Negotiating participation and identity in second language academic communities. *TESOL Quarterly* 38 (4), 573–603.
Morris, F. and Tarone, E. (2003) Impact of classroom dynamics on the effectiveness of recasts in second language acquisition. *Language Learning* 53 (2), 325–368.
Nakahama, T. and VanLier, L. (2001) Negotiation of meaning in conversational and information gap activities: A comparative discourse analysis. *TESOL Quarterly* 35 (3), 377–405.
Newman, D., Griffin, P. and Cole, M. (1989) *The Construction Zone: Working for Cognitive Change in School*. Cambridge: Cambridge University Press.
Nguyen, H.T. (2006) Sequence organization as local and longitudinal achievement. Paper presented at the *International Conference of Conversation Analysis*, Helsinki.
Norrick, N.R. (1998) Retelling stories in spontaneous conversation. *Discourse Processes* 25 (1), 75–97.
Nystrand, M. (1997) *Opening Dialogue*. New York: Teachers College Press.
Norton, B. (2001) Non-participation, imagined communities, and the language classroom. In X. Bonch-Bruevich, W.J. Crawford, J. Hellermann, C. Higgins and H. Nguyen (eds) *Selected Proceedings of the 2000 Second Language Research Forum* (pp. 167–180). Somerville, MA: Cascadilla Press.
Norton, B. (2003) *Identity and Language Learning: Gender Ethnicity and Educational Change*. London: Longman.
Ochs, E. (1997) Narrative. In T.A. Van Dijk (ed.) *Discourse as Structure and Process* (pp. 185–207). London: Sage.
Ohta, A. (2000) Rethinking recasts: A learner-centered examination of corrective feedback in the Japanese language classroom. In J.K. Hall and L.S. Verplaeste (eds) *Second and Foreign Language Learning Through Classroom Interaction* (pp. 47–71). Mahwah, NJ: Lawrence Erlbaum Associates.
Ohta, A. (2001a) *Second Language Acquisition Processes in the Classroom*. Mahwah, NJ: Lawrence Erlbaum.
Ohta, A. (2001b) A longitudinal study of the expression of alignment in Japanese as a foreign language. In K.R. Rose and G. Kasper (eds) *Pragmatics and Language Learning* (pp. 103–120). Cambridge: Cambridge University Press.
Peters, A.M. and Boggs, S.T. (1986) Interactional routines as cultural influences upon language acquisition. In B. Schieffelin and E. Ochs (eds) *Language*

Socialization Across Cultures (pp. 80–96). New York: Cambridge University Press.
Pica, T., Young, R. and Doughty, C. (1987) The impact of interaction on comprehension. *TESOL Quarterly* 21 (4), 737–758.
Platt, E. and Brooks, F.B. (2002) Task engagement: A turning point in foreign language development. *Language Learning* 52 (2), 365–400.
Polanyi, L. (1985) Conversational storytelling. In T.A. van Dijk (ed.) *Handbook of Discourse Analysis* (pp. 183–201). London: Academic Press.
Poole, D. (1990) Contextualizing IRE in an eighth grade quiz review. *Linguistics and Education* 2 (2), 185–211.
Poole, D. (1992) Language socialization in the second language classroom. *Language Learning* 42 (4), 593–616.
Preston, D. (1996) Variationist linguistics and second language acquisition. In W.C. Ritchie and T.K. Bhatia (eds) *Handbook of Second Language Acquisition* (pp. 229–265). San Diego, CA: Academic Press.
Rampton, B., Roberts, C., Leung, C. and Harris, R. (2002) Methodology in the analysis of classroom discourse. *Applied Linguistics* 23 (3), 373–392.
Reddy, M. (1979) The conduit metaphor. In A. Ortony (ed.) *Metaphor and Thought* (pp. 284–324). Cambridge: Cambridge University Press.
Reder, S. (2005) The 'Lab School'. *Focus on Basics* 8 (A), 1–7.
Reder, S., Harris, K., Hellermann, J., Kurzet, R., Brillanceau, D. and Banke, S. (forthcoming) *Adult Learners of English: A Final Project Report*. National Center for the Study of Adult Learning and Literacy.
Reder, S., Harris, K. and Setzler, K. (2003) A multimedia adult learner corpus. *TESOL Quarterly* 37 (3), 546–557.
Resnick, L.B., Levine, J.M. and Teasley, S.D. (eds) (1991) *Perspectives on Socially Shared Cognition*. Washington, DC: American Psychological Association.
Richards, K. and Seedhouse, P. (eds) (2005) *Applying Conversation Analysis*. London: Palgrave.
Ritchie, W.C. and Bhatia, T.K. (1996) (eds) *Handbook of Second Language Acquisition* (pp. 414–468). New York: Academic Press.
Robinson, J.D. (2001) Asymmetry in action: Sequential resources in the negotiation of a prescription request. *Text* 21 (1/2), 19–54.
Rogoff, B. (1990) *Apprenticeship in Thinking: Cognitive Development in Social Context*. New York: Oxford University Press.
Rogoff, B., Turkanis, C.G. and Bartlett, L. (eds) (2001) *Learning Together: Children and Adults in a School Community*. Oxford: Oxford University Press.
Sacks, H. (1972) On the analyzability of stories by children. In J.J. Gumperz and D. Hymes (eds) *Directions in Sociolinguistics: The Ethnography of Communication* (pp. 329–345). New York: Holt, Rinehart and Winston.
Sacks, H. (1974) On the analyzability of stories by children. In R. Turner (ed.) *Ethnomethodology* (pp. 216–232). Harmondsworth: Penguin.
Sacks, H. (1992) *Lectures on Conversation* (Vol. I and II) Oxford: Blackwell.
Sacks, H. and Schegloff, E.A. (1979) Two preferences in the organization of reference to persons in everyday conversation and their interaction. In G. Psathas (ed.) *Everyday Language: Studies in Ethnomethodology* (pp. 15–21). New York: Irvington.
Sacks, H., Schegloff, E. and Jefferson, G. (1974) A simplest systematics for the organization of turn-taking for conversations. *Language* 50 (4), 696–735.

Schegloff, E.A. (1968) Sequencing in conversational openings. *American Anthropologist* 70 (6), 1075–1095.

Schegloff, E.A. (1980) Preliminaries to preliminaries: 'Can I ask you a question?'. *Sociological Inquiry* 50 (3–4), 104–152.

Schegloff, E.A. (1987a) Between macro and micro: Contexts and other connections. In J. Alexander, B. Giesen, R. Munch and N. Smelser (eds) *The Micro-Macro Link* (pp. 207–234). Los Angeles: University of California Press.

Schegloff, E.A. (1987b) Some sources of misunderstanding in talk-in-interaction. *Linguistics* 25 (1), 201–218.

Schegloff, E.A. (1991) Conversation analysis and socially shared cognition. In L. Resnick, J. Levine and S. Teasley (eds) *Perspectives on Socially Shared Cognition* (pp. 150–171). Washington, DC: American Psychological Association.

Schegloff, E.A. (1992) Repair after next turn: The last structurally provided defense of intersubjectivity in conversation. *American Journal of Sociology* 95 (5), 1295–1345.

Schegloff, E.A. (1998) Body torque. *Social Research* 65 (3), 535–596.

Schegloff, E.A. (2000) When 'others' initiate repair. *Applied Linguistics* 21 (2), 205–243.

Schegloff, E.A. (2002a) Beginning in the telephone. In J.E. Katz and M. Aakhus (eds) *Perpetual Contact: Mobile Communication, Private Talk, Public Performance* (pp. 285–299). Cambridge: Cambridge University Press.

Schegloff, E.A. (2002b) Opening sequencing. In J.E. Katz and M. Aakhus (eds) *Perpetual Contact: Mobile Communication, Private Talk, Public Performance* (pp. 326–385). Cambridge: Cambridge University Press.

Schegloff, E.A. (2007a) *Sequence Organization in Interaction: A Primer in Conversation Analysis 1*. Cambridge: Cambridge University Press.

Schegloff, E. (2007b) A tutorial on membership categorization. *Journal of Pragmatics* 39 (3), 462–482.

Schegloff, E.A. and Sacks, H. (1973) Opening up closings. *Semiotica* 8 (4), 289–327.

Schegloff, E.A., Jefferson, G. and Sacks, H. (1977) The preference for self-repair in the organization of repair in conversation. *Language* 53 (2), 361–382.

Schiffrin, D. (1977) Opening encounters. *American Sociological Review* 42 (5), 679–691.

Scribner, S. and Cole, M. (1973) Cognitive consequences of formal and informal education. *Science* 182, 553–559.

Searle, J. (2002) End of the revolution. *New York Review of Books*, 27 June.

Seedhouse, P. (1997) The case of the missing 'No': The relationship between pedagogy and interaction. *Language Learning* 47 (3), 547–583.

Seedhouse, P. (1999) The relationship between context and the organization of repair in the L2 classroom. *IRAL* 37 (1), 59–80.

Seedhouse, P. (2004) The interactional architecture of the language classroom: A conversation analysis perspective. *Language Learning* 54 (supplement 1), 1–300.

Seedhouse, P. (2005) 'Task' as research construct. *Language Learning* 55 (3), 533–570.

Selinker, L. (1972) Interlanguage. *International Review of Applied Linguistics in Language Teaching* 10 (3), 209–231.

Sfard, A. (1998) On two metaphors for learning and the dangers of choosing just one. *Educational Researcher* 27 (2), 4–13.

Sfard, A. (2005) Discourse in flux. *Mind, Culture, and Activity* 12 (3–4), 233–250.

Siegler, R.S. and Crowley, K. (1991) The microgenetic method: A direct means for studying cognitive development. *American Psychologist* 4 (6), 606–620.
Silverman, D. (1999) Warriors or collaborators: Reworking methodological controversies in the study of institutional interaction. In S. Sarangi and C. Roberts (eds) *Talk, Work, and Institutional Order: Discourse in Medical, Mediation, and Management Settings* (pp. 401–425). Berlin: Mouton de Gruyter.
Silverstein, M. (1993) Metapragmatic discourse and metapragmatic function. In J.A. Lucy (ed.) *Reflexive Language: Reported Speech and Metapragmatics* (pp. 33–58). Cambridge: Cambridge University Press.
Sinclair, J.M. and Coulthard, R.M. (1975) *Towards an Analysis of Discourse: The English Used by Teachers and Pupils*. London: Oxford University Press.
Skehan, P. (2003) Task-based instruction. *Language Teaching* 36 (1), 1–14.
Smith, J. (1989) Topic and variation in ITA oral proficiency: SPEAK and field-specific tests. *English for Specific Purposes* 8 (2), 155–167.
Stokoe, E.H. (2000) Constructing topicality in university students' small-group discussion: A conversation analytic approach. *Language and Education* 14 (3), 184–203.
Streeck, J. (1993) Gesture as communication I: its coordination with gaze and speech. *Communication Monographs* 60 (4), 275–299.
Streeck, J. (1995) On projection. In E.N. Goody (ed.) *Social Intelligence and Interaction* (pp. 87–110). Cambridge: Cambridge University Press.
Streeck, J. and Hartge, U. (1992) Previews: Gestures at the transition place. In P. Auer and A. di Luzio (eds) *The Contextualisation of Language* (pp. 135–157). Amsterdam: John Benjamins.
Swain, M. (1985) Communicative competence: Some roles of comprehensible input and comprehensible output in its development. In S. Gass and C. Madden (eds) *Input in Second Language Acquisition* (pp. 235–256). Rowley, MA: Newbury House.
Swain, M. (1995) Three functions of output in second language learning. In G. Cook and B. Seidlhofer (eds) *Principles and Practice in the Study of Language* (pp. 125–144). Oxford: Oxford University Press.
Szymanski, M.H. (1999) Re-engaging and dis-engaging talk in activity. *Language in Society* 28 (1), 1–23.
Tarone, E. (1988) *Variation in Interlanguage*. London: Edward Arnold.
Tarplee, C. (1996) Working on young children's utterances: Prosodic aspects of repetition during picture labelling. In E. Couper-Kuhlen and M. Selting (eds) *Prosody in Conversation: Interaction Studies* (pp. 406–435). Cambridge: Cambridge University Press.
ten Have, P. (1999) *Doing Conversation Analysis: A Practical Guide*. London: Sage.
Toohey, K. (1996) Learning English as a second language in kindergarten: A community of practice perspective. *The Canadian Modern Language Review/LaRevue Canadienne des langues vivantes* 52 (4), 549–576.
Toohey, K. (2000) *Learning English at School: Identity, Social Relations and Classroom Practice*. Clevedon: Multilingual Matters.
Tracy, K. (2002) *Everyday Talk: Building and Reflecting Identities*. New York: Guilford.
van Lier, L. (2000) From input to affordance: Social-interactive learning from an ecological perspective. In J. Lantolf (ed.) *Sociocultural Theory and Second Language Learning* (pp. 245–259). New York: Oxford University Press.

van Lier, L. (2002) An ecological-semiotic perspective on language and linguistics. In C. Kramsch (ed.) *Language Acquisition and Language Socialization: Ecological Perspectives* (pp. 140–164). London: Continuum.

van Lier, L. and Matsuo, N. (2000) Varieties of conversational experience: Looking for learning opportunities. *Applied Language Learning* 11 (2), 265–287.

Vine, E.W. (2003) 'My partner': A five-year-old Samoan boy learns how to participate in class through interactions with his English-speaking peers. *Linguistics and Education* 14 (1), 99–121.

Varonis, E. and Gass S. (1985) Non-native/non-native conversations: As model for negotiation. *Applied Linguistics* 6 (1), 71–90.

Wagner, J. (1996). Foreign language acquisition through interaction – A critical review of research on conversational adjustments. *Journal of Pragmatics* 26 (2), 215–235.

Watson-Gegeo, K. (2004) Mind, language, and epistemology: Toward a language socialization paradigm for SLA. *Modern Language Journal* 88 (3), 331–350.

Wells, G. (1999) *Dialogic Inquiry: Toward a Sociocultural Practice and Theory of Education*. Cambridge: Cambridge University Press.

Wenger, E. (1998) *Communities of Practice: Language, Learning, and Meaning*. Cambridge: Cambridge University Press.

Wenger, E., McDermott, R. and Snyder, W. (2002) *Cultivating Communities of Practice: A Guide to Managing Knowledge*. Cambridge, MA: Harvard Business School Press.

Wetherell, M. (1998) Positioning and interpretative repertoires: Conversation analysis and post-structuralism in dialogue. *Discourse and Society* 9 (3), 387–412.

White, L. (1985) The 'pro-drop' parameter in adult second language acquisition. *Language Learning* 35 (1), 47–62.

White, L. (1989) *Universal Grammar and Second Language Acquisition*. Amsterdam: John Benjamins.

Willett, J. (1995) Becoming first graders in an L2: An ethnographic study of L2 socialization. *TESOL Quarterly* 29 (3), 473–503.

Willis, D. (1996) Accuracy, fluency and conformity. In J. Willis and D. Willis (eds) *Challenge and Change in Language Teaching* (pp. 44–51). Oxford: Heinemann.

Wittgenstein, L. (1958) *Philosophical Investigations*. (2nd edn) New York: Macmillan.

Wong, J. (2000) Repetition in conversation: A look at 'first' and 'second' sayings. *Research on Language and Social Interaction* 33 (4), 407–424.

Wootton, A.J. (1997) *Interaction and the Development of Mind*. Cambridge: Cambridge University Press.

Wootton, A. (2005) Interactional and sequential configurations informing request format selection in children's speech. In A. Hakulinen and M. Selting (eds) *Syntax and Lexis in Conversation: Studies on the Use of Linguistic Resources in Talk-in-interaction* (pp. 185–207). Amsterdam: John Benjamins.

Wortham, S.E.F. (2001) Interactionally situated cognition: A classroom example. *Cognitive Science* 25 (1), 37–66.

Wortham, S.E.F. (2005) Socialization beyond the speech event. *Journal of Linguistic Anthropology* 15 (1), 95–112.

Young, R.F. (1991) *Variation in Interlanguage Morphology*. Bern: Peter Lang.

Young, R.F. (1999) Sociolinguistic approaches to SLA. *Annual Review of Applied Linguistics* 19, 105–132.

Young, R.F. (2000) Interactional competence: Challenges for validity. Paper presented at the American Association for Applied Linguistics, Vancouver, BC.
Young, R.F. (2002) Discourse approaches to oral language assessment. *Annual Review of Applied Linguistics* 22, 243–262.
Young, R.F. and Miller, E.R. (2004) Learning as changing participation: Discourse roles in ESOL writing conferences. *Modern Language Journal* 88 (4), 519–535.
Zimmerman, D. (1978) Ethnomethodology. *The American Sociologist* 13 (1), 6–15.
Zimmerman, D.H. (1992) Achieving context: Openings in emergency calls. In G. Watson and R.M. Seiler (eds) *Text in Context: Contributions to Enthomethodology* (pp. 35–51). Newbury Park, CA: Sage Publications.
Zuengler, J. (1989) The influence of the listener in L2 speech. In S. Gass, C. Madden, D. Preston and L. Selinker (eds) *Variation in Second Language Acquisition: Discourse and Pragmatics* (pp. 245–279). Clevedon: Multilingual Matters.
Zuengler, J., Ford, C. and Fassnacht, C. (1998) *Analysts Eyes: Data Collection as Theory* (11006) SUNY Albany: Center on English Learning and Achievement.
Zuengler, J. and Miller, E. (2007) Apprenticing into a community: Challenges of the Asthma Project. In K. Cole and J. Zuengler (eds) *The Research Process in Classroom Discourse Analysis: Current Perspectives*. Mahwah, NJ: Lawrence Erlbaum Associates.

Index

Authors

Anderson, J. 15
Antaki, C. 103
Appel, G. 4
Au, K. 10

Bhatia, T. 3
Bamberg, M. 3
Bardovi-Harlig, K. 103, 105, 106
Barton, D. 28
Bateson, G. 16, 27
Bayley, R. 3, 4
Beach, W. 71, 101, 112, 150
Berger, P. 14
Billig, M. 35
Boggs, S. 6, 44, 151
Breen, M. 18
Brillanceau, D. 1, 10, 25, 150
Brooks, F. 4
Brouwer, C. 4, 31, 36, 38
Brown, A. 36
Brown, J. 6, 145
Bucholtz, M. 7
Button, G. 113, 124

Cazden, C. 1, 10
Cekaite, A. 5
Chafe, W. 44
Chaiklin, S. 28, 161
Chomsky, N. 13
Cicourel, A. 5
Clayman, S. 23, 160
Cole, E. 153
Cole, K. 1
Cole, M. 2, 6, 14, 26, 144
Coughlin, P. 17, 18, 144
Coulthard, R. 1, 142, 147
Couper-Kuhlen, E. 32
Creese, A. 9, 28
Crowley, K. 3

Davila, E. 50
Dewey, J. 26
Donato, R. 4

Doughty, C. 3
Duff, P. 17, 18, 144
Duranti, A. 161

Eglin, P. 35, 38
Ellis, R. 26
Erickson, F. 1, 10, 17, 27, 49, 50, 116
Eskildsen, S. 25

Fernandez Aguero, M. 88
Firth, A. 4
Fisher, E. 1, 17
Flynn, S. 3
Ford, C. 25, 32, 36, 76, 89
Forrester, M. 37, 39, 40
Foster, P. 17, 144
Fox, B. 32,
Frawley, W. 4
French, P. 32

Garfinkel, H. 13, 19, 28, 29, 30, 38
Garland, J. 25
Gass, S. 3, 4, 5, 13, 26
Gee, J. 9, 17
Glenn, P. 32, 111
Goffman, E. 29, 42, 43, 46, 49, 50, 105, 108, 148
Goldberg, J. 103
Goodwin, C. 2, 5, 16, 23, 32, 50, 77, 161
Green, J. 1
Greeno, J. 13, 15, 40
Gregg, K. 13,
Grice, H. 30
Gumperz, J. 50, 161

Hall, J. 4, 5, 37, 147
Hanks, W. 6
Hardy, I. 4
Harris, K. 1, 17, 18, 93, 156
Hartfod, B. 103, 105, 106
Hartge, U. 50
Hayashi, M. 32
He, A. 37
Heap, J. 2, 27, 29, 144

178

Index

Heath, C. 32, 105
Hellermann, J. 1, 4, 5, 17, 18, 25, 36, 37, 39, 111, 142, 147, 153
Heritage, J. 6, 23, 37, 60,
Hester, S. 1, 35, 38
Hopper, R. 42
Hosoda, Y. 36
House, J. 103
Hutchby, I. 23, 30, 160
Hutchins, E. 2, 7, 161
Huth, T. 31

Jacoby, S. 37
Jayyusi, L. 13, 30
Jefferson, G. 31, 32, 38, 83, 84, 85, 103, 161
Jeon, M. 105
Jones, S. 46, 105, 106

Kanagy, R. 5, 44, 151
Kasper, G. 4, 5, 27, 31, 32, 36, 37, 38, 44, 143
Kidwell, M. 50
Knapp, M. 105
Koole, T. 36
Korobov, N. 3
Koshcmann, T. 32, 37, 50
Kramsch, C. 4, 5, 88
Krashen, S. 26
Kress, G. 50
Kumaravadivelu, B. 17, 144

Lado, R. 3
Lantolf, J. 4, 16, 22
Larsen-Freeman, D. 37
Lave, J. 2, 6, 14, 15, 18, 28, 45, 144, 152, 153, 154, 155, 161
Lazaraton, A. 3
Lebaron, C. 32, 46, 50, 105, 106
Lee, K. 101
Lee, Y. 36, 147
Leki, I. 7, 8
Lerner, G. 36, 75, 84,
Lindstrom, A. 101, 150
Levinson, S. 161
Local, J. 32
Long, M. 3, 4, 13, 26, 88
Luckmann, T. 14
Lynch, M. 33

Macbeth, D. 2, 19, 27, 36
Mandelbaum, J. 84
Markee, N. 1, 4, 5, 31, 37, 38, 156, 160
Matsuo, N. 27, 144
Maynard, D. 23, 63, 81, 160
McDermott, R. 7, 35

McHould, A. 36, 95
McNamara, T. 5, 36, 37, 157
McNeill, D. 50
Mead, G. 29
Mead, M. 6
Mehan, H. 1, 27, 36, 95, 111, 147
Miller, E. 5, 7, 38
Moerman, M. 35
Mohatt, G. 10
Mondada, L 4, 7, 19, 26, 38, 108
Moore, J. 4
Mori, J. 27, 32, 37
Morita, N. 7, 8
Morris, F. 144

Nakahama, T. 140
Newman, D. 1
Nguyen, H.T. 37
Norrick, N.R. 84
Nystrand, M. 1
Norton, B. 7, 8, 10

Ochs, E. 83
Ohta, A. 1, 4, 17, 22, 151
O'Neill, W. 3

Pekarek Doehler, S. 4, 7, 19, 26, 38, 108
Peters, A. 6, 44, 151
Pica, T. 26
Platt, E. 4
Polanyi, L. 84, 88
Poole, D. 4
Preston, D. 3

Rampton, B. 35
Reason, D. 37, 39, 40
Reddy, M. 14
Reder, S. 1, 2, 22, 146
Resnick, L. 2
Richards, K. 37
Ritchie, W. 3
Robinson, J. 105
Roever, C. 5, 157
Rogoff, B. 6, 8, 10, 156

Sacks, H. 23, 29, 33, 38, 39, 43, 44, 46, 63, 81, 84-87, 93, 100, 103, 104, 106, 136, 147, 161
Schachter, J. 3
Schecter, S. 4
Schegloff, E. 28, 30, 33, 35-38, 42, 43, 58, 97, 103, 104, 106, 116, 133, 136, 158, 160, 161
Schiffrin, D. 42

Schultz, J. 49, 50, 116
Scribner, S. 6
Searle, J. 30
Seedhouse, P. 4, 18, 30, 32, 36, 37, 144, 160
Selinker, L. 14, 156
Sfard, A. 13, 19, 28
Siegler, R.S. 3
Silverman, D. 36
Silverstein, M. 15, 16, 35
Sinclair, J. 1, 142, 147
Skehan, P. 26
Smith, J. 88
Stokoe, E. 63, 81
Streeck, J. 49, 50
Swain, M. 13, 26
Szymanski, M. 103, 105, 118

Tarone, E. 3, 144
Tarplee, C. 40
ten Have, P. 30, 160
Thompson, S. 76, 89
Thorne, S. 4
Toohey, K. 4, 5, 7, 155
Tusting, K. 28

Van Lier, L. 4, 14, 15, 27, 144
Varonis, E. 4, 26
Vine, E. 4

Wagner, J. 4, 25, 31, 36, 38, 161
Wallat, C. 1
Watson-Gegeo, K. 4
Wells, G. 1
Wenger, E. 2, 6, 7, 11-14, 18, 28, 45, 108, 150, 152, 155
Wetherell, M. 35
White, L. 3
Willett, J. 4
Willis, D. 17
Wooffitt, R. 23, 30, 160
Wong, J. 36
Wootton, A. 7, 26, 37, 39, 40
Wortham, S. 2, 15, 16, 145

Yanez, M. 22
Young, R. 3, 5, 8, 10, 38

Zimmerman, D. 38, 42, 50, 63, 81
Zuengler, J. vii, 1, 7, 88

Subjects

affinity spaces 17
assessments
– by learners 119-123
– of learning 156

closings 104-106
community of practice 6-13
– characteristics of 9-13
– economies of meaning 12-13
– language learning 7-9
– learner agency 16
– overlapping 150-154
– reification and participation 11-12, 45
contact signals 42
conversation analysis 27-28, 29-40
– context 35-36
– critiques 35
– membership 36-39
– situated learning 39-40

disengagements
– Jorge, week 2 125-130
– Jorge, week 40 130-139
– participation structure 107-110

humor 62-63

interaction
– dyadic 25
interactional competence 5-6

'lab school' 22, 160
learning
– indexicality 16-17
– membership 37-39
– participation and acquisition 13-14
– situated 14-17

openings
– direct launch 51-52
– face-to-face 43-44
– greetings 46
– Jorge, week 2 73
– Jorge, week 40 80
– language development 65-68
– task clarification 58
– telephone 43

participation

Index

– peripheral-core 139-141; 152-154
posture 49-50; 116
professional vision 2, 24

routines 6, 44-45

second language acquisition (SLA)
– object of study 26
– socio-cultural perspectives 4-5
story telling
– conversation 84-86

– characteristics of language learners 92-97
– language development 97-100
– teacher 95

task 144-146
– process and workplan 18-19
– serial dyadic 69-81; 123-140
technology
– data collection 2
– video recording 23-24
turn allocation 53-54; 146-147

For Product Safety Concerns and Information please contact our EU Authorised Representative:

Easy Access System Europe

Mustamäe tee 50

10621 Tallinn

Estonia

gpsr.requests@easproject.com

www.ingramcontent.com/pod-product-compliance
Ingram Content Group UK Ltd.
Pitfield, Milton Keynes, MK11 3LW, UK
UKHW022217250326
4937IPUK00005B/30